MW00587927

Loc, Calvinism

CALVIN'S
DOCTRINE OF MAN

CALVIN'S DOCTRINE OF MAN

by

T. F. TORRANCE
M.B.E., B.D., D.THEOL., ABERDEEN

Wipf and Stock Publishers
150 West Broadway • Eugene OR 97401

Calvin's Doctrine of Man
by Thomas F. Torrance
Copyright© 1997 Thomas F. Torrance

ISBN: 1-57910-091-0

Printed by   **WS** WIPF & STOCK PUBLISHERS   1997

PREFACE

WHEN I came to Alyth in 1940 I was generously presented by my friend, the Rev. R. B. Hastie, of Blairgowrie, with a complete edition of Calvin's *Commentaries* in English. Constant reading of these many volumes in the course of sermon preparation, and of the *Sermons* in the *Corpus Reformatorum*, in addition to the study of the *Institutes*, convinced me that Calvin's own theological position was very different from the hardened system that has long passed under the name of Calvinism. It is a sad reflection that the Reformer's thought should have been crusted over for so long by a species of Aristotelianism, the very *damnosa hereditas* against which Calvin himself revolted with the full impetus of his mind and soul.

A request from the *Scottish Church Theology Society* to give them a lecture on Calvin's doctrine of man started me on the work of assembling material on the subject. So much material came to hand that, on the encouragement of the Rev. Dr. John McConnachie, of Dundee, I have prepared it for publication in this volume. It has been my attempt to lay bare Calvin's own thought and to present it as far as possible in his own way and in his own words. Traditional Calvinism I have studiously avoided, and have made no reference to works on Calvin, ancient or modern, so that this presentation might be free from the imputation of partisanship in any of the different schools, such as that of the Dutch Calvinists, or that of W. Niesel and the late Peter Barth. Consequently, the bulk of the book consists of citations gathered from all over Calvin's works, and arranged together with as little explanatory material of my own as was necessary. I am conscious that in the very arrangement of this material, as also in the exposition, interpretation has been unavoidable, but it is, I believe, in the direction in which Calvin's own thought moves as it is drawn out, particularly in its relevance to the modern theological debate.

One of the calamities of traditional exposition and interpretation of Calvin's theology has been, by means of arid logical forms, to make Calvin's own distinctions too clean and too rigid. This has resulted in an over-simplification which has obscured the flexibility as well as the range and profundity of his thought.

7

There is no doubt that Calvin was at times himself guilty of this procedure, particularly in his more systematic treatises when he was engaged in debate, as in regard to the problems of predestination and providence, but in the vast bulk of his work where he sticks closely to the Scriptures there is much profound theology that has never been sufficiently brought to light.

This is particularly true in regard to Calvin's teaching about the *imago dei*. There is a great deal of his thought on this difficult subject which has not yet found its way into exposition, and still lies buried in the cumbrous tomes of the *Corpus Reformatorum*. This is so varied that it is not easy to reduce to a concise and orderly account. Indeed that may be quite impossible, because in the nature of the case it is not possible to put fully into clear and distinct ideas just how a human creature may image the glory of God. I have tried, however, at the cost of repetition, to give some progression to this exposition, and at the same time to present before the reader something of the actual fullness and width of Calvin's own teaching. At times, the account has necessarily been circular, but becomes clearer, I think, when the whole matter has been set forth.

Against the constant temptation to eliminate certain elements of his thought as inconsistent with his main position, I have tried to handle these apparent contradictions as sympathetically as possible, on the assumption that Calvin could not have been as self-contradictory as he would at first appear, and that in the nature of the case a good deal of paradox was unavoidable. This procedure I have found to pay a good dividend, for again and again new passages and new ideas have come to my notice which throw light upon these earlier problems, and serve to show that in John Calvin the Reformed Church has had a theologian, with magnitude in mind and depth in understanding, second to none in the history of the Christian Church.

As it has been my aim to set forth Calvin's teaching on the doctrine of man in its own light, I have not attempted much in the way of criticism. Doubtless I have been at times too kind to the Reformer, though it is easy to criticize after centuries of discussion of problems which were not acute and demanded no immediate solution in the sixteenth century. Many of these questions which concern us to-day deal with aspects of the doctrine of man which did not greatly agitate the Reformers, but I feel sure that the modern theologian can find no better solution to them than he will reach through a careful study of Calvin's thoroughly Biblical position, and his searching understanding of human nature. It has not been my business to point out here any of these solutions, but I shall consider myself amply rewarded if I have succeeded in setting before the modern student much in Calvin's thought which is seldom brought to light, but which is extremely relevant to the present hour. For purposes of further study, as well as for verification, I have taken pains to provide ample references to passages beyond those actually cited or paraphrased, while for purposes of convenience to most readers, to whom the *Corpus Reformatorum* is rarely available, I have given these citations and references according to the chapter and paragraph or chapter and verse.

Besides the *Ioannis Calvini Opera* in the *Corpus Reformatorum*, edited by G. Baum, E. Cunitz, and E. Reuss (Brunswick, 1869-96), I have made use of A. Tholuck's edition of the *Commentarii in Novum Testamentum* (Berlin, 1833-34), and of the *Institutio Christianæ Religionis* (Edinburgh, 1874); the *Opera Selecta*, edited by P. Barth and W. Niesel (München, 1926-36), particularly for the edition of the 1536 *Institutio;* the English version of the *Institutes, Commentaries, and Tracts,* including some *Sermons,* published by the Calvin Translation Society (Edinburgh, 1843-55); H. Cole's translation of Calvin's treatise on *The Eternal Predestination of God,* and *The Defence of the Secret Providence of God* (1856); A. Golding's translation of the *Sermons on Job* (1584 edition), *Sermons on Deuteronomy* (1581), *Sermons on Galatians* (1574), *Sermons on Ephesians* (1577); and L. Tomson's translation of the *Sermons on Timothy and Titus* (1579). Though these translations have been most useful, I have allowed myself the freedom of altering them as occasion arose, either in order to express the original more accurately, or to erase archaic expressions.

I owe more than I can say to the constant encouragement and patient help of my wife during months of arduous research. To my brother-in-law and sister, the Rev. and Mrs. R. S. Wallace, of Pollok Church, Glasgow, and to the Rev. Professor David Cairns, Aberdeen, I am very grateful for much invaluable criticism and help. To the Lutterworth Press I am indebted for many useful suggestions and unfailing kindness. I thank them all very warmly.

T. F. TORRANCE.

ALYTH,
June, 1947.

CONTENTS

Chapter One

MAN'S KNOWLEDGE OF HIMSELF

Man's true knowledge of himself is reflexive of his knowledge of God. He is made to know God, and to live in dependence on God's grace. Therefore, only when a man so responds to the Word of grace that he becomes what he is made to be, can he begin to know his true nature. Christian self-knowledge differs from secular self-knowledge. The latter ministers to man's pride; the former ministers to his humility by revealing his creaturehood and wretchedness, but does not allow him to despair, or to despise his humanity, for he is a creature of God. This Biblical knowledge of man is gained: (a) Through the law, which enables man to see himself as he really is in comparison with his original truth which is the law of his being. This may easily lead to a despairing and unhealthy knowledge of depravity, though it may be used didactically with much profit; (b) Through the Gospel, which not only reveals to man what he actually is, but brings him regeneration so that he may become what he is meant to be. Here we have a revelation of the original truth of man which does not bring despair, but kindles hope and gratitude. The doctrine of depravity must be considered only within this context of grace.

FEW theologians are more concerned than John Calvin to provide the Church with a carefully articulated knowledge of man and at the same time to weave that into the context of our knowledge of God. "We cannot clearly and properly know God," he says, "unless the knowledge of ourselves be added."[1] By this he does not mean that anthropology of itself can contribute to or condition our knowledge of God, but that unless there arises within our knowledge of God a real knowledge of man our knowledge of God itself is not real. The purpose of a Christian anthropology is twofold: by pointing the believer to his original creation in the image of God to produce gratitude, and by pointing him to his present miserable condition to produce humility.[2] Only in a life of gratitude before the grace of God and of humility before the glory of God can man know God in such a

[1] *Instit.* I. 15. 1: *non potest liquido et solide cognosci Deus a nobis, nisi accedat mutua nostri cognitio.* Also *Comm. on Jer.* 9 : 23 f.: "We cannot know God without knowing ourselves. These two things are connected."
[2] *Instit.* 1. 15. 1; 2. 1. 1 f.

13

way as in his knowing actually to image the grace and glory of God.[1] That is to know God indeed. Therefore, while the knowledge of man has no independent status, in Calvin's theology it is regarded as an essential function of our knowledge and worship of God.

On the other hand, Calvin lays it down from the very start that there is no true knowledge of man except within our knowledge of God. "It is evident that man never attains to a true self-knowledge until he has previously contemplated the face of God, and come down after such contemplation to look into himself."[2] That is the essential direction of all Christian theology, and Calvin does not deviate from it. True knowledge of man must be grounded in the acknowledgment of a revelation, but in this instance the knowledge involved is essentially reflexive of a Word of God about the creative action of His love. The expression *come down* has, for Calvin, particular importance, for it means that a true knowledge of man is not only reflexive of the divine self-revelation but also of the divine action in grace. There is no true knowledge of man, therefore, unless it is conceived as grounded upon the downward motion of grace. As we shall see, Calvin thinks of the creation of man as such that only when he lives his *esse* over again in a true *cognoscere* does man's *esse* in grace come to its true intention.[3] Man is only an image of God, though to be in the image of God belongs to his true nature. Man can have true self-knowledge only when he knows God truly, and when in knowing God he so images Him as to be what he was made by God to be, man in complete dependence on God.[4] What Calvin would have us note at the outset of a doctrine of man is, that the direction and motion of our knowing must correspond to the essential direction and motion of grace, for that is the ground of man's being. Therefore, in formulating a doctrine of man we must make sure that our activity actually corresponds to the motion of grace, and does not invert it.[5]

---

[1] *Instit.* 2. 1. 1 f.; *Comm. on* 1 *Cor.* 1. 31. [2] *Instit.* 1. 1. 2.

[3] This is particularly clear in Calvin's doctrine that man's true *life* is *light*; unless he thankfully traces this *light* back to its source in the Word of grace, man turns *light* into *darkness* and alienates himself from the *fountain of life*. See below, especially on *John* 1 : 5; on *Gen.* 2 : 9.

[4] Cf. *Comm. on Isa.* 6 : 5: "Until God reveal Himself to us, we do not think we are men, or rather, we think that we are gods; but when we have seen God, then we begin to feel and know what we are. Hence springs true humility, which consists in this, that a man makes no claim for himself, and depends wholly on God."

[5] Cf. *Comm. on John* 11 : 25, where Calvin contrasts *motus natura* with *gratia*, and also *Comm. on* 2 *Cor.* 10 : 4.

Concretely, this means that we can know man only in answer
to God's Word of grace. "For there is none but He alone who
may be a competent judge to know what we are, or that has
authority to say it."[1] In every judgment about man, God Himself
must preside,[2] for He is the only standard of our judgment.[3]
Where God does not preside and the essential motion is inverted,
man's self-knowledge will only serve to inflate his pride.[4] The
antithesis to the motion of grace is man's self-assertion and
innate self-love, and that necessarily becomes the essential
motion of independent self-knowledge, so that man is unable to
descend humbly into himself to learn the truth about himself.
To learn the truth he must go in the direction opposite to that
which as a sinner he is naturally prone to take. No doubt,
says Calvin, "he who is most forward in extolling the excellence
of human nature, is received with loudest applause. But be this
heralding of human excellence what it may, by teaching man to
rest in himself it does nothing more than fascinate by its sweet-
ness, and at the same time so delude as to drown in perdition all
who assent to it. . . . Whosoever, therefore, gives heed to
those teachers who merely employ us in contemplating our good
qualities, so far from making progress in self-knowledge, will be
plunged into the most pernicious ignorance."[5] And so Calvin
points out that though, like the philosophers, Christian theology
makes self-knowledge "the second part of wisdom", yet "they
differ greatly as to the method by which this knowledge may be
acquired."[6] In theology we must proceed not *natura duce et
magistra*,[7] but *Scriptura duce et magistra*.[8]

Because man is blinded by self-love and unable to reach true
knowledge of himself by natural law, God has given us His
written Law in order that by it we may descend into ourselves
and see ourselves as we really are. "In this way we arrive at two

[1] *Serm. on Job* 11 : 7 f.; cf. *Comm. on Jer.* 17 : 11: "The recesses of the heart are so
hidden, that no judgment can be formed of man by any human being."
[2] *Comm. on* 1 *Cor.* 4 : 3: *Præsidet Deus* means *ex veritate et verbo Domini.* See also
on *Matt.* 18 : 5.
[3] *Instit.* 1. 1. 2: *Non autem convincimur si in nos duntaxat ipsos respicimus, et non in
Dominum quoque; qui unica est regula ad quam exigendum est istud iudicium.* Cf. *Instit.*
1. 6. 3: *Non ex iudicii nostri pravitate, sed æternæ veritatis regula æstimantur.*
[4] *Instit.* 2. 1. 2 f.; 2. 8. 1.   [5] *Instit.* 2. 1. 2.   [6] *Instit.* 2. 1. 3.
[7] *Introd. Arg. to Comm. on Gen.; Comm. on Gen.* 3 : 6; *Instit.* 1. 6. 2; *Comm. on Heb.*
3. 11; cf. *on Jonah* 1 : 5: We may make some progress in the knowledge of God,
natura duce et magistra, but we go astray immediately if we neglect the Word.
[8] *Comm. on Deut.* 8. 3 : 11. 8 f.: *Ergo quoniam non satis proficiunt homines natura duce et
magistra, quin potius in operum Dei intuitu cæcutiunt documentum semel in miraculo hoc
statui oportuit.*

results: First, contrasting our conduct with the righteousness of the Law we see how very far it is from being in accordance with the will of God, and therefore how unworthy we are of holding our place among His creatures, far less of being accounted His sons; and, secondly, taking a survey of our powers we see that we are not only unequal to fulfil the Law but are altogether null. The necessary consequence must be to produce distrust of our own ability, and also anxiety and trepidation of mind."[1] "He who tries himself by the standard of divine justice finds nothing to inspire him with confidence; and hence the more thorough his self-examination the greater his despondency. Abandoning all dependence on himself he feels that he is utterly incapable of duly regulating his conduct. It is not the will of God however that we should forget the primeval dignity which He bestowed on our first parents—a dignity which may well stimulate us to the pursuit of goodness and justice.[2] It is impossible for us to think of our first original or the end for which we were created without being urged to meditate on immortality, and to seek the Kingdom of God. But such meditation, so far from raising our spirits, rather casts them down and makes us humble. For what is our original? One from which we have fallen. What the end of our creation? One from which we have altogether strayed so that weary of our miserable lot we groan, and groaning sigh for a dignity now lost."[3]

Calvin is at pains to point out, however, that we must not build up a knowledge of man from the bare Word of God by bringing him under the light of the Law, for there can be an unhealthy knowledge of man over against the knowledge of God in His wrath, which is nothing but a bottomless pit of despair.[4] No doubt the Word of God in this way tells us what man actually is: a fallen creature, bereft of the image of God, and with his natural gifts thoroughly corrupted. At the same time we may see why man cannot be understood out of himself, because he has been bereft of his spiritual image, and because what remains in the natural gifts that distinguish him from the beasts is but a miserable

---

[1] *Instit.* 2. 8. 3. Cf. *Institutio* (1536) 29: *Quoniam autem homo adhuc arrogantia et ambitione sic turgidus et sui amore excæcatus est ut se perspicere non possit et velut in se descendere, quo se deiicere et submittere discat suamque miseriam fateri, Dominus legem nobis scriptam posuit.* . . . See also *Instit.* 2. 7. 7; *Serm. on Gal.* 3 : 19 f.
[2] Cf. *Comm. on John* 3 : 27: *Hæc nostra omnium mensura est, ut simus quales esse nos Deus voluit.*
[3] *Instit.* 2. 1. 3.
[4] *Comm. on Jer.* 9 : 23 f.; *Instit.* 2. 16. 1; *Serm. on Job* 7 : 7 f.; 14 : 1 f.

ruin. But any understanding of man starting from man as he is could only be "within the confines of human pollution",[1] and that would do dishonour to God the Creator.[2] No doubt also, and Calvin insists upon this point, "he who is most deeply abased and alarmed by the consciousness of his disgrace, nakedness, want, and misery has made the greatest progress in the knowledge of himself",[3] but it is of no avail if it is left there. God did not create man to be nothing, nor does God "despoil us with a view to leaving us bare",[4] for "He does not delight in the degradation of men".[5] God made man erect, unlike the other creatures, that he might know and worship God.[6] Thus Calvin has no concern in a doctrine of man's creaturehood as such or in a doctrine of human depravity in itself. The knowledge of man in his humble creaturehood, and the knowledge which strips him bare of his pride and self-righteousness are not intended "that he should lie down in disgrace",[7] but are only of avail if they lead men to the acknowledgment of the pure grace of God, and the adoration of His glory.[8] Therefore it is not to the bare Word of God's Law that we must go, but to the Word of grace, to the Gospel where man is not simply stripped of all his glory and pretensions, but where he is renewed and set forth in his true nature.[9] "When God has cast down His people, immediately He raises them up and restores them . . . Let not men therefore faint or be discouraged by the knowledge of their nakedness and emptiness; for the eternal Word is exhibited to them by which they may be abundantly supported and upheld."[10] It is only when we relate our self-knowledge to the merciful will of God in the Gospel, and not to the bare Law, that we have a knowledge of self which, while deflating man's pride and inverting the motion of self-assertion in accordance with the motion of grace, does not only show us man's degradation before God but prevents us from seeing man in his mere degradation.[11] A citation which Calvin makes from Bernard illustrates admirably his own position here:

---

[1] *Instit.* 1. 1. 2.
[2] *Instit.* 2. 1. 10 f.; 2. 2. 15; 3. 2. 25; *Comm. on* 1 *Cor.* 1 : 31; *on* 2 *Pet.* 1 : 3.
[3] *Instit.* 2. 2. 10.   [4] *Comm. on* 1 *Cor.* 1 : 31.
[5] *Comm. on Jer.* 9 : 23   [6] *Comm. on Isa.* 40 : 26.
[7] *Comm. on Jer.* 9 : 23.
[8] *Serm. on Job* 7 : 7 f. We must be careful to use the language of self-abasement "only to the glory of God", and we must not let it "hinder us from magnifying God's gracious goodness, although we know our state to be vile and abject". See also *Instit.* 2. 2. 1.
[9] *Instit.* 2. 7. 7-9; 4. 17. 2, 42; *Comm. on Rom.* 6 : 21.
[10] *Comm. on Isa.* 40 : 8.   [11] *Comm. on Rom.* 7 : 24-25.

B

"What then? Man doubtless has been made subject to vanity—man has been reduced to nothing—man is nothing. And yet how is he whom God exalts utterly nothing? How is he nothing to whom a divine heart has been given? Let us breathe again, brethren. Although we are nothing in our hearts, perhaps something of us may lurk in the heart of God. O Father of mercies! O Father of the miserable! how plantest Thou Thy heart in us? Where Thy heart is, there is Thy treasure also. But how are we Thy treasure if we are nothing? All nations before Thee are as nothing. Observe *before* Thee; not *within* Thee. Such are they in the judgment of Thy truth, but not such in regard to Thy affection."[1] That takes us to the very heart of Calvin's doctrine of man which, he insists again and again, we can formulate truly only from the standpoint of the grace of God in Jesus Christ.[2]

Calvin does, however, point out the value of thinking of ourselves apart from grace, so that after despairing of ourselves we may learn "how we are beholden to God for all that we have", and then turning to the gifts of grace may learn to say: "This is not my own. I have this not of myself; my possessing of it is only because He lends it to me. Therefore I must do Him homage for it."[3] Indeed Calvin asserts that the Scripture itself goes out of its way to speak about the hostility of God against us, and of the fact that we are cursed until our iniquity is expiated by the sacrifice of Christ, although God actually "prevents us with His mercy". "For how could He have given us in His only begotten Son a singular pledge of His love, if He had not previously embraced us with free favour?" That means that "such modes of expression are accommodated to our capacity, that we may the better understand how miserable and calamitous our condition is without Christ . . . since our mind cannot lay hold of life through the mercy of God with sufficient eagerness or receive it with becoming gratitude, unless previously impressed with fear of the divine anger, and dismayed at the thought of eternal death, we are so instructed by divine truth as to perceive that without Christ God is in a manner hostile to us, and has His arm raised

---

[1] *Instit.* 3. 2. 25.

[2] E.g. *Instit.* 3. 9. 3: "When once we have concluded that our earthly life is a gift of the divine mercy, of which in accordance with our obligation it behoves us to have a useful remembrance, *we shall then properly descend to consider its most wretched condition,* and thus escape from that excessive fondness for it to which we are naturally prone." See also *Serm. on Deut.* 6 : 4 f.

[3] *Serm. on Job* 7 : 7 f.

for our destruction".[1] "Though this is said in accommodation to the weakness of our capacity, it is not said falsely . . . for there is a perpetual and irreconcilable repugnance between righteousness and iniquity."[2] In the same way Calvin constantly employs a didactic purpose in his theology,[3] and employs the Law as a device to impress the truth upon his readers. Unless we keep in view this didactic purpose behind his theology, Calvin's position will appear more inconsistent than it actually is. Thus, for example, there are times when he says that "there is not a single drop of uprightness in us",[4] while at other times he admits that there are splendid virtues even in fallen man, and that whatever of good we see there we must attribute to divine action.[5] Both are correct, on Calvin's position, if they are regarded from the point of view of grace; but it must be admitted that, for the purpose of effect, Calvin does engage in moral denunciations of man, apart from the context of grace, which do not stand up to his own investigations. But of this there can be no doubt: that, from a dogmatic point of view, Calvin's doctrine of the fall of man and of sin is a corollary of the doctrine of grace in forgiveness and salvation.[6] Justification by grace alone carries with it the doctrine that the *justitia originalis* has been wholly and irrevocably lost.[7] That is the great Reformed inference, and however much Calvin may from time to time turn aside to force home by means of the Law the conviction of human depravity, he does not change his fundamental standpoint.[8] Indeed, it is just because Calvin holds so firmly that grace completely undercuts all our claims to righteousness and wisdom, and that we do not allow grace to strike home to us until we have renounced all our righteousness and wisdom, that he employs every didactic

---

[1] *Instit.* 2. 16. 2.   [2] *Instit.* 2. 16. 3.

[3] *Preface to Instit.*, 1539, and 1559. Calvin says that the purpose of the *Institutes* is to send the student of theology back to the Bible with renewed understanding. Cf. *Instit.* 1. 14. 21.

[4] *Comm. on John* 3 : 6.

[5] *Instit.* 2. 2. 13 f.; 2. 3. 3 f.; 1. 5. 6; 3. 14. 2.

[6] *Comm. on Matt.* 9 : 12: "Here Christ begins with reproof, but if we wish to make progress in His *doctrine*, what He has put in the second place must receive our first attention: He came to quicken the dead, to justify the guilty and condemned" . . . etc.

[7] *Comm. on 1 Cor.* 1 : 30: *Nam dum Christum iustitiam nostram appellat, subaudienda est antithesis, quod in nobis nihil sit nisi peccatum.* See also *on Rom.* 1. 18 f.; *on Col.* 2 :3; *on John* 17 : 3; *Instit.* 2. 31; 2. 36; 2. 15. 19: *The True Method of giving Peace and Reforming the Church* (Eng. tr., *Tracts*, vol. 3, p. 242), etc. C. R. 35.594.

[8] Cf. *Comm. on Micah* 7. 19, where Calvin calls the argument from the mercy of God "the true logic of religion".

method he can think of to deflate man's self-esteem and pride in his own integrity and achievements.

Unfortunately, later Calvinist theology too often turned Calvin's didactic devices into dogmatic procedure, producing a doctrine of the fall of man and of human depravity apart from the context of grace, and interpreting grace as God's answer to human depravity. This does violence to the doctrine of total depravity, because, when cast in moralistic and legalistic terms, it does not do justice to the undoubted elements of virtue and good in the unregenerate man, which Calvin himself recognized; and it slanders man's natural gifts, thus, as Calvin said, insulting the Creator. The unfortunate thing is that this procedure has been imputed to Calvin himself, and by obscuring his fundamental position it has made him out to be the author of a thoroughly pessimistic view of man. Nothing is further from the truth. It must be regretted that from a dogmatic point of view Calvin was not thoroughly consistent, though there can be no doubt about his real position: natural goodness and natural knowledge are both admitted, but they are persistently placed under the judgment and action of grace, which puts them totally out of court for the Christian in life and faith. Fundamentally, it is only from this point of view that the dogmatic theologian must produce his doctrine of total depravity—"total" because grace "totally" undercuts all human righteousness and wisdom as based upon independence and self-will. The amazing thing to the modern theologian is that Calvin could advance such a total judgment upon man as he is, and yet be so utterly free from a morbid view.[1] Take away from Calvin his basic position in regard to grace, and his great comprehensive inference from grace, and then translate his total judgments into merely moralistic terms, and the result can only be called pessimistic and black. In actual fact, he refused to advance any doctrine of man, apart from God's original intention of grace in creating him in the image of God, and apart from God's supreme act of grace in Jesus Christ for our salvation. Within these two brackets, and only within these two brackets, does Calvin give us an account of man's fallen nature and his sin. Never does he attempt to give a philosophical account of man's depravity. His position in this respect is very clearly brought out in a denunciation of Origen who, Calvin says, "disputes philosophically and profanely of the corruptions of mankind, and does

[1] See especially *Serm. on Eph.* 2 : 1-13; *on Gal.* 5 : 19-23.

not only enervate the grace of Christ but in a manner wholly destroys it".[1] If in the order of his discussion in the *Institutes* he gives an account of man and sin before an account of our salvation, he does that only by taking his stand entirely within the gracious redemption of man in Christ, and makes the argument from grace regulative throughout. The same procedure governs his *Commentary on Genesis*. In his introductory argument to the Commentary, he sums up the scriptural account of man's creation and destiny thus: "After the world had been created man was placed in it as in a theatre that he, beholding above and beneath him the wonderful works of God, might reverently adore their Author. Secondly, that all things were ordained for the use of man that he, being under deeper obligation, might devote and dedicate himself entirely to obedience towards God. Thirdly, that he was endued with understanding and reason, that being distinguished from brute animals he might meditate on a better life and might even directly tend towards God whose image he bore engraven on his person. Afterwards followed the fall of Adam whereby he alienated himself from God; whence it came to pass that he was deprived of all rectitude. Thus, Moses represents man as devoid of all good, blinded in understanding, perverse in heart, vitiated in every part, and under sentence of eternal death; but he soon adds the history of his restoration where Christ shines forth with the benefit of redemption." That last sentence shows Calvin's standpoint here. He does not try to place himself in understanding or judgment artificially at a point before the fall of man, but views the whole doctrine of creation and the fall from man's actual position in the redemption of Christ. Therefore, though he expounds the doctrine in the order of creation in original integrity, the miserable ruin of the fall, and the redemption of grace, yet he insists that inasmuch as man has fallen from his original, and has been redeemed in Christ, and so restored to God's original intention, we can only make headway in a doctrine of man by viewing the whole from the point of view of our restoration or renovation in Christ. That is a point which I shall be concerned to bring out again and again, though I shall follow Calvin's general order of exposition which he gives thus: "In considering the knowledge which man ought to have of himself, it seems proper to divide it thus, first, to consider the end for which he was created, and the qualities—by no means con-

[1] *Comm. on Rom.* 5 : 14.

temptible qualities—with which he was endued, thus urging him to meditate on divine worship and the future life; and, secondly, to consider his faculties or rather the want of faculties—a want which, when perceived, will annihilate all his confidence, and cover him with confusion. The tendency of the former is to teach him what his duty is; of the latter, to make him aware how far he is able to perform it."[1]

[1] *Instit.* 2. 1. 3; cf. 1. 15. 1.

Chapter Two

MAN'S PLACE IN CREATION

Man is not created because of the world, but the world is created because of man. As man was created for God, the whole order of creation must be regarded as designed to incite man to respond to the Father in love and gratitude, in worship and in adoration of His glory. It is as he reflects the glory of God in this way that man has his rightful place in the universe. The doctrine of creation speaks of man's nobility, for he is the crown of creation, but at the same time it reminds him of his humble origin in the dust. Man is in no sense a supernatural being, but is created out of nothing, body and soul, and is maintained in dependent being by the gracious will of God. In contrast to all other earthly creatures, man has been endowed with intelligence that he may have a special and familiar relation to God through the Word which addresses him personally and calls him to a life of communion with the Father. It is in this communion, maintained by the constant communication of the Word, that man lives as creature in the image of God. Man's true life consists in light. Thus in distinction from all other earthly creatures, for man, knowing (God) and being (man) are bound up together, so that he possesses his life only as deposited in the Word of God.

THE Word of God tells us that man is not here because of the world, but the world is here because of man. Man is the crown of creation, and all things have been made with a purpose subordinate to his life and destiny. "The whole order of this world is arranged and established for the purpose of conducing to the comfort and happiness of men."[1] "In the very order of the creation the paternal solicitude for man is conspicuous, because He furnished the world with all things needful, and even with an immense profusion of wealth, before He formed man."[2] Therefore "the Lord Himself by the very order of creation has demonstrated that He created all things for the sake of man".[3] Thus the world is to be understood only in relation to man, and in relation to man who himself has been made for God. Man cannot be understood by his relation to the world. It is not from below man that man can be understood but from above man. "Therefore we must not commence with the elements of the world, but with

[1] *Comm. on Psalm* 8 : 6; cf. 103 : 4.
[2] *Instit.* I. 14. 22; also I. 14. 2; I. 16. 6, etc.
[3] *Comm. on Gen.* I : 26.

23

the Gospel which sets Christ alone before us with His Cross and holds us to this one point."[1] That means of course that there can be no naturalistic understanding of man, for that would involve an inversion of the very order of creation, and would run directly counter to the divine purpose of grace upon which the whole of creation depends.[2]

As the chief work in God's creation man has "a singular honour and one which cannot be sufficiently estimated, that mortal man as the representative of God has dominion over the world, as if it pertained to him by right, and that to whatever quarter he turns his eyes, he sees nothing wanting which may contribute to the convenience and happiness of his life".[3] If to-day we see anything opposed to man in heaven or in earth, that is not a slight upon creation but means that "the beautiful order which God had established in the world at the beginning is now thrown into confusion".[4] But apart from the disorder of sin we must be quite clear in our minds about God's supreme intention, for God does not wish us ever to lose sight of our primeval dignity,[5] that the whole universe has been created and endowed as a habitation for man in such a way as to serve his true destiny in the worship and adoration of God. Therefore God has created such a wonderful universe that in it abound evident tokens of His fatherly love for man by which he may be incited to confide in God, to invoke Him, to praise Him, and love Him as His cherished child.[6] "If we do not submit ourselves wholly to God, it is for want of considering the good things which He has given us. For if we feel Him liberal, as He shows Himself toward us, surely it will draw us wholly to Him. So then let us consider that God's making of us so excellent as to have His image imprinted in us, was for no other purpose than that we should do Him homage for His precious gifts, and by that means be the more moved to love Him, and to keep ourselves from defiling such gifts as reason, will, discretion, and all the other powers of our souls which He has given to us."[7] In other words, God has deliberately created this world in such a way as to lead man to adore the glory of God in His kindness and grace.[8] By

---

[1] *Introd. Arg. to Comm. on Genesis.*
[2] *Instit.* 1. 14. 21 f.
[3] *Comm. on Ps.* 8 : 6.
[4] *Ibid.*
[5] *Instit.* 1. 14. 21.
[6] *Instit.* 1. 14. 21. 22; *Serm. on Deut.* 28. 46 f.
[7] *Serm. on Deut.* 6 : 4 f.
[8] *Instit.* 1. 5. 1 f.; 1. 5. 6; 1. 5. 14; 1. 6. 1 f.; *Comm. on Heb.* 11 : 3; *on Ps.* 103 : 4; *on Gen.* 1 : 26. Calvin really identifies the grace of God with His glory. Therefore, he says, "While God should be praised for all His works, it is His mercy principally that we should glorify", *on Ps.* 136 : 3. See also *on Rom.* 3 : 23; *on 1 John* 1 : 21.

living in a world so created and daily maintained, in surroundings in which grace presents itself in an immeasurable abundance, man is intended to live in utter and thankful dependence on the kindness of God alone. And that is the precise way in which he is destined to reflect the divine glory, and to be a man in the image of God. He can do that and be that in no other way.[1] It is thus too that man exercises rightly his dominion over the earth—if he gladly and gratefully submits to the gracious dominion of God over all, for then his dominion over the world becomes part of the way in which he as man images the glory of God.[2]

Thus we see that in Calvin's view the key to the whole doctrine of man in creation and destiny is the idea of thankful response to the unbounded grace of God. Nor can we understand the doctrine of creation unless we too are evoked to a grateful adoration of the perfections of God.[3]

When Calvin deals with the creation of man himself, he lays special emphasis upon three things: (a) the nobility of man; (b) the creaturehood of man; and (c) his peculiar relation to the Word of God.

(a) The order of creation itself points to the nobility of man. "Heaven and earth being thus most richly adorned, and copiously supplied with all things, like a large and splendid mansion gorgeously constructed and exquisitely furnished, at length man was made—man, by the beauty of his person and his many noble endowments, the most glorious specimen of the works of God."[4] Apart altogether from being placed in a world designed daily to manifest tokens of God's unbounded grace, man is such a world in himself, a veritable microcosm, "because he is above all creatures a token of God's glory, replenished with infinite miracles".[5] If only man has eyes to see it, he reflects in himself the wonderful grace of God displayed throughout the universe. He is indeed "a rare specimen of the divine power, wisdom, and goodness . . . having within himself undoubted evidences of the heavenly grace by which he lives, and moves, and has his being".[6] To live in accordance with that grace is, Calvin maintains, to be a man, but to be ungrateful and to plume oneself on these divine endowments, basely transferring to nature what

---

[1] *Comm. on Acts* 17 : 26-29.   [2] *Comm. on Gen.* 1 : 26.
[3] *Instit.* I. 2. 1-3; I. 5. 9; I. 14. 20 ff.   [4] *Instit.* I. 14. 20.
[5] *Comm. on Acts* 17 : 27; also *Comm. on Gen.* 1 : 26; *Instit.* I. 5. 1.
[6] *Instit.* I. 5. 3; *Comm. on Gen.* 1 : 26; cf. *Instit.* I. 14. 22.

belongs to grace, is to descend to the level of the beasts.[1] "But herein appears the shameful ingratitude of men. Though they have in their own persons a factory where innumerable operations of God are carried on, and a magazine stored with treasures of inestimable value—instead of bursting forth in His praise, as they are bound to do, they are, on the contrary, the more inflated and swelled with pride. They feel how wonderfully God is working in them, and their own experience tells them of the vast variety of gifts which they owe to His liberality. Whether they will or not, they cannot but know that these are proofs of His Godhead, and yet they inwardly suppress them. They have no occasion to go farther than themselves, provided they do not, by appropriating as their own that which has been given them from heaven, put out the light intended to exhibit God clearly to their minds."[2]

(b) Man has been created out of the dust of the earth. That was especially designed to remind him of his creaturehood and creaturely kinship with the rest of the world, as a curb to his pride and self-exaltation, and lest he should read more than he ought into the fact that he was made in the image of God.[3] Man is not in any sense a supernatural creature, though he does have a supernatural destiny.[4] The soul is as much a creature as the body. Both depend for their being entirely on the grace of God.[5] Man has not been given a bit of God as his soul, nor is his soul in any sense a transfusion of God in man.[6] Man, body and soul, is a creature, created *ex nihilo*.[7] Certainly as compared to the body the soul must be regarded as having *something essential* by which it survives the body and is distinguished from it, as that which inhabits or is imprisoned by the body.[8] But this does not mean

---

[1] *Instit.* I. 5. 2-4; *Tracts*, Eng. tr., Vol. 3, p. 242; *Instit.* 2. 2. 1; 2. 2. 27.
[2] *Instit.* I. 5. 4.
[3] *Comm. on Gen.* 2 : 7; *Instit.* I. 15. 1. It is at this point that self-knowledge plays such an important part. "We cannot properly estimate the divine goodness unless we take into consideration what we are as to our condition, as we can only ascribe to God what is due unto Him by acknowledging that His goodness is bestowed upon undeserving creatures." *Comm. on Ps.* 144 : 3-4.
[4] A supernatural life is possessed only in faith, *Comm. on Eph.* 4 : 18. It is quite clear that when Calvin uses such expressions as "something divine engraven on the mind" (*Instit.* I. 15. 2) or "something of divinity in man", he is simply referring to the *imago dei. Instit.* I. 5. 5. 6; I. 15. 2. 4; *Comm. on Ps.* 8 : 5. This does not mean that the soul is a "secret influx of divinity", *Instit.* I. 15. 5.
[5] *Comm. on Ps.* 103 : 15 f.; *Instit.* I. 15. 5; *Serm. on Job* 27 : 1 ff.
[6] *Instit.* I. 15. 5; *Serm. on Job* 27 : 1 ff.
[7] *Instit.* I. 15. 5: *Creatio non transfusio est, sed essentia ex nihilo exordium.*
[8] *Instit.* I. 15. 2; *Comm. on Gen.* 2 : 7.

that the immortality of the soul is to be confused with eternity,[1]
as if there were an eternal soul-substance in the universe. The
soul survives the death of the body only at the mercy of God, and
has no durability in itself.[2] "Although the soul after it has
departed from the prison of the body remains alive, yet its so
doing does not arise from any inherent power of its own. Were
God to withdraw His grace, the soul would be nothing more
than a puff or a blast, even as the body is dust; and thus there
would doubtless be found in the whole man nothing but mere
vanity."[3] "It behoves us to understand that our souls are not
immortal of their own power, nor is the life in them enclosed in
themselves, as though it had its roots there. Where is there life
then? In God."[4] "The soul of man perishes not in death; it is not
put out. But if we mark how our souls are immortal, it is not of
their own nature, for this virtue of life is not shut up in them,
but is borrowed and comes another way. Inasmuch then as it
pleases God to maintain our souls with His virtue, in this respect
do they have being and have continuance: hence comes this
immortality."[5] Commenting on the words "As the Lord liveth,
that made us this soul", Calvin says: "The word *liveth*, when
applied to God, denotes a life different from what is in men or in
brute animals; for men live by the will of another, that is, while
God gives them life. It belongs then to God alone to live, for
we do not live, or move, nor have any being but in Him, as Paul
says. And hence he teaches in another place, that God alone is
immortal."[6] "Our true immortality is to cleave to God."[7] That
means that it is really through faith that the soul is maintained in
its life. "Faith is the soul of our souls, and as our bodies are
quickened by the soul, so is the soul by faith. So then we are in
death, we are rotten in the grave, until God call us to the knowledge of His truth."[8] The same thing is expressed by saying:
"Because the soul is made in the image of God it cannot but be

[1] *Instit.* 1. 15. 5.
[2] *Comm. on* 1 *Tim.* 6 : 16; *Serm. on Deut.* 4 : 15 f.; *on Job* 12 : 11 f.
[3] *Comm. on Ps.* 103 : 15 f.
[4] *Serm. on Job* 10 : 7 f. *Serm. on Deut.* 28 : 65 f.
[5] *Serm. on* 1 *Tim.* 1 : 17-19. Cf. also on 6 : 15, 16: "This quality (immortality)
characterizes our souls, but it is *not natural*. For whatsoever had a beginning may
have an end, and may come to decay, and even perish utterly."
[6] *Comm. on Jer.* 38 : 16; cf. 10 : 10; *Comm. on John* 6 : 35; *Simplex doctrina est: non
vivere animas nostras intrinseca ut ita loquar virtute, sed vitam a Christo mutuari.*
[7] *Serm. on* 1 *Tim.* 6 : 15, 16.
[8] *Serm. on* 1 *Tim.* 3 : 14, 15. Compare *Comm. on Rom.* 8 : 10: *anima adeo vita non est,
ut ne ipsa quidem vivat.*

immortal."[1]   The life of the soul depends entirely upon the gracious will of God, who in His desire to create a noble creature excelling the animals, brought man into a peculiar relation to Himself by which he survives bodily dissolution and continues to be responsible to God,[2] even after death,[3] though the man who has been alienated from God does not know it.[4] Only the believer may rejoice in it through the witness of the Word and the Spirit of God.[5]

As regards the distinction between the soul and the spirit Calvin says: "Though the two terms while they are used together differ in their meaning, still, when spirit is used by itself, it is equivalent to soul, as when Solomon speaking of death says that the spirit returns to God who gave it (Eccles. 12 : 7). And Christ in commending His spirit to the Father, and Stephen his to Christ, simply mean that when the soul is freed from the prison-house of the body, God becomes its perpetual keeper. Those who imagine that the soul is called a spirit because it is a breath or energy divinely diffused into bodies, but devoid of essence, err too grossly, as is shown both by the nature of the thing and the whole tenor of Scripture."[6] And in regard to the question of life in man and creatures Calvin says: "There are three kinds of life in this world. The first is animal life, which consists only of motion and the bodily senses, and which we have in common with the brutes; the second is human life, which we have as children of Adam; and the third is that supernatural life, which believers alone obtain. And all of them are from God, so that each of them may be called *the life of God*. As to the first, Paul in his sermon at Athens says (Acts 17 : 28): 'In Him we live and

---

[1] *Serm. on 2 Tim.* 4 : 5, 6.

[2] *Serm. on Job* 7 : 7 f.: *L'homme n'est qu'un esprit ou un vent qui passe, et qui ne revient plus: il semble bien que l'homme soit accomparé aux bestes brutes, voire: et de fait il seroit semblable, si Dieu n'y mettoit la main. Car d'ou procède l'immortalité qui est en nos ames, si ce n'est d'une faveur speciale que Dieu nous a porté ? Il est dit par sainct Paul (1 Tim. 6 : 16), que Dieu seul est immortel: nous sommes donc caduques, nous ne ferons que nous escouler: et nos ames quoy ? Les Anges mesmes de paradis seroyent aussi bien mortels: mais d'autant que Dieu leur a inspiré sa vertu, il faut qu'ils subsistent en luy. Voila d'où procède leur immortalité, ie di, dès Anges et aussi il faut que de nostre costé nous puisions de ceste fontaine-la: comme il en est parlé au Pseaume (36 : 10), Seigneur c'est en toy que gist la fontaine de vie, et en ta clarté nous serons illuminez. Nous voyons maintenant commes les hommes estans considerez en eux mesmes, n'ont rien que defaillance: comme il est dit en un autre passage au Pseaume 104 (v. 29 s.), Seigneur retire ton Esprit et toutes choses seront aneantis et reduites à neant.*

[3] *C. R.* 53. 61.

[4] This *alienation* is the *death of the soul. Comm. on John* 11 : 25: *Nam mors animæ alienatio est a Deo.*

[5] *Comm. on 2 Cor.* 5 : 1-3.   [6] *Instit.* 1. 15. 2.

move and have our being'; and the Psalmist says: 'Send forth Thy Spirit, and they shall be created; and Thou wilt renew the face of the earth' (Ps. 104 : 30). Of the second, Job says: 'Thou hast granted me life, and Thy visitation hath preserved my spirit' (10 : 12). But the way of believers is called by way of eminence, *the life of God*, when He governs us by His Spirit. Of this all men who are not creatures in Christ are declared by Paul to be destitute."[1]

At this point it may well be stated that Calvin obviously makes an entire break from the Scholastic conception of creation and existence, particularly in the case of man. It represents a return to the essentially dynamic conception of God's relation to the world which we have in the Bible, but which mainly under the influence of Aristotelian thought had been translated into a logical and static relation of being.[2] For Calvin, all secondary causation is highly suspicious, and has no real place in theology. We must think of man therefore as created and maintained in being by direct and continuous relation to the will of God who kills and makes alive. And so Calvin thinks of human existence as being continually consumed and renewed by the Spirit of God. If God were for one instant to withdraw the presence of His Spirit we would drop into the nothingness from which we are called into being. That is just as true of the soul of man as of his body, for both depend from moment to moment in being and endowment on an immediate relation to the gracious and creative will of God.

(c) Man has a special relation to the Word of God through which he receives a peculiar dignity and a peculiar creaturehood. Here Calvin stresses the fact that man was not created by a mere word of command but through divine consultation and gradual transformation. This is the highest honour with which God has dignified man.[3] It is not that there is any distinction of "quality" between man and the beasts, but that God relates Himself to us in a special way.[4] "Three gradations are to be noted in the creation of man; that his dead body was formed out of the dust of the earth; that it was endued with a soul, whence it should receive

---

[1] *Comm. on Eph.* 4 : 18.
[2] It is significant that to the question "What is God's Being?" Calvin answers only with *verbs*—see, for example, *Serm. on Deut.* 32 : 32 f. In other words, Calvin's Biblical doctrine of *the living God* is in complete contrast to the Aristotelian and Scholastic conception of the divine Being.
[3] *Comm. on Gen.* 1 : 26; 2 : 7; *Serm. on Ps.* 27 : 4.
[4] *Serm. on Job* 40 : 20 ff.

vital motion; and that on this soul God engraved His own image, to which immortality is annexed."[1] It is in this way that man is made to outshine all other creatures which the earth has produced, so that there may be a distinct difference between them and him. That difference consists in a special relation to the Word in which man is made uniquely in the image of God. All the world, and all creatures in the world, image the glory of God inasmuch as they are the *workmanship* of God. And inasmuch as man is the workmanship of God, he images God in the same way, though doubtless in a higher degree since he is the noblest of all God's creations. But man images the glory of God in a fashion peculiar to himself alone among all the creatures of the earth. He responds to something that is more than a bare word. He lives upon the *communication* of God's Word.[2] The Word is his very life.[3] The world of things and creatures images the glory of God in that they bear in themselves evident tokens of God's wonderful grace, but man is made in order to be conscious of all these evident tokens. "Here it is another Word that is spoken of . . . for God speaks in a different way to the insensate works of His hands, which He silently subordinates to His will by secret laws impressed upon them, than He does to men who are endued with understanding, for these He teaches with *articulate language*, so that they may obey Him *intelligently and with consent.* . . . This is the grand proof of His love that He has set before us in His Word the light of eternal life."[4] "God created us after His own image in order that His *truth* might shine forth *in us*. It is not God's purpose that men should abolish and destroy the grace which He has put in them, for that would be utterly to deface His image in spite of Him, but rather that as He comes nearer to us, and we to Him, so He will have His image known in us and His truth shine forth in us all the more. Let us understand then that it is not the intention of God that we should be ignorant of Him, but to utter Himself in such a way, that we may be able to distinguish Him from forged idols, that we may take Him for our Father, and assure ourselves that we are called to the knowledge of His truth, and that we may

---

[1] *Comm. on Gen.* 2 : 7.
[2] *Comm. on Gen.* 2 : 9; 3 : 23. Cf. *on Luke* 11 : 27: "Without the Word He has no intercourse with us, nor we with Him. Communicating Himself by His Word, He rightly and properly calls us to hear and keep it, that by faith He may become ours." See also *Instit.* 4. 17. 8.
[3] *Serm. on Deut.* 32 : 44 f.; *Comm. on John* 1 : 4, 9.
[4] *Comm. on Ps.* 147. 19. This is what Calvin constantly calls God's *familiar Word.* See *Serm. on Job* 35 : 8 f.; 37 : 1 f.; *Instit.* 1. 5. 9; 1. 6. 1.

boldly resort to Him to call upon Him and seek succour at His hand."[1] Man is intended, then, to image the glory of God in his grateful acknowledgment of God's kindness and mercy, and in recognition of his utter dependence upon God the Father.[2] That is why God made man a living soul, not only in the sense in which he has a living body, but in the sense that he has a mind in order to meditate on the heavenly life in which he finds the true destiny of his being in the image of God.[3] It is this knowledge which forms man into the image of God.[4] Therefore "nothing is more absurd than that men should be ignorant of their Author who are endued with understanding principally for this use."[5] Men have being in God in the same sense as all other created being, and they have motion or animation in the same sense as other living creatures, but they have a higher life in God peculiar to them as men which can only be described in terms of *light*. And here Calvin laid great stress upon the words of John's Gospel: "And the life was the light of men."[6] "John speaks here of that part of *life* in which men excel other animals; and informs us that *the life* which was bestowed on *men* was not of an ordinary description, but was united to the *light* of the understanding . . . As it is not in vain that God imparts His *light* to their minds, it follows that the purpose for which they were created was, that they might acknowledge Him who is the Author of so excellent a blessing. And since this *light*, of which the *Word* was the source, has been conveyed from Him to us, it ought to serve as a mirror, in which we may clearly behold the divine power of the *Word*."[7] By the power of the Word this "*light* was originally bestowed on men",[8] and by the life-giving power of the Word man is sustained as a creature, and enlightened as a man, though it can be maintained as *light* in man, that is as spiritual *life*, only by acknowledging the blessing of the Creator, and it is turned into *darkness*, that is spiritual death, by revolt and perversity.[9] Therefore man's true life consists in the light of his understanding in so far as that is reflexive of the glory of God revealed through His Word. It is thus that men resemble God.[10]

[1] *Serm. on Deut.* 4 : 10 f.
[2] *Comm. on Acts* 17 : 28.
[3] *Comm. on Acts* 17 : 27.
[4] *Comm. on John* 17 : 3.
[5] *Comm. on Acts* 17 : 27; cf. *on Ps.* 96 : 10.
[6] *Comm. on John* 1 : 4; *on Acts* 17 : 28.
[7] *Comm. on John* 1 : 4.
[8] *Comm. on John* 1 : 5.
[9] *Ibid.* Cf. *Comm. on Gen.* 2 : 9.
[10] *Comm. on Acts* 17 : 28; *on Ps.* 36 : 9; 119 : 73; *Instit.* 1. 15. 3. Calvin thinks of goodness, righteousness, holiness, and truth as the *fruit of light* in the understanding, and therefore as the way in which men may resemble God (*Serm. on Eph.* 5 : 8-11).

It is just here that self-knowledge plays its part, for man must be prevented from burying the noble qualities which distinguish him from the beasts, in order to pursue his true life and destiny in the Kingdom of God.[1] In order to live, man must be conscious of his creaturehood, and conscious of his intellectual endowments, so that over and above his creaturely relation to the Word, he might have a knowledgeable relation in which his existence in the bare Word is raised to the level of a celestial life in being familiarly united to God: hence the different method God adopted in fashioning man. Therefore "if all men are born and live for the express purpose of learning to know God, and if the knowledge of God in so far as it fails to produce this effect is fleeting and vain, it is clear that all those who do not direct all the thoughts and actions of their lives to this end fail to fulfil the law of their being".[2] "And, indeed, man would want the principal use of his understanding if he were unable to discern his felicity, the perfection of which consists in being united to God. Hence the principal action of the soul is to aspire thither, and accordingly the more a man studies to approach to God, the more he proves himself to be endued with reason."[3] We may state this in other words by saying that only when a man knows himself to be a creature utterly dependent on the grace of God is he able in his knowledge of God so to live in a thankful fashion corresponding to the motion of grace that he reflects in the mirror of his intelligent life the glory of God. Or again, man has been created an intelligent being in order to know God in such a way that in the act of knowing (*acknowledgment*, as Calvin would say) man is brought to re-live consciously and in a qualitatively new fashon (*celestial* is Calvin's word) the very movement of grace in which he is created and maintained in being, so as to be carried beyond himself in responsible union with God, in whom he finds his true life and felicity, *i.e.*, in the image of God.[4] "The true happiness of men is to have the favour and love of God. And we are sure of His fatherly goodness toward us, if when He calls us by His Word, we accept that grace by faith. The inseparable bond then between God and man is that they receive the Word of His goodness which He gives to them, and that serves equally for this present life as for their everlasting life."[5]

[1] *Instit.* 2. 1. 1, 3: *Serm. on Job* 14 : 1 f.; 19 : 26 f.
[2] *Instit.* 1. 3. 3.
[3] *Instit.* 1. 15. 6.
[4] *Instit.* 1. 15. 3; *Serm. on Deut.* 6 : 4 f.
[5] *Serm. on Deut.* 32 : 28 f.

Calvin goes on to point out that this "life is termed a passage or a path";[1] Even before his fall man's life "had no firm and settled constancy", for he had not as yet attained celestial life.[2] As we have already noted, man has been designedly placed in this world with its evident tokens of divine solicitude and mercy that his whole mind and soul might be directed toward God, and that his true life should consist precisely in carrying out that relation to God. "When a man knows not wherefore God created him, nor has the skill to perceive to what end he is set in the world, I pray you, ought it to be said properly speaking that he lives?"[3] In other words, we do not really possess a life different from that of the beasts unless we know that our being and knowing are due to God alone. We must be able to trace the light of our under-standing wherein we resemble God back to its source in God, realizing that in so doing we are brought into immediate relation to the very fountain of life. Otherwise the light shines in darkness, and the darkness comprehends it not. But no man can be said to live in the proper sense of the word in that condition.[4]

Because "our minds are unable to pierce so far, having nature only for our guide",[5] and because of the "inefficacy of God's image imprinted on the fair form of the universe",[6] man is given the assistance of the Word so that through it the evident but mute tokens[7] of God's grace in the creation of the world may be witnesses to God's glory in such a way that His speech goes out to the very ends of the earth.[8] Without the Word the splendid representation of the glory of God in the world would profit man nothing.[9] Therefore his "special duty is to give ear to the Word".[10] According to Calvin, therefore, man had a primeval revelation which enabled him to live in communion with the Creator of the world, which indeed was continued to a certain extent after the fall of man.[11] Of this original Word Calvin thinks the tree of life planted in the garden was the sacramental symbol, so that it was

[1] *Serm. on Ps.* 27 : 4.
[2] *Comm. on Gen.* 2 : 7; *Serm. on Deut.* 28 : 65 f.
[3] *Serm. on Job* 14 : 1 f.
[4] This is the substance of Calvin's argument in passages such as *Comm. on John* 1 : 4 f.; *on Acts* 17 : 27, 28.　　　　　　　　[6] *Instit.* 1. 6. 3.
[5] *Comm. on Acts* 17 : 27.
[7] *Ibid.; Introd. Arg. to Comm. on Gen.; Comm. on Acts* 14 : 17; *Serm. on Job* 2 : 1 f. Cf. 12 : 7 f.: "When it is said that the beasts teach us, that is not by their examples, but because we have to behold the glory of God in them."
[8] *Comm. on Ps.* 19 : 7.
[9] *Ibid.; Introd. Arg. in Comm. on Gen.*
[10] *Instit.* 1. 6. 2; 1. 15. 6; *Serm. on Job.* 33 : 29 f.; 34 : 16 f.
[11] *Instit.* 1. 6. 2.

intended by God that "as often as man tasted of the fruit of that tree, he should remember whence he received his life, in order that he might acknowledge that he lives not by his own power, but by the kindness of God alone; and that life is not (as they commonly say) an intrinsic good, but proceeds from God".[1] Thus "the life of all things was included in the Word, but especially the life of men, which is conjoined with reason and intelligence. . . . Wherefore by this sign Adam was admonished that he could claim nothing for himself as if it were his own, and might not seek life anywhere but in Him. . . . *He possessed life only as deposited in the Word of God, and could not otherwise retain it than by acknowledging that it was received from Him.*"[2] This means that like all other creatures man lives in the continual renewal of the creative Word,[3] but unlike other creatures he has special endowments which he must use in continual acknowledgment of and response to God's gracious self-communication in which alone he finds his true life and destiny.[4] In that life of thankful relation to God, man reflects the divine glory in an image which is the *internal good* of the soul.[5] For a man to be ungrateful in a refusal to acknowledge the grace of God is to deface the image of God in him, to un-man himself, and to become a beast or a creature without *light* in his understanding.[6] It is in the doctrine of the *imago dei* that Calvin brings together his teaching about the relation of man, as an intelligent being, to the Word and grace of God.

[1] *Comm. on Gen.* 2 : 9; cf. *on Matt.* 4 : 4.
[2] *Comm. on Gen.* 2 : 9; cf. *on Gen.* 3 : 6; 3 : 22; *on Eph.* 1 : 10; *Instit.* 2. 2. 10.
[3] *Comm. on Gen.* 2 : 2; *on Ps.* 104: 29.
[4] *Serm. on Job* 10 : 7 f.
[5] *Instit.* 1. 15. 4. But Calvin makes it quite clear that this *bonum internum* is also *a bonum adventitium; Comm. on Gen.* 2 : 7.
[6] *Serm. on Deut.* 28 : 46 f.

Chapter Three

THE IMAGE OF GOD (1)

Calvin uses imago dei *in a twofold sense: (1) In a general sense, in which all creation is said to reflect (as in a mirror) the glory of God. God images Himself in nature, by beholding the works of His hands. This workmanship, however, may be regarded as a mute reflection of His glory, until it is made to speak of God by means of the Word which, properly speaking, is the image of God. It is by this Word that man is really able to see the glory of God imaged in creation. (2) In a particular sense, in which man specially is said to reflect (as in a mirror) the glory of God, by an intelligible response to the Word. Strictly speaking, it is God who images Himself in man, and that means that He graciously embraces man as His child in Christ the express Image of His glory. It is as man answers this gracious decision in love and faith that he bears the image of God. As a parallel to this imago-relation between man and God, Calvin points to the relation of Adam and Eve in their mutual society, and just proportion, and in the response and obedience of one to the other. The characteristic order of this imago-relation Calvin calls rectitude. In its general sense, rectitude refers to constant dependence upon God, the order of grace in which the world was made, the order of creation. This is particularly reflected by man in his obedience to the familiar Word of God, and in his filial response to the Father who is pleased to look upon him as His son, and to image Himself in him. Because men have been created for such intercourse and communion with God, they have intercourse and society among themselves so that their life in community, characterized by rectitude, may image the glory of God. This is the legitimate and original order of creation, but it has been overthrown by the ingratitude of men and perverted through sin. That is the cause of the present disorder in the world and the alienation between man and man, as well as between man and God. This can be repaired only by an act of grace in which the original order of creation is restored, and which may be realized among men as they respond in obedience, and become nothing but vessels of the mercy of God. In such children of obedience God reflects Himself again in men as in a mirror.*

I T is in his teaching about the *imago dei* that Calvin sets forth his doctrine of the creaturehood of man in relation to God.[1] In the nature of the case, that is possible only from the standpoint

---

[1] Calvin does not make any distinction between *image* and *likeness*; *Comm. on Gen.* 1 : 26; *Instit.* 1. 15. 3.

of the man renewed in Jesus Christ. If man does not truly know himself until he knows God truly, and until in that knowing of God he becomes a true man, then it is only from the standpoint of renewed man face to face with God in Christ that we may understand the significance of the fact that man is made in the image of God. Moreover, the coming of God in Christ and His self-communication to man have taken such a form in the incarnation that it is there only that we may see human nature set forth in its truth as creature made for a filial relation to the heavenly Father. Thus there can be no question of trying to understand man out of himself or from his relation to the world. He must be understood exclusively from the Word made flesh. It is while we behold the Word made flesh to be the glory of the only begotten of the Father, full of grace and truth that we know not only that we are born to be sons of God, but that our relation as sons to the Father rests, not on the will of man or on any natural character belonging to him, but, in faith, on the will and power of God alone. Again it is when we see Christ to be the express image of God, that is in substance and reality, that we understand what it is for man in conformity to Christ to reflect that image so that while he is in the image of God he is only an image in regard to God. It is the *imago dei* interpreted in this light that carries in the theology of Calvin his view of man.

Calvin's use of the expression *imago dei*, however, is much wider than his doctrine of the image of God in man which expresses man's peculiar relation to God as a conscious witness to His grace and glory. This has been a fruitful source of confusion in the understanding of Calvin's thought; and not without some justification, for it is difficult to see how Calvin is always consistent himself. No doubt, once we grasp his use of *imago dei*, a great deal of the apparent inconsistency will disappear.

reflection There is no doubt that Calvin always thinks of the *imago* in terms of a *mirror*. Only while the mirror actually reflects an object does it have the image of that object. There is no such thing in Calvin's thought as an *imago* dissociated from the act of reflecting. He does use such expressions as *engrave* and *sculptured*, but only in a metaphorical sense and never dissociated from the idea of the mirror.[1] Where the thought is of the mirroring of

---

[1] Calvin can also speak of God's covenant as *engraven* on the bodies of children in baptism (*Instis*. 4. 16. 9). Faith is said to be *engraven* on our hearts (*Comm. on Matt.* 13 : 21). This is the metaphor of the *seal*, for which *see below*, p. 37.

God, properly speaking the mirror is always the Word. "The Word itself, whatever be the way in which it is conveyed to us, is a kind of mirror in which faith beholds God. In this, therefore, whether God uses the agency of man or works immediately by His own power, it is always by His Word that He manifests Himself to those whom He designs to draw to Himself."[1] It is not often that Calvin uses the expression *imago dei* except in this intimate association with mirror and word. "God was never willing to be disjoined from His Word, because He is Himself invisible, and never appears otherwise than in a mirror."[2] This gives us, I believe, the key to Calvin's apparent confusion of thought.

In what we have called the wider sense of the *imago, imago dei* may be used of anything in the universe created by God. Both the world as a whole and the tiniest creature are said to image the glory of God. Thus he says: "God has been pleased so to manifest His perfections in the whole structure of the universe, and daily place Himself in our view, that we cannot open our eyes without being compelled to behold Him. His essence indeed is incomprehensible, utterly transcending all human thought, but on each of His works is engraven in characters so bright, so distinct, and so illustrious, that none however dull and illiterate can plead ignorance as their excuse. Hence with perfect truth, the Psalmist exclaims (Ps. 104 : 2), 'He covereth Himself with light as with a garment', as if He had said that God for the first time was arrayed in visible attire when in the creation of the world He displayed those glorious banners on which, to whatever side we turn, we behold His perfections visibly portrayed. In the same place the Psalmist aptly compares the expanded heavens to His royal tent, and says, 'He layeth the beams of His chambers in the waters, maketh the clouds His chariot, and walketh upon the wings of the wind', sending forth the winds and lightnings as His swift messengers. And because the glory of His power and wisdom is more refulgent in the firmament, it is frequently designated as His place. And, first, wherever you turn your eyes there is no portion of the world, however minute, that does not exhibit at least some sparks of beauty; while it is impossible to

[1] *Instit.* 3. 2. 6.
[2] *Comm. on Ezek.* 13 : 19. Cf. *also on John* 1 : 1: "*Word* is said to be, among men, the *image of the mind;* so it is not inappropriate to apply this to God, and to say that He reveals Himself to us by His *Word.*" Sometimes Calvin uses instead of the *mirror* the metaphor of a *seal*, e.g., *on John* 17 : 11, 22.

contemplate the vast and beautiful fabric as it extends around
without being overwhelmed by the immense weight of glory.
Hence, the author of the Epistle to the Hebrews elegantly
describes the visible worlds as images of the invisible (Heb. 11 : 3),
the elegant structure of the world serving as a kind of mirror in
which we may behold God, though otherwise invisible. For the
same reason the Psalmist attributes language to celestial objects, a
language which all nations understand (Ps. 19 : 1), the manifestation of the Godhead being too clear to escape the notice of any
people however obtuse. The Apostle Paul stating this more
clearly says: 'That which may be known of God is manifest in
them, for God hath showed it unto them. For the invisible things
of Him from the creation of the world are clearly seen, being
understood by the things that are made, even His eternal power
and Godhead (Rom. 1 : 20)' ".[1] In the following sections of the
Institutes from which this citation is taken, Calvin goes on to
point out that the shameful ingratitude and pride of man mean
that he employs this very manifestation of God "to put out the
light intended to exhibit God clearly to their minds" . . .
"minds which are not afraid to employ the seed of Deity deposited
in human nature as a means of suppressing the name of God."[2]
Consequently, "bright as is the manifestation which God both
gives of Himself and His immortal Kingdom in the mirror of His
works, so great is our stupidity, so dull are we in regard to these
bright manifestations, that we derive no benefit from them"[3];
that is, apart from the Word.[4] Calvin's position, however, is
that "if man had not fallen" he would be able to see the imaging
of God in the universe as God originally intended.[5]

Under this wider sense, *imago dei* refers to the *workmanship*[6] of
God in the universe, and that includes man himself as the pre-
eminent specimen of God's handiwork.[7] Calvin attacks the
suggestion of Osiander that when the Bible speaks of man being
made in the image of God it refers to his bodily form,[8] but in this
sense he has no hesitation in attributing *imago* even to the physical

[1] *Instit.* I. 5. 1. See also *Comm. on Rom.* 1 : 19; 10 : 18.
[2] *Instit.* I. 5. 4. [3] *Instit.* I. 5. 11.
[4] *Instit.* I. 5. 14; I. 6. 3; *Comm. on Heb.* 11 : 3.
[5] *Instit.* I. 2. 1: "*Atque hic nondum attingo eam notitiæ speciem, qua homines in se perditi ac maledicti Deum redemptorem in Christo mediatore apprehendunt; sed tantum de prima illa et simplici loquor, ad quam nos deduceret genuinus naturæ ordo si integer stetisset Adam.*"
[6] *Comm. on Rom.* 1 : 19 f.; 10 : 18.
[7] *Instit.* I. 5. 3; I. 14. 20. [8] *Instit.* I. 15. 4.

person of man inasmuch as he has been fashioned by the hands of God and in the wonders of his body bears evident tokens of God's grace.[1] But apart from the body as such, rays of God's glory can be seen reflected in all man's natural gifts and faculties.[2] That applies particularly to man as an intelligent being with his marvellous faculties of thought and imagination by which his mental glance transcends the body and reaches out to heaven and earth, the past, present, and even in a sense to the future.[3] Thus *imago dei* in its wider reference to man refers to "the perfection of our whole nature . . . as appeared when Adam was endued with a right judgment, had affections in harmony with reason, had all his senses sound and well regulated, and truly excelled in everything good.[4] Thus the chief seat of the divine image was in his mind and heart where it was eminent; yet there was no part of him in which scintillations of it did not shine forth. For there was an attempering of it in the several parts of the soul which corresponded with their various offices. In the mind perfect intelligence flourished and reigned, uprightness attended as its companion, and all the senses were prepared and moulded for due obedience to reason; and in the body there was a suitable correspondence with this internal order."[5] Here Calvin's wider sense of *imago* begins to pass over into the narrower sense, but the reason for that will become clear later.

At this point we are forced to ask ourselves a question. If *imago dei* in this wider sense refers to the reflection of God's glory in His workmanship when it is used as a mirror, who is it that does the beholding? Strictly speaking, there can be no image where there is no one beholding. And that is the point of Calvin's thought. Primarily, it is God Himself who beholds His own glory in the works of His hand,[6] or rather who images Himself in these works.[7] "It is certain that He acknowledges His own work. God looks upon Himself, as one might say, and beholds Himself in men as in a mirror"[8]—and here Calvin is speaking of

---

[1] *Instit.* 2. 12. 7; 3. 20. 31.
[2] *Comm. on Gen.* 1 : 26; *Instit.* 1. 15. 3 f. [3] *Instit.* 1. 15. 2.
[4] This is what Calvin so often calls *integrity*. Cf. *Brief Confession of Faith*, Eng. tr. by Beveridge, p. 131: "I confess that man was created in the image of God, *i.e.*, endued with full integrity of spirit, will, and all parts of the soul, faculties and senses." See also *Instit.* 1. 15. 3, 4.
[5] *Comm. on Gen.* 1 : 26. See also *Instit.* 1. 15. 3-5.
[6] *Serm. on Job* 10 : 7 f. [7] *Instit.* 1. 15. 3.
[8] *Serm. on Job* 10 : 7 f.: "*Il est certain qu'il recognoist son ouvrage. Dieu par maniere de dire se mire et se contemple aux hommes: ce n'est point sans cause qu'il a regardé tout ce qu'il avoit fait et qu'il l'a trouvé bon.*"

men as God's workmanship.[1] But man looks into the mirror of creation, too; and he also beholds the image of God there, only he does it through the Word, which, properly speaking, is the image of God.[2] Thus, for example, Calvin says: "When it is said that the beasts teach us, that is not by their examples but because we have to behold the glory of God in them."[3] The works of creation teach us, doubtless by their "mute instruction",[4] but all this is of no avail apart from the Word. Therefore "it is in vain for any to reason as philosophers upon the workmanship of the World".[5] "We must not therefore commence with the elements of this world", but "keep to this one point", namely, "the eternal Word of God" which is "the lively and express image of God".[6] Even Adam needed the Word in order to know God as Creator, apart altogether from knowing Him as Redeemer.[7] The reasons for this are not difficult to find.

Because the image of God imprinted on the fair form of the universe was *inefficacious*[8] and because it is difficult to hear God's Word when it is merely *uttered in the air*,[9] Calvin maintains, God gave man the Word and special symbols to attest the Word.[10] It is here that Calvin brings in his interesting doctrine of the ancient sacraments which God gave to Adam and Eve in such symbols as the tree of life and the tree of the knowledge of Good and Evil, and to fallen man in such natural events as the rainbow— a doctrine which helps to make clear to us the relation which Calvin envisaged between the Word and both the *dumb teachers*[11] of nature and the *common light of nature*[12] which is essential to man as his true life. Speaking of these natural symbols, Calvin says: "They had a mark engraven on them by the Word of God, to be proofs and seals of His covenant. The tree was previously a tree, and the bow a bow; but when *inscribed with the Word of God*, a new form was given to them: they began to be what they previously were not. . . . God as the Lord and Governor of nature, at His pleasure, makes all things subservient to His glory. If He had impressed memorials of this description on the sun, the stars, the earth, and stones, they would all have been to

---

[1] Ibid. "Il regarde à son œuvre et à sa fracture."
[2] Introd. Arg. in Comm. on Gen.   [3] Serm. on Job 12 : 7 f.
[4] Introd. Arg. in Comm. on Gen.   [5] Ibid.
[6] Introd. Arg. in Comm. on Gen.; cf. Comm. on John 1 : 18; on Heb. 1 : 3.
[7] Instit. 1. 6. 1.   [8] Instit. 1. 6. 3.   [9] Instit. 1. 6. 4.
[10] Instit. 1. 6. 2: Semper enim Deus indubiam fecit verbo suo fidem, quæ omni opinione superior esset.
[11] Instit. 1. 6. 1.   [12] Comm. on John 1 : 5, 8.

us as sacraments. For why are the shapeless and the coined silver not of the same value, seeing they are the same metal? Just because the former has nothing but its own nature, whereas the latter, impressed with the public stamp, becomes money and receives a new value. And shall the Lord not be able to stamp His creatures with His Word, that things which were formerly bare elements may become sacraments? . . . The ancient sacraments had the same end in view as our own, viz., to direct and almost lead us by the hand to Christ, or rather, were like *images* to represent Him and hold Him forth to our knowledge."[1]

If these selected elements of nature need a *special* relation to the *Word* before they are able to *image* God as He is familiarly exhibited to us in Christ the *Word*, how much more do the general elements of nature need the *Word* before they can in a less familiar fashion *image the glory of God to men?* "It is very true that we are not sufficiently instructed by that bare and simple, but magnificent, testimony which the creatures bear to the glory of their Creator."[2] "Therefore He has added the light of His Word."[3] Calvin employs several times in this connection the metaphor of spectacles, for man needs the Word as a pair of spectacles in order to be able to see the imaging of the glory of God in nature.[4] "It is by faith alone that we know that it was God who created the world."[5] "But faith is not conceived by the bare beholding of heaven and earth."[6] "We profit little in the contemplation of universal nature if we do not behold with the eyes of faith that spiritual glory of which an image is presented to us in the world."[7] "It is thus manifest that God, foreseeing the inefficacy of His image imprinted on the fair form of the universe, has given us the assistance of the Word."[8] All this means that behind Calvin's wider sense of the *imago dei* he thinks of the image as the reflection

---

[1] *Instit.* 4. 14. 18, 20. These ancient sacraments, however, did not give the *same familiar* knowledge as we have in Christ and the Christian sacraments (4. 14. 22). But at the same time through the Word and these ancient sacraments the patriarchs were able to gain a familiar knowledge of God; such was impossible to unbelievers (1. 6. 1).

[2] *Instit.* 1. 5. 15: *Verissimum tamen est, nuda ista et simplici testificatione, qua Dei gloria a creaturis magnifice redditur, nequaquam nos sufficienter erudiri.*

[3] *Instit.* 1. 6. 1. Cf. *Comm. on Ezek.* 2 : 3: "If signs only are permitted to our eyes, they will be, as it were, *dead images.* The Word of God, then, throws life into the sacraments." Also *on Jer.* 27 : 1 f.: "All signs are as it were dead, except life is given them by the Word. As then an image avails not so much, whatever signs may be set before our eyes they would be frivolous and without meaning, were no doctrine added as the life."

[4] *Introd. Arg. in Comm. on Gen.*; *Instit.* 1. 6. 1; 1. 14. 1.

[5] *Comm. on Hebrews* 11 : 3.

[6] *Comm. on Acts* 14 :17.

[7] *Comm. on Ps.* 104 : 4.

[8] *Instit.* 1. 6. 3.

seen by the eye of man who, coming down from his knowledge of God, reads it into nature, or who by means of the Word makes the *mute* creation speak of the glory of God.[1] Therefore Calvin's wider use of the *imago dei* is grounded upon the special relation of man to the Word of God, that is, upon the narrower sense of the *imago dei*. This narrower sense of the image is the important one, and it is in this sense that the expression *imago dei* should most properly be used. "Though the divine glory is displayed in man's outward appearance, it cannot be doubted that the proper seat of the image is the soul. . . . Let it be understood that the image of God which is beheld or made conspicuous by these external marks is *spiritual*."[2] By this, man is sharply distinguished from the rest of God's creation. "It is certain that in every part of the world some lineaments of the divine glory are beheld, and hence we may infer that when His image is placed in man there is a kind of tacit antithesis, as it were, setting man apart from the crowd, and exalting him above all other creatures."[3]

It is important to note, however, that even in the narrower sense it is, fundamentally, God who does the beholding of the image. He images Himself in man. "Man was created therefore in the image of God, and in him the Creator was pleased to behold as in a mirror His own glory."[4] It is a corollary to this that the image of God in man is really Christ, the Son of God; that is, the express image or the lively image of God.[5] "Christ was even then the image of God and accordingly whatever excellence was engraven on Adam had its origin in this, that by means of the only begotten Son he approximated to the glory of His Maker. . . . To this degree of honour he was exalted by the kindness of the only begotten Son."[6] This means, however, that the image of God is really more in Christ than in men; more therefore in the favour and grace of God than in the being of man.[7] "God accepts and takes pleasure in His children, in whom He sees the traces and lineaments of His own countenance. We have said

---

[1] *Comm. on Ps.* 19 : 7; 145 : 10; *Instit.* 1. 6. 1.　　　　[3] *Instit.* 1. 15. 3.
[2] *Instit.* 1. 15. 3; see also 1. 15. 4; *Comm. on James* 3 : 9.
[4] *Instit.* 2. 12. 6.
[5] *Comm. on Matt.* 22 : 11: *Scimus non aliter reformari nos in imaginem Dei, nisi dum Christum induimus.* See especially *Serm. on* 1 Tim. 2 : 15, 16.
[6] *Instit.* 2. 12. 6.
[7] Cf. *Comm. on Rom.* 2 : 11: *Si quis autem cavilletur, non esse igitur gratuitam Dei electionem: respondendum, esse duplicem hominis acceptionem coram Deo, primam, qua nos ex nihilo vocatos gratuita bonitate cooptat: quum nihil sit in natura nostra, quod illi probari queat, alteram, qua ubi nos regeneravit, etiam cum suis donis amplectitur: ac quam in nobis recognoscit Filii sui imaginem, favore suo prosequitur.*

elsewhere that regeneration is a renewal of the divine image in us. Since God, therefore, whenever He beholds His own face, justly loves it and holds it in honour, the life of believers when formed to holiness and justice is said not without cause to be pleasing to Him. But because believers when encompassed with mortal flesh are still sinners and their good works only begun savour of the corruption of the flesh, God cannot be propitious either to their persons or their works, unless He embraces them more in Christ than in themselves."[1] That is spoken of the redeemed man, but it is also true of man in his original state. Whether in man originally or in man renewed in Christ, the image of God is basically that which God sees and fashions by His grace, the garment or ornament or badge with which He adorns men to mark them out as His sons.[2]

It may help us to understand this if we examine what Calvin has to say about the relation between Adam and Eve as man and wife. God so created them that "Adam was taught to recognise himself in his wife as in a mirror; and Eve in her turn to submit herself willingly to her husband."[3] This image Adam did not see in any of the other creatures which God had made; there was no "affinity of nature", nor "just proportion" between them and him.[4] And so he was not able to choose for himself out of them a "companion for life".[5] God created Eve out of Adam in such a way that the two should be one, and that each should be incomplete without the other,[6] and that the two together might "cultivate mutual society between themselves".[7] Thus a man's wife is intended by God to be "a kind of counterpart, for the woman is said to be *opposite to* or *over against* the man because she responds to him".[8] This was designed that there might be "a friendly connection" between them.[9] And so man "obtained a

---

[1] *Instit.* 3. 17. 5.
[2] *Instit.* 3. 17. 6. The metaphors ornament, garment, etc., in relation to the *imago dei* make it clear that it does not refer to man's natural being. Hence the sonship which it confers is one of adoption. "That we are sons of God we have not from nature, but from adoption and grace only." *The Catechism of the Church of Geneva*, Eng. tr. by Beveridge, p. 43. See also *Comm. on Matt.* 10 : 31: "The sons of God possess a far higher right than they derive from creation. The rank which belongs to men arises solely from the undeserved kindness of God."
[3] *Comm. on Gen.* 2 : 21.
[4] *Comm. on Gen.* 2 : 19. The expressions are *naturæ affinitas* and *æquabilis proportio*.
[5] *Comm. on Gen.* 2 : 20.
[6] *Comm. on Gen.* 1 : 27; 2 : 23 f.; *Comm. on Malachi* 2 : 15; *on* 1 *Cor.* 11 : 10; *Serm. on Eph.* 5 : 31-33.
[7] *Comm. on Gen.* 2 : 18; *on* 1 *Cor.* 11 :12.   [8] *Ibid.*
[9] *Comm. on* 1 *Cor.* 11 : 12: *Ita hæc erit ratio amicæ coniunctionis.*

faithful associate of life, for he now saw himself who before had been imperfect rendered complete in his wife. And in this we see a true resemblance of our union with the Son of God. For He became weak that He might have the members of His body endued with strength."[1] Calvin draws out this resemblance a little more when he comments on Paul's statement that the woman is the glory of man as he is the image and glory of God.[2] There is a relation of proportionality (to borrow a word from Aquinas) between the imago-relation between Christ and the Father on the one hand and the imago-relation between the woman and man on the other hand. And this imago-relation is also seen in the relation of man, and man and woman together, to God through union with the Son. Calvin does not quite say that it is as man and woman are one in a mutual society that they image the glory of God, but that seems to be implied again and again. The particular element in this imago-relation which Calvin singles out for comment is the *sacred bond* of union or *government* or *order* or *superiority* between man and wife and between God and man.[3] Here, he says, "the question is respecting that glory of God which peculiarly shines forth in human nature where the mind, the will, and all the senses, represent the divine order".[4] In the same connection Calvin thinks of man's dominion over the creatures in which he is designed to reflect the order and government of God.[5] The favourite expressions he uses for this order or relation are *temperatura* and *rectitudo*. Being made in the image of God means being brought into a holy and sacred bond of order with God, to whom we are to submit ourselves obediently and thankfully, and in which the whole of our human nature receives its inner and outer *temperature*, and *rectitude* and *integrity*. When the image is defaced the *order of nature is inverted*,[6] and decay and ruin set in. The life and integrity of man depend on keeping the divinely appointed order:[7] complete dependence on God the heavenly Father.

We may now say that the image of God in Calvin's special sense has to do with man's unique relation to God in His self-

---

[1] *Comm. on Gen.* 2 : 21.   [2] *Comm. on* 1 *Cor.* 11 : 7 f.
[3] Cf. *Serm. on Job* 10 : 7 f.: "The image of God is imprinted in us . . . because men are born to have some common order and society among themselves". See also on *Eph.* 4 : 17-19.
[4] *Comm. on Gen.* 1 : 26.
[5] *Ibid.; Comm. on Rom.* 8 : 21; *Serm. on Deut.* 16 : 18 f.
[6] *Comm. on Gen.* 2 : 18.   [7] *Comm. on Gen.* 2 : 16 f.; *on Ps.* 8 : 5.

communication and His glory, not just through the bare Word of command but through a *familiar* Word which brings man into a friendly relation with the Father.[1] "God sends His Word to us in order to be joined to us and that we also may be united to Him, so that He requires nothing but obedience that we may be His children and He show Himself to be our Father. . . . Seeing we have God's Word, we have a record of the fact that He desires to be one with us, and to do the duty of a father, and to maintain us all in prosperity—if we bury not His grace, nor withhold the thing that is due on our part."[2] That was the distinction and dignity conferred on man in the mode of his creation and in his gradual formation through the Word. He was created an intelligent being capable of response to and communication with God, and created such that his true life depends on the maintenance of that communication. At the same time such a creation meant that men are made for intercourse with one another. Man is essentially a "social animal".[3] To this end all men are bound together by the sacred bond of the *imago dei*,[4] and must treat each other in a mutual society only as in the image of God.[5] Though Calvin does not state it as expressly as this, no doubt because such language was not so familiar to him as it is to us, this is his thought. It is in this community of man with God and man with man that we have been created to image the glory of the Godhead. In other words, it is as believers are bound together in the mutual relations of the Body of Christ, so that, while many, they are one in the perfect Man, that through the Spirit of unity and love and Truth they image the unity of the Father and the Son. Commenting upon the words "That they may be one as We are", Calvin says: "This points the way in which they shall be kept, for those whom the heavenly Father has decreed to keep, He brings together in a *holy unity* of faith and of the Spirit. But as it is not enough that men be agreed in some manner, He adds, *As We are.* Then will our unity be truly happy, when it shall bear the image

[1] *Instit.* 2. 6. 1; cf. *Comm. on Micah* 7 : 20: "Except God speak we cannot form in our minds any idea of His grace but what is uncertain and vanishing. But when He declares that He will be merciful to us, then every doubt is removed." *On Jer.* 38 : 23 f.: "The true and right knowledge of God begins here, when we know Him to be merciful toward us." It is a thankful response to this familiar Word that images the grace and glory of God.

[2] *Serm. on Deut.* 5 : 28 f.

[3] *Comm. on Gen.* 2 : 18; 2 : 21 f.; *Introd. Arg. in Comm. on Gen.; Comm. on Gal.* 5 : 15; *Instit.* 2. 2. 13; 2. 8. 39; 3. 7. 6.

[4] *Comm. on Ps.* 8 : 5.   [5] *Comm. on Gen.* 9 : 6; *on Ps.* 8 : 5.

of God the Father and of Christ, as wax takes the form of the seal which is impressed upon it."[1] Schism in the Christian community detracts from the glory of God, and divides Christ asunder. That is what happened at the fall of man when men were alienated from God and alienated from one another, although all men were made to be in the image of God. Therefore the true glory and image of God in men will not be restored until Christ as the Head *gathers all together in Himself* and restores the original rectitude between God and man, and man and man.[2] As regards the image of God in general, we must say that only as man maintains his original relation with God in which he finds his true being, is he also in a true relation with other men. When he becomes alienated from God so that the *imago dei* is defaced in him, he becomes alienated both from himself and from his fellows.[3]

In his *Introductory Argument to the Commentary on Genesis* Calvin sums up the account of the creation of man thus: "After the world had been created, man was placed in it as a theatre that he, beholding above him and beneath the wonderful works of God, might reverently adore their Author. Secondly, that all things were ordained for the use of man that he, *being under deeper obligation*, might devote and dedicate himself entirely to obedience towards God. Thirdly, that he was endued with understanding and reason, that being distinguished from brute animals he might meditate on a better life, and might even tend directly towards God, whose image he bore engraven on his own person."[4] The thought of Calvin is that in distinction from the animals man has been created with far greater endowments than they, and therefore with greater attestations of God's grace, and that he has been made to be conscious of the grace of God not through mere intelligence and reason but by means of a living communication in which he is brought into close relation with God, so that as man is under far deeper obligation to God than the other creatures, he is bound to yield to God a response of gratitude for His grace in a far deeper way, that is, by *imago*—it is for that very purpose that he has been created, and that response is his very life. "God in creating man gave a demon-

---

[1] *Comm. on John* 17 : 11. See also on verses 21, 22; and *on Eph.* 4 : 3-6, 11-16.
[2] See *Comm. on John* 17 : 21; *Serm. on Eph.* 4 : 6-8.
[3] *Comm. on Gen.* 3 : 1 f.; 9 : 6 f.
[4] He goes on to say: "Afterwards followed the fall of Adam whereby he alienated himself from God; whence it came to pass that he was deprived of all rectitude."

stration of His infinite grace and Fatherly love towards him."[1]
"He bears towards him a fatherly love, defends and cherishes him,
and extends His providence towards him."[2] It is man's duty to
"stir himself up to celebrate the free and undeserved goodness
of God" who "though He was under no necessity of choosing
men who are dust and clay" yet "condescended to adorn him
with numerous blessings". "How is it that God . . . stoops
down to us, poor worms of earth, if it is not to magnify and to
give a more illustrious manifestation of His goodness?" That is
what Calvin calls "the legitimate order which God originally
established".[3] When man in his special and familiar relation with
God responds to that order and partakes of it, then he is in the
image of God. That is the *rectitude* that characterizes true human
nature.

The whole conception of order and rectitude plays such an
important rôle in Calvin's thought that it may be well to draw
together at this point his thought on the matter, much of which
has already passed through our discussion. By the legitimate
order of nature Calvin means the order of utter dependence on
the mercy of God. Dependence on the mercy of God is order;
independence is disorder, wherever it may be found. And so,
speaking of the superiority which man has over woman, Calvin
says: "In this superior order of dignity the glory of God is seen,
as it shines forth in every kind of superiority."[4] The whole
universe therefore has been created so that in the ordering of it
all, whether in the marvellous order of the heavens,[5] which
constantly calls forth Calvin's admiration, or in "the order
established in nature, that all animals are brought to a dependence on their Maker",[6] or in the dominion of man over the world
of animals and nature,[7] the glory of God is seen. The only principle of order that pervades the whole of the universe is utter
dependence on the mercy of God.[8]

All this is especially mirrored in man, who is under much

---

[1] *Comm. on Ps.* 8 : 7 f.   [2] *Comm. on Ps.* 8 : 3 f.   [3] *Ibid.*
   [4] *Comm. on* 1 *Cor.* 11 : 7. At the same time Calvin insists on the equality of man
and woman who, as we have seen, both image the glory of God. "Any inequality
which is contrary to this arrangement is nothing else than a corruption of nature
which proceeds from sin " (*on Gen.* 1 : 26). As a matter of fact this order of nature
is inverted by sin (*on Gen.* 2 : 18).
   [5] E.g., *Comm. on Ps.* 19 : 1 f.; *on Jer.* 10 : 1 f.
   [6] *Comm. on Ps.* 145 : 15, 16.
   [7] *Comm. on Gen.* 1 : 28 f.; 2 :15 f.; *on Ps.* 8 : 6; *on Heb.* 2 : 5, etc.
   [8] But this does not mean that grace is bound to the accustomed order of nature.
Comm. on Gen. 48 : 17.

deeper obligation to the Creator,[1] and whose dependence on the mercy of God is of a profounder order: the dependence of a son on the Father. The whole order of creation's dependence on the mercy of God is designed to "image forth the continual care which God has over us",[2] but to believing men "the inestimable grace of God appears in that He exhibits Himself to them as a Father."[3] By dependence on the mercy of God, by obedience to the Creator, by gratitude to the Father, it is intended that man should image forth this order — that is his *rectitude*.[4] "The glory of God peculiarly shines forth in human nature where the mind, will, and all the senses, represent the divine order."[5] That is to say, in man, rectitude is essentially the order of *spiritual* rule, and can only be understood in terms of *spiritual jurisdiction*. Speaking of this spiritual Kingdom, Calvin says: "As it is spiritual, the justice and judgment do not belong only to civil and external order, but rather to that rectitude by which it comes that men are reformed according to God's image, which is in righteousness and truth."[6] At the same time, this order "may be set forth under the image or form of an earthly and civil government".[7] That is supremely the case in the relation of superiority that man bears to the whole of creation. It is his *right of nature* that, in obedience to the divine dominion over him, he exhibits dominion over the rest of creation.[8] But in the relation between himself and God the order is preserved only as he acknowledges that he is utterly dependent on the grace of God. The order of creation points the way towards that, and helps by inciting wonder and admiration for the Maker, but God has given the Word to man so that through the Word he might have a familiar knowledge of God and be a *dear friend*.[9] It is his special duty therefore to give ear to the Word — indeed it is part of the order of nature that he has been given an ear for this purpose.[10]

The whole of this order of creation has been overturned by the disobedience of man and his will to be independent. "What

---

[1] *Introd. Arg. in Comm. on Gen.*   [2] *Comm. on Ps.* 147 : 7.
[3] *Comm. on Ps.* 145 : 18; *Serm. on Eph.* 4 : 6-8.
[4] Rectitude, integrity, truth, justice, are all more or less synonymous in Calvin's usage—see, for example, *Comm. on Dan.* 4 : 37.
[5] *Comm. on Gen.* 1 : 26. Calvin also calls this the *spirit of rectitude—on Ezek.* 18: 20.
[6] *Comm. on Jer.* 32 : 15; see also *on Matt.* 6 : 10.
[7] *Ibid.* Cf. *on* 1 *Pet.* 2 : 14: "Magistrates ought to bear the image of God."
[8] *Comm. on Heb.* 2 : 5.   [9] *Serm. on Job* 37 : 1 f.
[10] *Serm. on Job* 33 : 14 f.

more monstrous disorder can be conceived of than exists where the Creator is not acknowledged?"[1] The whole of nature has been dragged down into disorder by the fall of man. "Since Adam by his fall destroyed the proper order of nature, the creatures groan under the servitude to which they have been subjected through sin."[2] "If it be found that men and others of His creatures often suffer and die of want, this is to be traced to the change which has come upon nature by sin. The fair order which subsisted in it by God's original appointment often fails since the fall through our sins, and yet in what remains of it, though marred, we may see the kindness of God, for in the severest failures of crop, there is no year so barren and unproductive, that God may not be said to open His hand in it."[3] "We throw heaven and earth into confusion by our sins. For were we in right order as to our obedience to God, doubtless all the elements would be conformable, and we should thus observe in the world an angelic harmony. . . . These two things then are both true: that God is not without a testimony as to His beneficence, for He gives rain, He gives suitable seasons, He renders the earth fruitful, so as to supply us with food, and also, that heaven and earth are often in great disorder, that many things happen unseasonably, as though God had no care for us, because we provoke Him by our sins and thus confound and subvert the order of nature."[4] Nevertheless it remains true that God's original intention is not set aside by the perversity of man, and He still maintains some order until the whole creation can be redeemed through Christ and the obedience of the Cross.[5] There is no doubt in Calvin's mind that the death of Jesus on the Cross has an efficacy for the whole of creation. "Out of Christ all things were disordered, and through Him they have been restored to order.[6] And truly, out of Christ, what can we perceive in the world but mere ruins? We are alienated from God by sin, and how can we but present a broken and shattered aspect? The proper condition of creatures is to keep close to God. Such a *gathering together* as might bring us back to regular order, the Apostle tells us, has been made in Christ. Formed into

---

[1] *Comm. on Ps.* 96 : 10; *Serm. on Deut.* 30 : 15 f. [2] *Instit.* 3. 25. 2.
[3] *Comm. on Ps.* 145 : 16. [4] *Comm. on Jer.* 5 : 25.
[5] *Comm. on John* 12 : 31 ; 13 : 31. As *rectitude* is restored by the Cross, the glory of God shines forth there more than anywhere else.
[6] There is a sense in which "all parts of our redemption are already accomplished" (*Instit.* 3. 25. 2), but "the final result is suspended until Christ the Redeemer appear" (3. 25. 6). Cf. also *Comm. on Eph.* 1 : 14; *on Rom.* 8 : 19 f.

D

one body, we are united to God, and closely connected with each other. Without Christ, on the other hand, the whole world is a shapeless chaos and frightful confusion. We are brought into actual unity by Christ alone."[1]

Until that final redemption when all things shall be restored to their original rectitude, the world is still perverted in its order; and corresponding to that world-perversion there is perversity in the heart of fallen man. The active principle of this perversity is what Calvin calls, as we shall have cause to see, *concupiscence*. That lies at the back of "the violent lawless movements which war with the order of God".[2] "In consequence of this corruption of nature, all our faculties are so vitiated and corrupted that a perpetual disorder and excess are apparent in all our actions."[3] The loss of this rectitude means the spiritual destruction and death of the whole soul, and whatever are left of natural gifts such as sense and understanding and will are so perverted that their only operation is one in further alienation from God. "That men live and breathe and are endued with sense and understanding and will, all this tends to their destruction, because there is no part nor faculty of the soul that is not corrupted and *turned aside from rectitude*. Thus it is that death everywhere holds dominion, for the death of the soul is nothing else than its being estranged and turned aside from God."[4] From this state man must be brought back to obedience and thankfulness and true rectitude, and that is done through the obedience of Christ unto death and by justi- fication (= rectification) through grace. "This is performed when in righteousness and holiness men bear a resemblance to their heavenly Father, and prove that they are not degenerate sons."[5] "Accordingly, through the blessing of Christ we are renewed by that regeneration into the righteousness of God from which we have fallen through Adam, the Lord being pleased in a manner to restore the integrity of all whom He appoints to the inheritance of life. . . . After Paul (Calvin continues) I make the image of God to consist in righteousness and true holiness . . . that the nearer any one approaches in resemblance to God, the more does the image of God appear in him."[6]

---

[1] *Comm. on Eph.* 1 : 10; *Serm. on Eph.* 1 : 7-10; *Comm. on Isa.* 65 : 25.
[2] *Instit.* 3. 3. 12.
[3] *Ibid.* Cf. *Comm. on Gen.* 6 : 3; and *Instit.* 2. 8. 1, where Calvin says that our present nature is continually opposed to the rectitude of God's rule.
[4] *Comm. on John* 11 : 25.
[5] *Instit.* 3. 18. 1.   [6] *Instit.* 3. 3. 9.

The wonderful grace manifested in Christ begets once again profound thankfulness in the believer,[1] while his eyes are opened to see the attestations of God's mercy in the whole government of the world, so that he gives God the glad response of utter dependence on His mercy. "While we submit ourselves to His righteousness He makes us partakers of His glory"[2]—that is to say, in so far as we are ready to cast ourselves on His mercy. "We must eventually become illustrations of the glory of God, *if we are nothing but vessels of His mercy*."[3] This points us back to the original creation, and the original relation which was the law of man's being in the order of nature: he was so formed in personal intercourse with God in a world which abounds with attestations of His mercy, and in the midst of a Church in which the familiar Word of God is heard, through which comes the special communication of God's grace and fatherly love, that he might bear witness to the grace and partake of the glory of God by a life of thankfulness and obedience. That is man's true rectitude: to be created in the image of God is to be opposite to or to respond to Him in such a way that God may be able to behold Himself in man as in a mirror.

[1] At the opposite pole to thanksgiving or blessing Calvin puts cursing—Cf. *Comm. on James* 3 : 11: "A cursing tongue is something monstrous and contrary to all nature, and subverts the order everywhere established by God."

[2] *Instit.* 3. 20. 42.

[3] *Comm. on Eph.* 1 : 12. The whole passage runs thus: *Ut simus in laudem gloriæ ipsius. Quia tunc demum illustratur in nobis Dei gloria, si nihil simus quam vasa eius misericordiæ. Ac nomen gloriæ κατ'ἐξοχὴν, peculiariter eam significat, qua elucet in Dei bonitate: nihil enim magis est illi proprium, in quo glorificari velit, quam bonitas.* For similar passages see *on John* 8 : 54; *on Rom.* 9 : 22, 23.

Chapter Four

THE IMAGE OF GOD (2)

A more precise knowledge of the imago dei *may be gained from the reparation of man's corrupt nature in Christ, i.e., in regeneration through the Spirit. This shows us that the image of God is not any natural property of the soul, but is a spiritual reflection in holiness and righteousness, in knowledge and truth, which should characterize all human nature. The* imago dei *is essentially spiritual, and is apparent in man's response to God the Father, in his witness to the Truth as it is sealed in his heart by the Word and the Spirit. It is grounded in the* testimonium internum Spiritus Sancti. *As such it is not a possession of the soul, though the soul may be said to be the seat of the* imago dei. *To think of this image, or to try to use it, as if it were a natural possession of the soul, is an act of impiety which does despite to grace. This image of God in man and his knowledge of God have a mutual relation. It is God's action on man by the imprint of the Truth upon his mind, and becomes man's possession only in the active response of love and obedience. Therefore the strength of the* imago dei *and its continued maintenance in man lie in the Word of God and not in the soul of man. In a real sense the image of God in man is the communicated Word in which God's glory shines forth. By means of this spiritual image man's whole person partakes of rectitude, so that his whole person may be said to image the glory of God.*

WE must now follow Calvin's thought as he goes on to deal more precisely with the *imago dei.* "The definition of the image seems not to be complete until it appears what the faculties are in which man excels, and in which he is to be regarded as a mirror of the divine glory. This however cannot be better known than from the reparation of our corrupt nature."[1] In other words, it is from our "spiritual generation" that we see what the *imago dei* really is and in what it truly consists.[2] Calvin admits that when a believer is regenerated by receiving the quickening Spirit from Christ, he receives a richer measure of grace than Adam when he was created a living soul, but that does not alter the fact that it is in regeneration, when we are formed anew in the image of God, that we can best see what that image is.

[1] *Instit.* 1. 15. 4; 2. 12. 6.   *Comm. on Gen.* 1 : 26.

"This principle cannot be overthrown that the leading feature in the renovation of the divine image must also have held the highest place in its creation."[1] Proceeding in this way, we see that "the image of God is spiritual",[2] and indeed that it "comprehends everything which has any relation to the spiritual and eternal life".[3] "Regeneration is like another creation, and if we compare it with the first creation, it far surpasses it. For it is much better for us to be made children of God, and reformed after His image within us, than to be created mortal: for we are born children of wrath, corrupt and degenerate (Eph. 2 : 3), since all integrity was lost when God's image was removed. We see, then, the nature of our first creation. But when God refashions us, we are not only born sons of Adam, but we are the brothers of angels, and members of Christ, and this our second life consists in rectitude, justice, and the light of true intelligence."[4]

It seems quite clear from this that when Calvin says that the proper seat of the image is in the soul,[5] he does not mean that the *imago dei* is the soul, or any natural property of the soul, but that the soul is the mirror which reflects in it or ought to reflect in it the image of God. In this way Calvin can say, on the one hand, that the *imago dei* is a *bonum adventitium*. "The image of God is incomparably the highest nobility; and lest men should use it as an occasion of pride, their first origin is placed immediately before them; whence they may learn that this good was adventitious; for Moses relates that man had been in the beginning dust of the earth. Let foolish men now go and boast of the excellency of their nature."[6] On the other hand, he can insist equally that the *imago dei* is a *bonum internum*. "The likeness must be within, in himself. It must be something which is not external to him, but is properly the internal good of the soul."[7] The soul has been fashioned by God in order to be the mirror to reflect the glory of God, but the soul does not possess the image so reflected as part of itself; rather does it possess it by way of spiritual ornaments or endowments such as wisdom, virtue, justice, truth, and holiness.[8]

---

[1] *Instit.* I. 15. 4.   [2] *Instit.* I. 15. 3.   [3] *Instit.* I. 15. 4.
[4] *Comm. on Ezek.* 18 : 32.
[5] *Instit.* I. 15. 3-5; cf. *Comm. on Gen.* I : 26, 27. Calvin can also say that *ideas* are seated in the mind; *Instit.* 4. 19. 1.   [7] *Instit.* I. 15. 4.
[6] *Comm. on Gen.* 2 : 7.
[8] *Instit.* 2. 1. 5; 3. 3. 9; 3. 18. 1; 3. 20. 42; *Institutio* (1536) 27; cf. *Comm. on Rom.* 13 : 14. *Induere Christum hic significat, virtute Spiritus eius undique nos muniri, qua idonei ad omnes sanctitatis partes reddamur. Sic enim instauratur in nobis imago Dei, quæ unicum est animæ ornamentum.*

These are not external endowments but are within the soul, but they are such endowments as are necessarily constitutive of true human nature. At other times Calvin speaks of these endowments as "supernatural gifts",[1] blessings which are not our own, but are "derived by divine communication",[2] i.e., are "communicated to us by the Spirit."[3] The presence of these gifts imaging God in the soul bespeak the very presence of God Himself within man.[4]

Of the Biblical expression *spirit* Calvin says it refers to that part of the soul which has been renewed or regenerated so as to bear the image of God. "Whatever in man is created anew in the image of God is called *spirit*. 'That which is born of the flesh is flesh; that which is born of the Spirit is *spirit*.' "[5] This he also calls the *inner man* renewed after the likeness of God.[6] No doubt we only begin to bear the image of God in Christ, but one day we shall be wholly renewed in body and in soul.[7] Meantime when we speak of the image of God we refer to our spiritual generation or our spiritual communion with God.[8] It was probably in reference to the *imago dei* in this sense that Calvin said in his letter to Sadolet: "There is nothing in which man excels the lower animals unless it be his spiritual communion with God in the hope of a blessed eternity."[9] This spiritual communion is through Christ, which entails in us such "a representation of Christ" that it becomes "the bond of our adoption".[10] In other words, that is the action of the Spirit in our hearts crying "*Abba Father*"—the *testimonium internum Spiritus Sancti*.[11] Calvin goes so far as to say: "The spirit is called the renewing of our corrupt nature, while God reforms us according to His image. Hence cometh that kind of speech, because that newness which is wrought in us is the gift of the Spirit."[12]

Enough has been said here to make it quite clear that, for Calvin, the *imago dei* is in no sense a natural possession, but a spiritual possession, and therefore above nature and the world.[13]

[1] *Instit.* 2. 2. 4; 2. 2. 12; *Comm. on John* 3 : 6; *on* 2 *Pet.* 1 : 3.
[2] *Instit.* 2. 2. 1; 3. 7. 4.
[3] *Instit.* 2. 2. 16; *Comm. on Eph.* 1 : 17.   [4] *Instit.* 1. 5. 6.
[5] *The Eternal Predestination of God* (Eng. tr. by H. Cole), p. 101. See also *Comm. on John* 3 : 6; *on Rom.* 7 : 18-23; *Serm. on Gal.* 3 : 1 f.; 5 : 14 f.
[6] *Comm. on Rom.* 7 : 23; *on* 2 *Cor.* 4 : 16; *on Eph.* 3 : 16.   [7] *Ibid.*
[8] See *Instit.* 3. 2. 24.
[9] Calvin's *Tracts*, Eng. tr., Vol. 1, p. 34; *Instit.* 2. 12. 6.
[10] *Instit.* 3. 6. 3.
[11] *Comm. on Rom.* 8 : 15; *on Gal.* 4 : 6; *on* 2 *Cor.* 1 : 22; 5 : 5; cf. *on John* 14 : 1.
[12] *Comm. on Rom.* 7 : 14. See also *on John* 6 : 26.
[13] See *Comm. on Heb.* 6 : 4.

The spiritual renovation in which the *imago* consists is secret, and invisible, by which Calvin appears to mean that it is not subject to psychological investigation.[1] It is essentially a "heavenly image" or a "celestial image".[2] Calvin does speak of it as a quality,[3] but it is quite clear that he does not mean any heightening of our physical existence.[4] Eventually, man will receive an entirely new nature, but until then he possesses that only in faith. Meantime, however, the renewal of the believer does partly restore him to his true and substantial *integrity, rectitude* and *temperature*, which were deformed by the loss of the spiritual image, and it does that because it brings with it knowledge, righteousness, and holiness. Hence we may argue, says Calvin, back to the original *imago* and its relation to the person of man in the light of the intellect and rectitude of the heart.[5] And that we see to be entirely due to the illumination of the Holy Spirit.[6] "Hence we may learn, on the one hand, what is the end of our regeneration, that is, that we may be made like God, and that His glory may shine in us; and, on the other hand, what is the image of God of which mention is made by Moses in Genesis 1 : 26 and 9 : 6, the rectitude and integrity of the whole soul, so that man reflects like a mirror the wisdom, righteousness, and goodness of God."[7] Returning, therefore, to Calvin's word that the proper seat of the *imago dei* is in the soul, we see that the image is not natural or substantival to the soul, but a reflection by the whole soul and in the soul of that which the soul is not in itself, and cannot claim to be without contumacy and ingratitude.[8] It was indeed the sin of Adam that "though he was formed after the image of God to have understanding of all things that pertained to him in such wise that he could wish for nothing more . . . he was not content to be so far enlightened in the knowledge of

---

[1] *Comm. on Rom.* 7 : 23. Cf. *Instit.* 1. 15. 4; *Comm. on Col.* 3 : 3; 3 : 10.

[2] *Instit.* 2. 1. 5. Cf. the "heavenly intelligence" of *Instit.* 2. 2. 13. It is celestial because it corresponds to *celestial truth*, or "the light of heavenly wisdom in which God manifests Himself to us that He may conform us to His image", *Comm. on John* 17 : 17.

[3] *Instit.* 2. 12. 6. Commenting on 2 *Pet.* 1 : 4 Calvin says: "Let us then mark that the end of the Gospel is to render us eventually conformable to God, and, if we may so speak, to deify us. . . . But the word *nature* is not here essence but quality." Contrast the *Serm. on Job* 40 : 20 f.: "Was not the Elephant created with us? Are we made of any more precious mould than he? Is there any quality in us why we should be more excellent? No, there is nothing that makes a difference between us but God."

[4] *Instit.* 1. 15. 4; *Comm. on Heb.* 11 : 27.

[5] *Instit.* 1. 15. 4.

[6] *Comm. on Col.* 3 : 10.

[7] *Comm. on Col.* 3 : 10.

[8] *Instit.* 2. 2. 1; 2. 2. 10; 3. 7. 4; *Comm. on Isa.* 29 : 16; 31 : 3; 48 : 5.

things by God's Spirit as was expedient for his welfare, but would needs become like unto God. And when he was so lifted up he could not but meet with God's mighty hand to cast him down into this horrible gulf of confusion wherein we are this day."[1] There is nothing upon which Calvin is more insistent than that we are "conformable to God *not by an influx of substance,* but by the grace and virtue of the Spirit."[2] Anything else would be to take advantage of the imago-relation we have to God and to turn it into a substantival one, that is, to a likeness of being, which, as we shall see, is for Calvin the very tap-root of original sin.

How then is the conformability in the *imago dei* produced and maintained? It is certainly not by any natural means such as achievement or inheritance. "Have we it through our effort? Have we it by inheritance from our ancestors? No. But we have it of God's free gift through His own mere goodness."[3] Calvin's answer is that we have it by grace and by the virtue of the Spirit through the Word.[4] *Imago dei* is essentially a reflection in and by the soul of the Word of God which is itself the lively or quickening image of God.[5] Therefore man has been made such that it is his "special duty to give ear to the Word of God";[6] while, on the other hand, it is the work of the Holy Spirit who "with a wondrous and special energy forms the ear to hear, and the mind to understand".[7] Commenting in the *Institutes* on the words of Psalm 119 : 18, "Open Thou mine eyes that I may behold wondrous things out of Thy law", Calvin says: "By this expression he certainly intimates that it is like sunrise to the earth when the Word of God shines forth; but men do not derive

[1] *Serm. on Job* 28 : 10 f.

[2] *Instit.* 1. 15. 5; cf. 3. 2. 21; *Comm. on John* 8 : 44. Christ alone has an imago-relation *in substance* to God, men only *by irradiation, on Heb.* 1 : 3.

[3] *Serm. on Job* 33 : 1 f. It is a *miracle* of grace (*on Eph.* 3 : 7-9).

[4] *Comm. on Hos.* 2 : 19, 20: "Since the knowledge of God is the special gift of the Spirit, we may with certainty conclude that what is said here refers not only to outward preaching but that the grace of the Spirit is also joined, by which God renews us after His image. . . . This He conveys not only by outward teaching but also by the illumination of our minds by His Spirit, yea, by the renewing of our hearts."

[5] *Comm. on 2 Cor.* 2 : 11; *on Ps.* 8 : 6; *Instit.* 1. 15. 4. Cf. 3. 2. 21: "The Word which is incorruptible seed produces faith which is similar to itself." See also *Comm. on Luke* 11 : 27; *on Matt.* 12 : 8.

[6] *Instit.* 1. 6. 2; 1. 15. 6

[7] *Instit.* 2. 2. 20; *Serm. on Job* 26 : 1 f.: "Until God enlightens us by His Word we are blind; until He opens our ears we are deaf; until He gives us faith we have neither soul nor heart. . . . Our Lord must make His Word available by the working of His Holy Spirit. He must bore into our ears or we shall never hear Him."

much benefit from it until He Himself, who is for this reason
called the Father of Lights (Jas. 1 : 17), either gives eyes or opens
them; because whatever is not illuminated by His Spirit is wholly
darkness."[1] It was only when Adam became "incredulous as to
God's Word" that "the heavenly image in man was effaced".[2]
Thus Calvin regards as a constitutive part of the *imago dei*, and of
its continuance in man, man's response to the Word by which
"he truly ascribes all his excellence to the admirable gifts of his
maker".[3] Just as Calvin thinks of the Word of God as making
the ineffective image of God in the world speak of His glory, so
the Word in man's grateful response to it makes him as an intelligent being reflect in his intellectual action the image of God's
glory. It is "knowledge which forms us anew into the image of
God from faith to faith".[4] Calvin thinks of the image of God and
man's knowledge of God as having a mutual relation. On the
one hand, he says, "man was framed after the image of God in
order to have understanding of all that pertained to Him";[5] but,
on the other hand, he says, "we cannot attain to the knowledge of
God until we are transformed into His image".[6] Thus, properly
speaking, it is only in man who has been made to know God and
hear His Word that the image of God is truly reflected. And all
the stress is laid by Calvin on the Word as mediated by Christ.
"There is no other way in which God is known but in the face of
Jesus Christ, who is the bright and lively image of Him."[7]
" 'Thy Word is Truth.' The Truth is here taken by way of
eminence for the light of heavenly wisdom in which God manifests Himself to us that He may conform us to His image. The
outward preaching of the Word, it is true, does not of itself
accomplish this, for that preaching is wickedly profaned by the
reprobate; but let us remember that Christ speaks of the elect,
whom the Holy Spirit efficaciously regenerates by the Word."[8]
It is clear from these passages that the *imago dei* is God's action
on man in the imprint of His Truth by the Word, and man's
action only in response to the communication of that Word.
"God created us after His own image in order that His Truth
should shine forth in us."[9] The "prerogative" in man's knowledge of God "is not ascribed to man as an individual, but to the

---

[1] *Instit.* 2. 2. 21.   [2] *Instit.* 2. 1. 4, 5.   [3] *Instit.* 1. 15. 3.
[4] *Comm. on John* 17 : 3; *on* 1 *John* 2: 3; 3 : 6; 4 : 7; *on* 2 *Cor.* 3 : 18; *on James* 1 : 23-25.
[5] *Serm. on Job* 28 : 10 f.
[6] *Serm. on Job* 21 : 22 f.; cf. 36 : 25 f.   [7] *Comm. on John* 17 :3.
[8] *Comm. on John* 17 : 17.   [9] *Serm. on Deut.* 4 : 10 f.

Word of God, which the spiritual follow in judging and which is truly dictated to them by God with true discernment".[1] It must be God who testifies of Himself in the Word. "As God alone can properly bear witness to His own words, so these words will not obtain full credit in the hearts of men until they are sealed by the inward testimony of the Spirit."[2] Thus Calvin uses the *imago dei* in the sense of *witness* by men to the glory of God. "God will use men for witnesses of His Truth, and He gives it to them to keep. . . . We are keepers of His precious image, of that which concerns the majesty of the doctrine of salvation, of the life of the world."[3] We understand how Calvin thinks of this witness when we remember that, for him, the power and substance lie in the object witnessed to and not in the witness itself.[4] In other words, the strength of the *imago dei* and its continued maintenance in the believer lie in the Word of God and not in the soul of man. In a real sense the image of God in man is the *communicated Word* in which God's glory shines forth.[5] This is not to confuse the *imago dei* in man with the original and lively image of God which is Christ Himself or the eternal Word.[6] Thus Calvin distinguishes two senses of the *imago dei* in Christ Himself. "Christ is not only the image of God, in so far as He is the eternal Word of God, but even on His human nature, which He has in common with us, the likeness of the glory of the Father has been engraved so as to form His members to the resemblance of it."[7] However, man's *imago dei* is generated only over against that prime image of God in a knowledgeable relation of faith and obedience, so that knowledge of the Word of God is an essential part of the *imago dei* in him.[8] "Paul also teaches us this: that we all with unveiled face by beholding the glory of God are changed into the same image (2 Cor. 3 : 18). Hence it follows that no one ought to be reckoned among the disciples of Christ, unless we perceive the glory of God impressed on him, as with a seal, by the likeness of Christ."[9]

[1] *Comm. on 1 Cor.* 2 : 15. See also *Instit.* 1. 6. 3; 1. 7. 5.
[2] *Instit.* 1. 7. 4.
[3] *Serm. on 1 Tim.* 3 : 14, 15.   [4] *Serm. on Job* 14 : 13 f.
[5] *Serm. on Titus* 2 : 3 f. Calvin goes on to say here that if by our lives we dishonour Word, instead of adorning it, so that the Word is evil spoken of, we actually betray the image of God.
[6] *Instit.* 3. 2. 6; *Introd. Arg. in Comm. on Gen.; Comm. on Rom.* 1 : 3; *on 1 Pet.* 1 : 23; *Serm. on 1 Tim.* 6 : 15, 16.
[7] *Comm. on John* 17 : 22.
[8] *Comm. on Gen.* 2 : 9; *on Eph.* 4 : 23 f.; *on Col.* 3 : 9 f.
[9] *Comm. on John* 17 : 22.

It may now be said that in a very fundamental sense the *esse* of the *imago dei* in man is constitutively bound up with its *percipi*, or on the part of man with his *percipere*. To know God in such a way as to be transformed into His likeness is to be a true man. "There is no true life but in God, and this is communicated to us by His Word. However fading then is the nature of man, yet he is made eternal by the Word; for he is re-moulded and becomes a new creature."[1] "Direct communication with God is the source of life to man."[2] "The knowledge of God is the true life of the soul."[3] That is to say, man's life is absolutely reflexive of the Word of God, and can be lived only in a motion of continued reflexion. Calvin's favourite expression, which we have already had cause to notice, is that man's *life* consists in *light*, and that is the major distinction between him and all the other creatures on the earth. The other creatures have their life in a relation of motion over against God who continually upholds them in being. But man's life consists in a knowledgeable or conscious motion in which he responds to the self-communication of God. The knowledge of God involved in this carries with it a knowledge of man's true self. He needs this self-knowledge to know that he has nothing of himself, and stands only by the mercy of God, so that as he possesses his life only in the grace of God he may learn to depend upon God and not seek life anywhere but in Him. He cannot indeed retain his life in any other way than by such an acknowledgment that he lives not by his own power but by the kindness of God alone.[4] Calvin's doctrine of the *imago dei* in man sums up the whole of this relation between man and God. Its being is to be found in the activity of this relation. The knowledge by which the *imago dei* is formed in the soul of man comes by obedience.[5] Therefore we must turn to examine in some further detail the relation of the *imago dei* to the will of God or to the action of His grace. But here in concluding this section it must be pointed out that though the kernel of the *imago dei* for Calvin is to be found in this relation which we understand truly from our regeneration in Christ, yet it carries with it the wider significance of the word. Through the image man partakes of the divine order, and when he is in the right with that, the whole of his person partakes of the imago-relation,

---

[1] *Comm. on* 1 *Pet.* 1 : 25.
[2] *Comm. on Gen.* 3 : 22; see also *on Gen.* 2 : 9; 3 : 6.
[3] *Comm. on Eph.* 4 : 18. See especially *Serm. on Eph.* 2 : 1 f.
[4] *Comm. on Gen.* 2 : 9. [5] *Instit.* 1. 6. 2; *Comm. on Gen.* 2 : 9.

so that the essential direction of the imago-relation, the *rectitudo*, characterize the whole man. Thus Calvin writes: "According to Paul, spiritual regeneration is nothing else than the restoration of the same image (Col. 3 : 10; and Eph. 4 : 23). That he made this image consist in 'righteousness and true holiness' is by the figure *synechdoche*, for though this is the chief part, it is not the whole of God's image. Therefore by this word the perfection of our whole nature is designated, as it appeared when Adam was endued with a right judgment, had affection in harmony with reason, had all his senses sound and well-regulated, and truly excelled in everything good. Thus the chief seat of the divine image was in his mind and heart where it was eminent: yet there was no part of him in which some scintillations of it did not shine forth. For there was an attempering of it in the several parts of the soul which correspond with their various offices. In the mind perfect intelligence flourished and reigned, uprightness attended as its companion, and all the senses were prepared and moulded for due obedience to reason; and in the body there was a suitable correspondence with this internal order."[1] It was in this sense, as we have seen, that Calvin thought of Christ as bearing the image of God in virtue of His human nature in addition to the fact that He was the image of God in the sense of the eternal Word. The former is true of man only so far as "he truly ascribes all his excellency to the admirable gifts of his maker".[2] But man has sinned through ingratitude and effaced the image of God in him, so that even in the elect who are regenerated it is only *partly* seen. "Its full lustre however will be displayed in heaven."[3]

[1] *Comm. on Gen.* 1 : 26. [2] *Instit.* 1. 15. 3.
[3] *Instit.* 1. 15. 4; cf. *Comm. on Matt.* 13 : 43.

Chapter Five

THE IMAGE OF GOD (3)

Calvin's conception of the imago dei *must be regarded in the context of his doctrine of the* creatio continua. *All creation owes its existence from moment to moment to the gracious will of God. Calvin constantly thinks of man, and of the* imago dei, *in terms of this dynamic relation to* [relational view] *God. The image of God is in no sense a static reflection of the being of God, but a dynamic reflection by way of active obedience to the Word and Will of God. It is man's intelligent life-answer to God's grace, and as such is a continuous relation of his mind and will in orientation toward God. This means that the* imago dei *must be understood teleologically and eschatologically, for it is only shadowed forth in man until he reaches perfection.* Imago dei *is thus man's destiny in God's gracious intention.* [intended reflection] *It is the original truth of his being which is also future. As such it cannot be interpreted as a natural heritage which can be handed on from man to man by the will of the flesh, but may be gained and possessed only in faith. As man's destiny the* imago dei *also hangs over fallen man as his judgment, as the law of his being. It is not, as such, a natural law, but that which has its ground in the creative Word of grace. The emphasis must be placed on the gracious will of God to regard men as His children, a will which cannot be set aside or thwarted by sin and depravity. Objectively, therefore, the image of God has its ground in the divine intention. Subjectively, it is grounded in a response of thankful* [Hmm...] *obedience, while ingratitude is the perversion of it.*

WE must now go back to Calvin's teaching that the creation of man, body and soul, was the result of the will of God to bring him into being out of nothing, and to preserve him in being according to His mercy. This means that the whole being and life of man continues to hang on the gracious will and decision of God from moment to moment. Man lives and moves and has his being in the unceasing visitation of the presence of God, and in the constant and continuous repetition of His pure grace. That is to say, Calvin thinks of man's being only in a dynamic relation to God, or rather only in a continuously dynamic relation from God to man. "It is certain that inasmuch as God sustains the world by His power, governs it by His providence, cherishes and even propagates all creatures, He is constantly at work. Therefore

61

that saying of Christ is true, that the Father and He Himself had worked from the beginning hitherto, because if God should but withdraw His hand a little, all things would immediately perish and dissolve into nothing as is declared in Psalm 104 : 29. And indeed God is rightly acknowledged as the Creator of heaven and earth only whilst their perpetual preservation is ascribed to Him."[1] "When God sets us in a good state, yet we cannot continue unless He have His hand continually stretched out over us. What is to be done then, that we may continue in that state wherein we be established? God must breathe His power into us without ceasing and be continually at hand with us."[2] Calvin also thinks of man as being consumed and renewed every instant of his being in the sense that he is continually being called out of non-being into being and life by the Word and Will of the Creator who is the Lord of life and death.[3] "We continue to live so long as He sustains us by His power; but no sooner does He withdraw His life-giving Spirit than we die. . . . The world is daily renewed, because God sends forth His Spirit. In the propagation of living creatures we doubtless see continually a new creation of the world. . . . When we see the world daily decaying and daily renewed, the life-giving power of God is reflected to us herein as in a mirror. All the deaths which take place among living creatures are just so many examples of our nothingness, so to speak; and when others are produced and grow up in their room, we have in that presented to us a renewal of the world. Since then the world daily dies, and is daily renewed in its various parts, the manifest conclusion is that it subsists only by a secret virtue derived from God."[4] "Men have God present with them not only in the excellent gifts of the mind but in their very essence; because it belongeth unto God alone to be, all other things have their being in Him. Also, we learn out of this place (i.e., Acts 17 : 28) that God did not so create the world once that He did afterward depart from His work; but that it standeth by His power, and that the same God is the

[1] *Comm. on Gen.* 2 : 2: *Certum enim est quatenus mundum sua virtute sustinet Deus, et providentia gubernat, fovet creaturas omnes, atque etiam propagat, esse in opere assiduum. Verum est ergo illud Christi, Patrem et Ipsum ab initio huc usque fuisse operatos, quia si paululum retrahat manum suam Deus, interibunt protinus omnia, et in nihilum diffluent: ut habetur* Ps. 104 : 29. *Nec vero probe Deus agnoscitur cæli et terra creator nisi dum perpetua illa vegetatio ei tribuitur.*

[2] *Serm. on Job* 10 : 7 f.

[3] "Our life hangs by a thread" (*Serm. on Deut.* 28 : 65 f.).

[4] *Comm. on Ps.* 104 : 29 f.; see also *Serm. on Job* 5 : 20 f.; 7 : 7 f.; 14 : 5 f.; *Comm. on Jer.* 17 : 1-5.

Governor thereof who was the Creator. We must think well
upon this continual impartation of life that we may remember
God every minute."[1] Thus Calvin can say: "We and all creatures
do not, strictly speaking, live, but only borrow life from God."[2]
"When God vouchsafes to look upon us, that look gives us life,
and as long as His serene countenance shines, it inspires all
creatures with life."[3]

All this means that from the point of view of his theology
Calvin has nothing to do with second causes.[4] All nature, and
the gifts and endowments of man, depend for their being upon
the immediate agency of God through His Spirit and His Word.
That does not encourage the Christian to overlook inferior causes,[5]
but it does mean that we can never think of the world of nature
as in any sense independent of the Creator. "Philosophers think
not that they have reasoned skilfully enough about inferior
causes, unless they separate God very far from His works. It is a
diabolical science, however, which fixes our contemplations on
the works of nature and turns them away from God. If any one
who wished to know a man should take no notice of his face, but
should fix his eyes only on the points of his nails, his folly might
justly be derided. But far greater is the folly of those philosophers
who out of mediate and proximate causes weave themselves veils
lest they should be compelled to acknowledge the hand of God
which manifestly displays itself in His works."[6] It is a sin of the
deepest ingratitude to transfer to nature what belongs to grace,
and so to suppress the name of God.[7] God must be regarded as
present and as active through His Spirit to all existing things,
maintaining them in existence, even in the case of the reprobate
and the wicked.[8] All creaturely endowments, such as wisdom
and craftsmanship, come directly as gifts from God whether they
are in unbelievers or believers.[9] All being and motion and life,
wherever found, are due to the immediate action of the Spirit of
God.

[1] *Comm. on Acts* 17 : 28; also *Instit.* 1. 5. 1 f.; 1. 16. 1 f.; *Comm. on Ps.* 33 : 6.
[2] *Comm. on* 1 *Tim.* 6 : 16.   [3] *Comm. on Ps.* 104 : 29.
[4] *Instit.* 1. 5. 4 f.; 1. 16. 1 f.; *Comm. on* 2 *Pet.* 3 : 5; *on Ps.* 147 : 15 f.; *on Jonah* 4 :
6-8: *Has medias causas gubernat Dei consilium.* See especially *Defence of the Secret
Doctrine of the Providence of God* (Eng. tr. by H. Cole).
[5] *Instit.* 1. 17. 8, 9.   [6] *Comm. on Ps.* 29 : 5.
[7] *Instit.* 1. 5. 1, 4; *Serm. on Job* 39 : 22 f.; *Instit.* 1. 16. 6; 2. 2. 1; 2. 2. 27; *Calvin's
Tracts* (Eng. Tr.), Vol. 3, p. 242.
[8] *Instit.* 1. 2. 2; 1. 9. 2; 2. 2. 15, 16; 2. 3. 3 f.; 3. 2. 15; 3. 14. 2; *Comm. on Acts* 17 :
27, etc.
[9] *Ibid.*

As a corollary to this dynamic view of the relation of man and God, Calvin held an essentially activist view of human life, particularly as opposed to the quietism of the Medieval Church. He vigorously attacked the so-called *contemplative life* which had not only become an excuse for idleness, but cast a slur upon the ordinary life and work of men.[1] God has not created men to be idle;[2] there is nothing more pleasing to God than that every man should diligently apply himself to his own calling.[3] In other words, Calvin taught the dignity of human labour as part of man's response to the active providence of the heavenly Father. "Let each of us remember that he has been created by God for the purpose of labouring, and of being vigorously employed in his work; and that not only for a limited time, but till death itself, and what is more, that he shall not only live but die to God."[4] The life of faith is a life of active and strenuous obedience.

If man's being and nature are to be understood only in the light of this dynamic relation to the will of God, then his being in the *imago dei* must be interpreted in the same light. We are not therefore to think of the image of God as in any sense a static reflection of the Being of God, but a dynamic reflection by way of active response to the Will of God and to the Word of God. It must entail "not merely a knowledge that God is, but a perception of His Will toward us. It concerns us to know not only what He is in Himself but also in what character He is pleased to manifest Himself to us."[5] It must be a continuous relation of man's mind and will in response to God. It must be a life-answer such that it characterizes the whole of man's being and action. Thus "the image of God resides in the whole of the soul inasmuch as it is not the reason merely that is rectified but also the will".[6] For that reason, continues Calvin in the same passage, the image of God has to do with righteousness and goodness. It is the obedient response of man's mind and will to God's Will by which we become conformable to God.[7] As we submit to His righteousness God makes us partakers of His glory,[8] for the glory of God includes His righteousness.[9]

This stress upon the will is of prime importance in Calvin's

---

[1] *Comm. on Luke* 10 : 38; *Serm. on Deut.* 5 : 12 f.
[2] *Serm. on Job* 29 : 18 f.; 34 : 16; 34 : 33 f.; 35 : 8 f.; 37 : 14 f.; *Serm. on Deut.* 1 : 22 f.; cf. *Instit.* 1. 14. 2; 2. 1. 8.
[3] *Comm. on Luke* 10 : 38. [4] *Comm. on Luke* 17 : 7. [5] *Instit.* 3. 2. 6.
[6] *Comm. on Col.* 3 : 10. [7] *Comm. on 2 Pet.* 1 : 4; on *Eph.* 4 : 24.
[8] *Instit.* 3. 20. 42; cf. 3. 18. 1. [9] *Instit.* 3. 23. 8.

theology, for it indicates how much he broke with the traditional
habits of the Schoolmen who used to think of the relations
between God and man in terms of a gradation of being, and so
inevitably of the *imago dei* in terms of a static analogy of being.
Calvin expressly repudiates the idea that the will is primary in
man,[1] but he insists that it is not an intellectual fiction. He thinks
of man's person in its totality as a person, and therefore gives
will, as distinguished from rational appetite, a proper place in
man's life and activity.[2] When the element of will is given its
true place in the *imago dei*, the *imago dei* is seen to be the con-
figuration formed in the person of man by the constant will of
God to communicate Himself to man through the Word. Thus
man's contemplation of God through which the image becomes
impressed on him is not a "dead contemplation" but an active
and continuous one in which man is transformed into the image
of God from glory to glory.[3] It "must be going forward in us
during our whole life".[4] That applied equally to Adam before he
fell, inasmuch as he had no firm and settled constancy, but had a
life maintained, as we have already seen, in the Word of continuous creation and communication, to the end that he might
attain to the celestial image and to eternal life.[5] Thus Calvin thinks
it to be true that "the image of God was only shadowed forth in
him, till he should arrive at perfection".[6] Therefore our life is
but "an empty image" unless we keep close to God.[7] When we
do, it becomes a "vital life".[8] There can be no doubt that Calvin
lays the stress therefore on the dynamic character of the image of
God which is maintained in man by continuous conformity to
God, by continuous obedience to the claim of the divine will
upon him.[9] In other words, the *imago dei* is interpreted teleologically as above and beyond man in terms of man's destiny

---

[1] *Comm. on Eph.* 4 : 17: "The mind holds the highest rank in the human con-
stitution, is the seat of reason, presides over the will, and restrains sinful desires."

[2] *Instit.* 1. 15. 7 f. But cf. his views on Aristotle here.

[3] *Comm. on 2 Cor.* 3 : 18; *Serm. on Titus* 1 : 15, 16. Therefore the image is renewed
in us by degrees (*Instit.* 3. 25. 45); cf. *Comm. on Matt.* 13 : 43; *on Luke* 17 : 20.

[4] *Comm. on 2 Cor.* 3 : 18; *on John* 17 : 17; cf. *on 1 John* 1 : 7: "He is said to be like
God who aspires to His likeness, however distant from it he may as yet be."

[5] Cf. *Institutio* (1536) 27 f.: *Quo in certam nostri notitiam veniamus, hoc prius habendum
est: parentem omnium nostrum Adam esse creatum ad imaginem et similitudinem Dei, hoc
est, sapientia, iustitia, sanctitate præditum, atque his gratiæ donis Deo ita hærentem, ut
perpetuo in eo victurus fuerit, si in hac integritate naturæ, quam a Deo acceperat, stetisset.*

[6] *Comm. on Gen.* 1 : 26; see *on Gen.* 2 : 7. Cf. *Serm. on Job* 15 : 11 f.: "*Nous sommes
seulement au chemin.*"

[7] *Comm. on Eph.* 4 : 18.   [8] *Ibid.*

[9] *Comm. on 2 Cor.* 3 : 18; *on 2 Pet.* 1 : 4; *on 1 John* 3 : 2; *on Gen.* 1 : 26; *on Ps.* 8:
5 f.; *Instit.* 3. 2. 35 f.

E

which is made known in the Word of God, and in the claim of the divine Will thus revealed upon man's life. The image of God hangs over man, so to speak, both as his destiny and as the law of his being — and that is seen in the Law of God. "The Law comprehends within it that new life by which the image of God is restored in us",[1] though no doubt "we have degenerated from our true origin and the Law of our Creator".[2] This brings the image of God into close association with predestination, for man is predestined to be conformed to the image of the Son.[3] Calvin seems a little perturbed about that relation,[4] though it follows very closely from his association of predestination with ethic. The reason seems to be that, for Calvin, predestination is essentially grounded upon the secret council of God, while the *imago dei* is essentially a knowledgeable relation to God the eternal Word.[5] But that only indicates a weakness in Calvin's doctrine of predestination which is not grounded wholly in Christ.[6] But if, as Calvin asserts, God insists on fulfilling His original intention for man, keeping in view the end of His creation,[7] and that divine insistence is seen in the continuous relation of God's gracious will toward us, then the image of God must be interpreted in terms of predestination, though certainly not in terms of a dead predestination,[8] for God is the living God, but in terms of a predestination that is itself to be interpreted eschatologically. At any rate, it is certain that Calvin thinks of the *imago dei* at times in eschatological terms. It is called a "heritage",[9] not in the sense of a natural hereditary endowment, for it rests only on the goodness of God so that we are constantly beholden to Him for it.[10] Man is "formed in God's image to the intent that he should hope for the inheritance of God's Kingdom, and so be partakers of the glory of His Son".[11] "The spring of this faith and hope

---

[1] *Instit.* 3. 6. 1, 3.   [2] *Ibid.*
[3] *Comm. on Rom.* 8 : 29; *on 2 Cor.* 4 : 10; *on Eph.* 1 : 4-12; *on 2 Pet.* 1 : 3; *on Ps.* 33 : 12.
[4] Cf. Calvin's hesitancy to admit that all men are "created unto salvation", *The Secret Providence of God*, Art. 1.
[5] *Instit.* 1. 15. 7; *Comm. on Col.* 3 : 10; *on Eph.* 4 : 24.
[6] The difficulty of Calvin's position is seen in that he makes "election precede grace" (*Instit.* 3. 22. 2), which cuts away the ground from such statements as in 2. 17. 1, and 3. 24. 5, where he says that we must not think of election apart from Christ.
[7] *Comm. on Gen.* 9 : 6.
[8] Here again Calvin is not true to his conception of the dynamic relation or the lively activity of the divine will over against man, and operates to a certain extent with a static conception of the divine Being.
[9] *Serm. on Job* 39 : 8 f.
[10] *Serm. on Job* 33 : 1 f.   [11] *Serm. on Job* 19 : 26 f.

which he has in God is not in the things that may be seen and comprehended by the natural reason, but it passes out of the world according as it is said, we must hope beyond hope, and that hope is of things hidden."[1] This is particularly true of the Christian, who, since Adam lost the image, possesses the image of God in faith so that until it is displayed in heaven it is only partly visible.[2] Since Adam lost the similitude of God, he can only beget men in his own image—*the spiritual image cannot be handed on.*[3] The spiritual image has to do with our *heavenly nature* and is gained only through our restoration in Christ. "For now we begin to bear the image of Christ, and are every day more and more transformed into it, but the image consists in spiritual regeneration. But then it will be fully restored both in body and soul, and what is now begun will be perfected and accordingly we will obtain in reality what we as yet only hope for."[4]

At this point we must relate the dynamic movement in which the *imago dei* has its being to the grace of God. It is not so much over against the will of God as law that Calvin thinks of the image of God as over against the will of God for man in mercy and kindness.[5] It is not with every kind of knowledge of the divine will that faith has to do, but with His gracious will.[6] And we must say the same thing of the image of God which Calvin relates to the gracious promise of God, that is, to His gracious will *toward us*.[7] Just as we live and move and have our being entirely in the grace of God,[8] so we are made conformable to God only through His grace.[9] Calvin's doctrine of creation as gracious act graciously maintained is all-important here, for it is only within that view of creation that he thinks of the *imago dei*. God has not made us in such a way that, having put us in the world, He lets us alone to walk as we can.[10] Rather does He abide with us continually so that "His hand is always stretched out toward us". We live by divine *visitation*.[11] "It behoves us to mark well this word *visitation* which signifies as much that when God has put us

---

[1] *Ibid.;* cf. *Serm. on Job* 14 : 1 f.
[2] *Instit.* I. 15. 4.
[3] *Comm. on Rom.* 5 : 12.
[4] *Comm. on* 1 *Cor.* 15 : 49.
[5] *Instit.* 3. 2. 6, 7; *Comm. on Heb.* 4 : 16; *Instit.* I. 10. 2.
[6] *Instit.* 3. 2. 7; 3. 2. 30; *Comm. on Heb.* 4 : 16; 11 : 11; *on Ps.* 19 : 8.
[7] *Instit.* I. 10. 2; 3. 2. 6, 7.
[8] *Instit.* I. 5. 3; *Serm. on Job* 5 : 20 f.
[9] *Instit.* I. 15. 4, 5.
[10] *Serm. on Job* 10 : 7 f. This thought is constantly repeated by Calvin. To leave us to ourselves would be a "sore scourge". "Behold God thunders against us when He says He will leave us in our own hand" (13 : 1 f.).
[11] The word is taken from *Job* 10 : 12; cf. *Comm. on Eph.* 4 : 18.

into this world, He does not leave us alone here, as if He should say, Walk every one as you can: but He abides with us continually, and has His hand always stretched out to pour His power into us to the intent that we may not miscarry. Therefore seeing we cannot continue except He have His eye always upon us to visit us and to look to us, we must learn to rule our life in such a way as if we were ever in His presence. And forasmuch as this assures us of God's infinite goodness which He shows toward us, let it enable us to walk in fear of Him, to magnify Him, and to yield Him His due praise."[1] God has deliberately created a world "stuffed with riches" that we may learn to attribute all to the love and mercy of God,[2] and to learn that what He gave at creation He continues graciously to give.[3] It was just for this reason, says Calvin, that the Scriptures indicate that God created man "in the image of God, thereby intimating that the blessings in which man's happiness consisted were not his own but were derived by divine communication".[4]

In this doctrine of the *imago dei*, Calvin agrees with the Roman Catholic view that the image of God must be related to a *supernatural gift*—though he points out that this is rarely understood properly.[5] To have been made in the image of God is an act of sheer kindness,[6] indeed of "infinite grace and more than fatherly love".[7] One of the difficulties in expounding the thought of Calvin here is that there are two important factors constitutive of the *imago dei*. One is the act of God's pure grace, and the other is the response of man to that act — and both are brought together in one in the doctrine of the *imago dei*. That applies to man's ordinary life. Even though the body is God's goodly and wonderful workmanship, it is nothing if it have not life shed into it. "For as much then as God has quickened us, therein He has uttered His great goodness, and we ought to glorify Him the more in it and acknowledge ourselves bound unto Him beyond all measure." This acknowledgment is constitutively part of the *imago dei*, as much as the workmanship of God. "But there is much more in men than life. That is the reason why Job says expressly

---

[1] *Serm. on Job* 10 : 7 f.   [2] *Serm. on Job* 11 : 7 f.
[3] *Instit.* 2. 1. 1.   [4] *Instit.* 2. 2. 1.
[5] *Instit.* 2. 2. 2, 4, 12, 16. Calvin disagrees, of course, with the Roman interpretation of this idea. See also *Comm. on Ezek.* 11 : 19, 20.
[6] *Comm. on Ps.* 8 : 3 f.; *Instit.* 2. 12. 6: "To this degree of honour he was exalted by the kindness of the Son."
[7] *Comm. on Ps.* 8 : 9 f.

that God had given him *life and grace*. For thereby he tells us that the life of men is matched with understanding and reason. And therefore it is said in the first chapter of St. John, *That life was the light of men*. When John declared that all things were quickened by the Word of God and that the said eternal wisdom which is in God is the wellspring of life and power, he shows that men have not only life, so that they can eat and drink, but that there is also a light shining in them. By this word *light* He means that the image of God is imprinted in us, because we have understanding and reason, because we discern between good and evil, and because men are born to have some form and order and common society among themselves, so that every man has a conscience of his own to tell him what is evil and what is good. Ye see then how God has granted men a prerogative which is not only that He has given them life, but also enlightened their minds, in such a way that they judge and discern and even take hold of eternal life. Thus ye see how God has endued man with a grace that cannot be valued sufficiently. And therefore let us learn to consider well what God has given us and we shall have cause enough to glorify Him, and we shall not need to pass beyond ourselves for it."[1] "We should be ravished with the knowledge of God's goodness and grace in making us such as we are and of so goodly and excellent a workmanship."[2] There are times when Calvin appears to say that the *imago dei* is equivalent to man's reason and understanding, but on examination that never turns out to be the case. It is always to the *light* of the understanding that he points, which is man's life as a child of God and which can only be maintained in him by thankfully responding to God's grace, and that response is thought of as part of the *imago-light* which God intends to be in his soul. There is then in Calvin's doctrine of the *imago dei* an objective basis which is the act of God's pure grace, and which may indeed be identified with Christ Himself.[3] In this aspect of it the image of God must be regarded as *above the common order of nature* and as consisting in supernatural gifts.[4] But just because it is such, that is above nature, it does not involve a supernatural heightening of our ordinary nature or our physical qualities.[5] On the subjective side, however, the *imago dei* has to

[1] *Serm. on Job* 10 : 7 f.   [2] *Ibid.*
[3] *Instit.* 2. 12. 6. This is doubtless not realized through our first creation, but is seen clearly in our restoration in Christ. See *Comm. on Gen.* 1 : 26; *on* 1 *Cor.* 15 : 44 f.
[4] *Comm. on* 2 *Pet.* 1 : 3.   [5] *Instit.* 2. 3. 6 f.

do with man's response to grace. Thus he was made in the image of God "with the object of extolling the singular grace of God",[1] and "of truly ascribing all his excellencies to the admirable gifts of his Maker".[2] On the subjective side, the *imago dei* may be defined as man's humble and adoring gratitude to God for His wonderful grace, in which motion of thankfulness man most truly reflects or images the glory of the Father so as to be himself a true child of the Father. It is grateful sonship.[3]

No theme recurs more constantly throughout Calvin's *Institutes*, *Commentaries*, and *Sermons* than man's duty of thankfulness, and his sin in ingratitude.[4] We shall see that more clearly when we come to deal with the way in which Calvin thinks of the fall of man, and the destruction of the *imago* through pride and unthankfulness, but Calvin cannot be truly understood there unless we see the emphasis he places here upon the element of thankfulness in man's inner life. God has graciously chosen man, though he is not worthy, to be the recipient of boundless grace and, as that recipient, to reflect God's glory back to Himself. "We are created to God's glory, to serve Him and worship Him. For although He has no need of us, nor is the better or the worse for our service, yet it is His will to have reasonable creatures which shall know Him and in knowing Him yield Him that which belongeth unto Him."[5] In thankful adoration we yield back to God the *imago dei*. "We have to consider how we ought to glorify God in all our life, and hereby see also to what end we are created and why we live. Therefore if we wish to maintain our life before God we must always aim at this mark: that He be blessed and glorified by us and that we have such a burning zeal and affection to serve His glory as to assure ourselves that it is an intolerable and even a most horrible thing in all respects that His name should be blasphemed and as it were cursed through us, that is to say, that we should cause His glory to be as it were defaced, especially since He has put His image in us to this end that it should shine forth in us."[6] Calvin thinks of God as having made man to be the conscious correlative of His grace in a life of

[1] *Instit.* 1. 15. 4.   [2] *Instit.* 1. 15. 3; 3. 7. 4.
[3] *Instit.* 3. 6. 3; *Comm. on* 1 John 4 : 17.
[4] See *Instit.* 1. 5. 1 f., 3 f.; 2. 1. 1 f.; 2. 2. 10, 15, 18; 2. 3. 5 f., 10; 3. 20. 41; *Comm. on Gen.* 2 : 9; 3 : 2-6; 8 : 21; *on John* 1 : 9; *on Heb.* 2 : 5; *on* 2 *Pet.* 1 : 3; *Serm. on Deut.* 28 : 46 f.; *on Job* 5 : 11 f.; 35 : 8 f., etc.
[5] *Serm. on Job* 1 : 1 f.
[6] *Serm. on Job* 1 : 6 f.

thankful response,[1] but in such a way that it is only as man reflects in thankfulness and praise the grace and glory of God that he himself becomes established as a man in the image of God. "It is intended that man should remember whence he received his life in order that he might acknowledge that he lives not by his own power but by the kindness of God alone and that life is not an intrinsic good, but proceeds from God. . . . He cannot otherwise retain it than by acknowledging that it was received from Him."[2] But inasmuch as man lives by the hand of God constantly stretched out to him in goodness, or by God's gracious and abiding visitation, so that he has his life not in himself but only in this gracious act of communication, therefore his *imago dei* which is thus *adventitious and above nature*[3] is grounded in the continual giving of God, and exists truly only in a motion that is essentially correlative to the motion of God's gracious will towards him.[4] *Imago dei* is not a dead but a living image, not a mute expression of the divine glory,[5] but a witness-bearing image evoked by the wonderful grace of God in calling man into communion with Himself, and having its own essential motion contrapuntal to the gracious and continual giving of the Father. "When Paul makes *the overflowing of God's gift* (i.e., grace) *consist in gratitude*, tending to the glory of its Author, he admonishes us that *every blessing that God confers upon us perishes through our carelessness if we are not prompt in rendering thanks*."[6]

At this point it will be sufficient to note that Calvin regards as the exact antithesis of the image of God in man, or as the total perversion of it, a motion that is characterized by pride or selfish

---

[1] *Instit.* 3. 19. 8: "By thanksgiving I understand that which proceeds from a mind recognizing the kindness and goodness of God in His gifts. For many indeed understand that the blessings which they enjoy are the gifts of God, and praise Him in their works; but not being persuaded that these have been given to them, how can they give thanks to God as the Giver?" See also *Comm. on Rom.* 1 : 8.

[2] *Comm. on Gen.* 2 : 9.

[3] Cf. *Instit.* 2. 2. 12; *Serm. on Eph.* 5 : 31-33.

[4] Cf. *Instit.* 2. 2. 1, 10; 2. 3. 5; *Comm. on Gen.* 2 : 9; 8 : 21; *on Col.* 3 : 10; *on John* 1 : 9.

[5] *Instit.* 3. 6. 3: "The Scripture exhibits God the Father, who, as He has reconciled us to Himself in His Anointed, has impressed His image on us, to which He would have us be conformed. . . . After showing us that we have degenerated from our true origin, viz., the law of our Creator, it adds that Christ through whom we have returned to favour with God is set before us as a model, *the image of which our lives should express*. . . . The Lord adopts us for His sons on the condition that our life be a *representation* of *Christ*, the bond of union."

[6] *Comm. on 2 Cor.* 4 : 16. Cf. *on Rom.* 11 : 22: *Gentes ergo Paulus ascitas hac lege esse docet in spem vita aterna, ut eius possessionem sua gratitudine retineant.* See also the 1536 *Institutio*, where Calvin practically equates the *imago* with the *actio* of gratitude.

possession or self-propelled activity,[1] for that would be a motion not correlative to, but counter to, the grace of God, and so far from reflecting the honour of God it does dishonour to Him and *does despite to* or *disgraces His grace*.[2] Then it is no longer the *imago dei* in man, for it does not reflect the truth of God which is His mercy,[3] but reflects sin and self-will. "We are covered with reproach, and whereas the image of God should shine forth in us, now we have the marks of sin."[4] "To whatsoever extent any man rests in himself to that same extent he impedes the beneficence of God."[5] For man to rest utterly upon God is to be a true child of His grace, but he can do that only in a life of thankfulness in which his mind and will, which are natural but rational endowments created for this very purpose, are given a total orientation over against God's gracious will such that man lives from beyond himself, and not from his own fancied momentum. To be conformable to God he must live *in God's wise*, in accordance with the motion of His grace and revelation, in recognition "that He is our Maker, our Maintainer, and one that has showed such fatherly goodness toward us that we of our duty ought to be as children towards Him if we would not be utterly unthankful".[6] "Nothing is more grateful to Him than obedience."[7]

---

[1] See *Serm. on Job* 7 : 7 f.

[2] *Serm. on Job* 3 : 2 f.; 5 : 20 f.; 10 : 7 f.; 33 : 1 f.; *Serm. on* 1 *Cor.* 10 : 12 f.; *Instit.* 2. 3. 10: *Imo nos ipsi eam (gratiam) obscuramus et extenuamus nostra ingratitudine.* Cf. *Instit.* 2. 2. 1.

[3] *Instit.* 3. 2. 7. For this reason, says Calvin, *mercy* and *truth* are joined together in the Bible. Cf. 3. 13. 4.

[4] *Serm. on Deut.* 28 : 46 f.

[5] *Serm. on Job* 1 : 1; see also 1 : 6 f.; 3 : 1 f.; 4 : 20 f.; *Comm. on Ps.* 33 : 12; 147 : 10: "For man to arrogate the very least to himself will only be a hindrance, in the way of the mercy of God by which alone we stand."

[6] *Instit.* 2. 3. 5-14. Calvin's thought reflects the New Testament relation between *eucharistia* and *charis*. See also 3. 6. 3.

[7] *Instit.* 3. 20. 4.

Chapter Six

THE IMAGE OF GOD (4)

The teaching of Calvin on the imago dei is set forth with particular fullness in the Sermons on Job, which also give us his mature views. Imago dei has to do fundamentally with God's beholding rather than with man's. It is grounded in the will of God to regard man with a fatherly eye, and is maintained by His constant and gracious visitation. God has made man to be aware of this grace, and to live in conscious dependence upon it. The image reflected in man is not a matter of his natural being, but is above nature, and is grounded in a special relation to the familiar presence of God which distinguishes man from all other created beings on the earth. On man's side, the image is grounded in his response to this familiar address of God, but it is not a response which he is able to make by virtue of his own nature. It is only possible through the quickening Word of the Spirit. It is here that God utters His Word to the full in the creation of man, in distinction from the utterance of the bare Word upon which all creation depends for being. This Word forms man in his obedience to respond to it in faith and love, and creates the spiritual capacity by which he knows God and reflects His image. To disdain this Word is to do despite to grace, to dishonour God, and to turn the imago dei into its opposite. In this way man denies his human nature, and becomes a beast.

IN the foregoing discussion frequent citations have been made from Calvin's *Sermons on the Book of Job*, where the text gives him ample opportunity to develop his teaching on the doctrine of man. Though he is constantly employing eristic, as he does in the *Commentaries* and in the *Institutes*, his discussion in the *Sermons* keeps very close to the Scripture, so that what doctrine we have in them is given in the form of Biblical theology. At the same time, his later *Sermons*, particularly on *Job, Deuteronomy*, and on *Ephesians*, are of particular value in giving us his mature teaching about man. It is not always easy to reach consistency in interpreting his thought in the *Institutes* and the *Commentaries*, but in the *Sermons on Job* particularly, we have in constant repetition, and without the bias due to systematic treatment, teaching which brings out in particular fullness and clarity his views about the

75

imago dei.[1] At the same time this helps us to understand the emphasis he placed upon elements already brought out in the foregoing discussion.

Here then it becomes quite clear that Calvin thinks of the *imago dei* as having to do first of all and fundamentally with God's beholding, rather than man's—that is, what I have called the objective basis of the image of God in grace. "God looks upon Himself, so to speak, and beholds Himself in man as in a mirror."[2] It is this gracious beholding by God that keeps man in existence, although as man he ever lives on the very verge of death. His "life is consumed from morning to evening",[3] and "were it not that God looks upon him with a fatherly eye, it is certain that he should be undone every minute of the hour".[4] God has made man to be aware of this utter dependence on the mercy of God in order that in his awareness he may be drawn to God the Father by bonds of love and thankfulness that he may be, as no other creature is, a real child of God. "He sends us into this world even to show Himself a Father toward us. For inasmuch as we are reasonable creatures and have the image of God implanted in our nature we have a record that He beholds us here as His children."[5] This is the act of His pure grace "that He accepts us as the work of His hand. Then we must not pretend to be loved at God's hand for any deserts of our own, but because He sees we are His workmanship."[6] We are unable to reach this consciousness by the aid of our natural reason, though the universe has been fashioned so as to direct us into a thankful and filial adoration of the Father. But we do understand and see the wonder of God's grace when we are reformed by the Holy Spirit and repaired after the image of God in Christ, and so adopted as the children of God.[7] Then we know too that when God beholds His image in us He does that "*not by looking at that which He has put into us by nature, but at that which He has put into us by grace*".[8] Man, in the image of God, is much more than the *groundwork of his being*.[9] He is what he is, a man made in the

---

[1] These sermons were written down as Calvin preached them, were seen by him, and published a year before his death in 1564. Ten years later they were done into English.

[2] *Serm. on Job* 10 : 7 f.   [3] *Serm. on Job* 5 : 20 f.   [4] *Serm. on Job* 10 : 7 f.
[5] *Serm. on Job* 5 : 20 f.   [6] *Serm. on Job* 14 : 16 f.
[7] *Serm. on Job* 10 : 7 f.; 14 : 1 f. Cf. *Comm. on Eph.* 2 : 10.
[8] *Serm. on Job* 10 : 7 f.; cf. *Comm. on Eph.* 1 : 17: "The gifts of the Spirit are not the gifts of nature."
[9] *Serm. on Job* 10 : 7 f.

image of God, over and above his ordinary creation, and indeed *above nature*, by an act of grace in which God continually acknowledges him as his child.[1] In the changes of human existence, in man's being continually consumed and renewed, there is a special renewing after the image of God in Christ by which men surmount ordinary life,[2] and continue bound to God by an inestimable bond.[3] "It is even as if He had changed us, and cast us new again into a mould, and as though He had put us once again to the making."[4] Commenting on Job's words, "Thou hast given me life and grace, and Thy visitation hath preserved my soul", Calvin says: "See why Job matches the word *life* with the word *grace*, meaning thereby that the brute beasts have no partaking of the life that is in man, but there is in men a dignity far greater, and of much more value."[5] Then when commenting on *John* 1 : 3, 4, he says: "All things have their life of God, and the same life has forever been enclosed in His eternal Word. Howbeit there is one life which is light, and that life serveth for men. . . . Forasmuch then as God so enlightens men, we see ourselves bound in a far greater and closer bond than if He had but simply made us His creatures. For if there were no more than that God created us with His hand, yet it would behove us to give Him thanks for it. But seeing it has pleased Him to make a difference between us and the brute beasts, and to give us so noble and excellent life as we may see, may we not well say: Lord what were we? And yet notwithstanding it has pleased Thee to set us here in the number of Thy children and to give us Thy *mark*. And whence does this come to us? Can we find anything in ourselves to say that we have moved Thee to this, or that Thou wert led to it by our worthiness? No, but all proceeds of Thine own free goodness."[6]

On the subjective side, as we have already seen, man's being in the image of God consists in his answer to the grace of God, and in particular in answer to the gracious decision of God to regard him as His child. Fundamentally, "God alone knows His Works",[7] but "He will have His glory shine in us",[8] and have us "yield what belongs to Him".[9] It is to this end that we have

---

[1] *Serm. on Job* 14 : 13 f.; 14 : 16 f.; 10 : 7 f.; 35 : 8 f.
[2] *Ibid.; Serm. on Job* 32 : 4 f.
[3] *Serm. on Job* 35 : 8 f. "And so we are bound in a far greater and narrower bond than if He had simply made us His children" (*Ibid.*).
[4] *Serm. on Job* 14 : 13 f. [5] *Ibid.* [6] *Serm. on Job* 35 : 8 f.
[7] *Serm. on Job* 2 : 1 f. [8] *Serm. on Job* 3 : 2 f. [9] *Serm. on Job* 1 : 1.

been created, that we may acknowledge His goodness, but acknowledge it in "His wise"[1] by knowing that He has accepted us as the work of His hand, and that He looks upon us with a fatherly eye,[2] and also "by being ravished with the knowledge of the goodness of God and His grace".[3] We are unable, however, to make this response by virtue of our own nature,[4] and in our natural state we do not know that God wishes to regard us with a fatherly eye, and therefore we cannot come to Him as He would have us. It is only a saving knowledge of God that can enable us to do that — and that we may have through His Word. Thus, "It is not enough for us to conceive God to be the Maker of the world, and to father all power upon Him: but we must know Him to be our Father because He draws us to Him with so gentle and loving a care as if we were His own children. What earthly father can do so much for those that are descended from him? Then to know God rightly we must taste of His goodness which He has uttered to us. . . . God's intent is to draw us unto salvation when He speaks unto us; but here He speaks gently and familiarly, He utters His heart unto us, He shows us which is the way of life; and He enlightens us with the brightness of His Word which shines upon us."[5] The Word itself however is a dead thing until by His Spirit God quickens our minds to understand it,[6] though of course God's Word is not dark of itself.[7] "True it is that when we come into this world, we bring some remnant of God's image wherein Adam was created: howbeit that same image is so disfigured that we are full of unrighteousness and there is nothing but blindness and ignorance in our minds. Ye see then what the state of men is at their birth. But God enlightens us by His Spirit and in such a way that we are able to behold Him, as far as we need for the transforming of us into His glory and for the reforming of us by His Holy Spirit."[8] This is a matter of faith. "We must always believe that God beholds His workmanship in us, that He will be moved and inclined to do us good, and to maintain us. For we know what is attributed to Him in Holy Scripture, namely that He preserves what He has made and brings the thing which He has once made

[1] *Serm. on Job* 7 : 16 f.; 1 : 1.   [2] *Serm. on Job* 14 : 13 f.; 14 : 16 f.
[3] *Serm. on Job* 10 : 7 f.
[4] *Serm. on Job* 10 : 7 f.; 19 : 26 f.; 32 : 4 f.; 14 : 13 f.: "Men of their own nature can never open their mouths to call upon God in truth."
[5] *Serm. on Job* 36 : 1 f.   [6] *Serm. on Job* 42 : 1 f.
[7] *Serm. on Job* 33 : 14 f.   [8] *Serm. on Job* 14 :13 f.

to perfection."[1] "However, we must not look only to our first creation, for the hope that we shall have thereby will be very slender, for God's image is as it were blotted out in us by Adam's sin. But forasmuch as God of His own infinite mercy has renewed us and adopted us to be His children in our Lord Jesus Christ, and imprinted His image again in us: therein we are His workmanship, and we may come with our heads upright to call upon Him, and to assure ourselves that He will not shake us off, and that we shall be welcome to Him."[2]

"And so we come to God not only as Him that created me, but also as Him that hath uttered a fatherly love toward me. For I am created after *His* image and likeness."[3] "We see in what wise we may answer God: that is to say, in what wise we may freely come to Him, namely, by knowing that He loves us and that He has accepted us as the work of His hand. . . . Therefore let us mark well that it behoves us to be persuaded of God's love towards us, that thereby we may conceive such trust as we may present ourselves to Him and be well assured that our sovereign welfare is to answer Him."[4] "When the Holy Ghost teaches us how to pray, He sets these words before us, 'Lord, we are Thy Workmanship'. . . . Ye see then whereof we ought to take occasion to trust in God."[5]

If in Calvin's thought the *imago dei* has thus to do first of all with God's gracious beholding of man as His child, which is the objective basis of the *imago*, and then with man's response to that decision of God's grace in coming to Him as a Father and yielding to Him the gratitude and honour which are due in such a filial relation, which is the subjective basis of the *imago*, it is implied throughout that God has created man just for this relationship with God and in that relationship has already given the *imago dei* its being in the sphere of man's understanding. It was thus in creating man that "God uttered His Word to the full".[6] "God uttered His great riches so that in effect man was a mirror of the excellent glory that shines fully in God."[7] In this act of creation God has specially made man with ears that he may give ear to that Word and know how, as a man in the image of God, he should answer Him. "The use of the tongue and ears is to lead

[1] *Serm. on Job* 10 : 7 f.　[2] *Serm. on Job* 14 : 16 f.
[3] *Serm. on Job* 35 : 8 f.　[4] *Serm. on Job* 14 : 16 f.　[5] *Ibid.*
[6] *Serm. on Job* 10 : 7 f. Cf. also "The infinite wisdom of God uttered itself in the shape of a man" (*Ibid*).
[7] *Serm. on Job* 14 : 1 f.

us into the truth by means of God's Word that we may know how we were created incorruptible and that when we are passed out of this world there is an heritage prepared for us above, and in short to bring us unto God. Faith cometh by hearing, as St. Paul says. Seeing then that God has ordained our ears to so excellent a use as to lift us up to heaven to behold our God, and to behold Him as our Father, and to witness unto us that He receives us as His children and to sow the seed of incorruptible life in us in the midst of the corruptions that are in us, should we play as deaf men and stop our ears?"[1] Not to give ear to God's Word, and not to give the answer of thankfulness to God's love is in fact to disclaim the image of God,[2] and to do despite to His grace.[3] This is what fallen man has actually done — he has "turned the image of God into dishonour"[4] and "turned truth upside down and converted it into falsehood".[5] That as we shall see is the way in which Calvin thinks of sin as destroying or utterly defacing the image of God in man. In this way man has become a "double beast", says Calvin. He was made with an animal nature as other beasts, but he was made with the image of God which distinguished him from the beasts. To deface the image of God is to return to beastliness, and that is what fallen man has done.[6] "Such as disdain to give ear to God and to His Truth to be taught by it, and seek not to be conformed more and more in the things that they have heard already, pervert the order of nature, and become as it were monsters, and worse than brute beasts. And why? For a beast follows his own kind, but behold, a man who calls himself wise, having reason and discretion, and who was created after the image of God to be enlightened in all truth, nevertheless gives his mind daily to eat and to drink, but not to profit in God's Word."[7]

Since this is actually the case with fallen men, they must learn to give God an answer that cuts across the grain of their present nature. "We must serve Him after a clean contrary fashion from that which pleases our nature."[8] But if so, God Himself must "bore into our ears" until we hear His Word and are enabled to give an answer corresponding to His grace and glory. No doubt God's Word comes to all men alike, to the reprobate as well as the

[1] *Serm. on Job* 33 : 29 f.; 34 : 1 f.   [2] *Serm. on Job* 31 : 9 f.
[3] *Serm. on Job* 3 : 2 f.; 5 : 20 f.; 33 : 1 f. Cf. *on* 1 *Cor.* 10 : 12 f.
[4] *Serm. on Job* 33 : 1 f.   [5] *Serm. on Job* 15 : 17 f.
[6] *Serm. on Job* 32 : 4 f.; 33 : 29 f.   [7] *Serm. on Job* 33 : 29 f.
[8] *Serm. on Job* 21 : 12 f.

elect, but even in the reprobate there must be "an opening of the ear insomuch that they may perceive, in spite of themselves, that God speaks to them."[1] Here Calvin must think of the reprobate as having the image of God in so far, at least, as they have their ears bored open to hear the Word of God — a point which we shall discuss later. But the elect are not able to give the answer that God requires, and that yields Him His glory, apart from the effective operation of the Holy Spirit through the Word in men's hearts. Therefore, "we must esteem the Word of God. For our chief felicity is that God draw near unto us, and we unto Him. And how shall this be done, and by what means? It is done when He on His part comes down to us, delivers His Word unto us, and testifies unto us that He will dwell amongst us: and when we receive this Word, it is as much as if we received God, and did Him homage to the end that He might reign over us. Forasmuch then as God is present with us by means of the Word . . . we must desire always to be in His presence. . . . What must we do then? We must acknowledge Him to be our Father as indeed He shows Himself unto us so. When we know Him to be so good and pitiful, it is certain that we shall seek boldly to come near to Him; and when we come near, we shall desire nothing else but to continue there to the end and by no means to swerve from Him in the world. Not only therefore should we have God before our eyes but we should desire Him to look upon us and guide us."[2] Our answer is to look to God as He looks to us, and that is the way we render unto God His due in honour and glory. The *imago dei* in Calvin's exposition has always to do with the glory of God, i.e., with His grace.[3] Only when a man seeks the glory of God, by acknowledging His Word and by responding to His grace thankfully and with the adoring love of a child for his father, does he reflect that Glory.[4] Otherwise he does God dishonour and turns himself doubly into a beast.

In gathering together Calvin's thought, so far as we have discussed it, we must say that Calvin does not think of the *imago dei*

---

[1] *Serm. on Job* 33 : 14 f.   [2] *Serm. on Job* 21 : 13 f.

[3] Cf. *Comm. on Rom.* 9 : 22, 23; *on Eph.* 1 : 12; *on John* 8 : 54.

[4] Cf. *Instit.* 2. 3. 4: "The principal part of rectitude is wanting when there is no zeal for the glory of God, and there is no such zeal in those whom He has not regenerated by His Spirit." Cf. *Comm. on Jer.* 13 : 16: "How can we ascribe glory to God, except by acknowledging Him to be the fountain of all wisdom, justice, and power, and especially by trembling at His sacred Word? Whosoever then does not fear and reverence God, whosoever does not believe His Word, robs Him of His glory."

in terms of being, that is, in terms of man's being this or that in himself, but in terms of a spiritual relation to the gracious will of God. Within the single thought of *imago dei* there is included a two-sided relation, but it is a relation which has only one essential motion and rhythm. There is the grace of God, and man's answer to that grace. Such an answer partakes of and subsists in the essential motion of grace — for even man's answer is the work of the Holy Spirit who through the Word forms the image anew in man, and forms his lips to acknowledge that he is a child of the Father. The *imago dei* is thus the conformity of an intelligent being to the will and Word of God, the imprint of the Holy Spirit who forms man's ear to hear and his eye to see the Glory of God. Man's answer corresponds in reflexive fashion, so far as it is true, to the essential character of grace which is the free and spontaneous act of divine love. That he can do only in thankfulness, for it is thankfulness that is the motion from man to God, reciprocating the downward motion of grace from God to man. He can be thankful only when he knows that even that answer is from the Lord. " 'The preparation of the heart in man and the answer of the tongue are from the Lord' (Prov. 16 : 1). It is a strange infatuation, surely, for miserable men, who cannot even give utterance except in so far as God pleases, to begin to act without Him."[1] Thus the *imago dei*, spiritually considered, has no momentum or security of its own, but depends entirely upon the grace of God and is maintained only in relation to that grace. To fulfil his destiny as made in the image of God man must live a life of thankful dependence on the goodness of God without seeking to arrogate anything of God's gifts to himself as if they were his own, and as if he did not have them only in divine communication. "Man cannot arrogate anything, however minute, to himself without robbing God of His honour, and through rash confidence subjecting himself to a fall."[2] "He cannot arrogate to himself one particle beyond his due without losing himself in vain confidence, and by transferring divine honour to himself becoming guilty of the greatest impiety. And assuredly whenever our minds are seized with a longing to *possess a something of our own, which may reside in us rather than in God*, we may rest assured that the thought is suggested by no other counsellor than him who enticed our first parents to aspire to be like gods, knowing good

[1] *Instit.* 1. 16. 6.
[2] *Instit.* 2. 2. 1; cf. *Comm. on Lam.* 1 : 7.

and evil."[1] "God bestows His grace upon us that we may know that we are nothing, that we stand only by the mercy of God."[2] Therefore a man must continually go beyond himself, and seek from God what he lacks in himself, which is how Calvin defines the life of faith. "Faith sets man before God emptied of all things, so that he seeks what he needs from God's gratuitous goodness. . . . He brings nothing before God except faith: then he brings nothing of his own, because faith borrows as it were through favour what is not in man's possession. He then who lives by faith has no life in himself, but because he wants it, he flies for it to God alone."[3] Faith is the motion of man's response to the Word by which he becomes comformable to God, that is, has *imago dei*, but thankfulness is the great characteristic of that motion. Man was not made with any settled constancy, but it was the intention of God that by living in this wise, in utter dependence on God's grace in a world which witnessed to him every day of how absolutely dependent he was on God's unmerited kindness, man should eventually be endowed with a more permanent *imago dei* and a more permanent life. God planted the tree of life in the Garden as a pledge of life, that man might learn to find his perfection in God Himself.[4] And so "it behoves God to stabilize that which He has once put into us, for if He maintains it not by His grace all will go to decay".[5]

All this we see truly only in Christ. In that man had conferred on him in Christ a *quickening Spirit*, we see that the state of man when he became a *living soul* was "not perfected in the person of Adam". "A peculiar benefit is conferred by Christ that we may be renewed to a life which is celestial, whereas before the fall of Adam, man's life was only earthly, seeing it had no firm and settled constancy."[6] Calvin really identifies the *imago dei* in the Christian with what Paul called the *inner man* which is created after the image and glory of Christ.[7] In Christ "the image of God is restored in holiness and righteousness to us for this end, that we may at length be partakers of eternal life and glory as far as it will be necessary for our complete felicity".[8] This image is "not what

[1] *Instit.* 2. 2. 10; *Serm. on Gal.* 5 : 2 f.
[2] *Instit.* 2. 2. 11. Cf. 3. 7. 4; *Serm. on Gal.* 5 : 2 f.
[3] *Comm. on Hab.* 2 : 4; cf. *Instit.* 3. 11. 7; 4. 17. 42, etc.
[4] *Comm. on Gen.* 2 : 9; 3 : 23.
[5] *Serm. on Job* 7 : 7 f.
[6] *Comm. on Gen.* 2 : 7; cf. on 1 *Cor.* 15 : 44 ff.
[7] *Comm. on Rom.* 7 : 23; on 1 *Cor.* 15 : 49; on *Eph.* 3 : 16; *Serm. on Gal.* 3 : 1 f.
[8] *Comm. on 2 Pet.* 1 : 4.

God puts into us by nature, but what He puts into us by grace".[1]
"Therefore it remains that men seek elsewhere for that which
they shall never be able to find within themselves. And surely
this is the office of faith to translate unto us what is proper to
Christ, and to make it ours by free participation. So that there is a
mutual relation between faith and the grace of Christ. . . . That
is given to men by the grace of God which they cannot give
themselves."[2] "Thus it is the property of faith to pass beyond
the whole course of this life and stretch toward a future immortality. Therefore since believers owe it to the favour of God
that enlightened by His Spirit they through faith enjoy the
prospect of heavenly life; there is so far from an approach to
arrogance in such glorying that anyone ashamed to confess it,
instead of testifying modesty or submission, rather betrays
extreme ingratitude by maliciously suppressing the divine goodness."[3]

[1] *Serm. on Job* 10 : 7 f.
[2] *Comm. on Acts* 15 : 9: *Superest ergo ut alibi quærant homines, quod intus apud se
nunquam invenient. Et certe fidei officium est, quod proprium habet Christus in nos transferre,
et gratuita communicatione efficere nostrum. Ita inter fidem et Christi gratiam mutua est
relatio . . . In summa, conferri hominibus per Dei gratiam significat, quod sibi dare ipsi
nequeunt.* This really means that the *imago dei* which, strictly speaking, is Christ, in
man subsists in the mutual relation of faith and grace. Cf. *on Heb.* 11 : 11; and *Instit.*
3. 2. 6, where Calvin says there is an "inseparable relation between faith and the
Word". See also *on John* 11 : 22.
[3] *Instit.* 3. 2. 40.

Chapter Seven

TOTAL PERVERSITY (1)

Calvin refuses to enunciate a doctrine of sin apart from the doctrine of creation, and except in the context of grace. To think of man as he is within the confines of pollution would lead to the contempt of man and to slander against the Creator. The doctrine of depravity is properly a corollary of the doctrine of grace, an inference from the Gospel of a new creation. Just because the Gospel speaks of man's salvation in total terms, the doctrine of depravity must be enunciated in total terms. This applies also to the doctrine of the imago dei. *Since the Gospel speaks of a new creation, and tells us that man can be restored to a being in the image of God only by going outside of himself to Christ, the express image of God, it follows that in himself man is bereft of that image, while, if anything of it remains, it is but a fearful deformity. The total terms required by the Gospel of a new creation provide Calvin with a problem. On the one hand, Calvin admits that the image has been wholly defaced from man, and that he is utterly dead in trespasses and sins. In this sense one cannot speak about a portion of the image remaining in fallen man. However, Calvin makes a distinction between the spiritual and the natural. At the fall, man was totally deprived of all spiritual gifts, and corrupted in his natural gifts, and that means the corruption of his whole nature. While he is completely despoiled of the spiritual image, that does not mean that his natural gifts are polluted or destroyed in themselves, though it is through the natural gifts, such as the mind, that the spiritual image is reflected. Sin does not mean an ontological break with God, for Calvin does not hold a doctrine of evil as the privation of being. Sin does mean, however, a total corruption of the whole person in a spiritual sense, which is quite consonant with the fact that man's natural gifts, while impaired, are still maintained in being by the will of God. This doctrine of Calvin is formulated under the concept of* perversity. *By this he means that the original order of grace upon which the* imago dei *was grounded is utterly perverted, though that does not mean that God's gracious intention has been set aside by sin. As far as man himself is concerned, therefore, the* imago dei *has been totally perverted, and if there is a remnant of it, it is now a dishonour to God, inasmuch as it can no longer image the divine glory. Three facts emerge here: (a) Any remnant of the image must refer to man's natural gifts, which indeed are used in the reflection of the spiritual image, but*

83

which are not in any sense the spiritual image or part of it. There is not a shred of the spiritual image left. If the distinction between good and evil remains, it has no relation to the spiritual image. (b) God does not let go His original intention in regard to man, i.e., the imago dei as grounded in the objective act of grace. Yet He disowns fallen men as His children, for He will not be Father of the children of disobedience who have turned His image into dishonour. (c) Nevertheless, some light and a seed of religion have been left in man, but in the nature of the case these partake of the total perversity, so that from the very start they are turned into the fountainhead of superstition. The light that is in man is turned into darkness, and the truth is held down in the form of falsehood. This remnant of truth turned into a lie can never be a predisposition for faith, or a basis for the knowledge of God.

So far, we have pursued Calvin's doctrine of man without taking much account of the doctrine of the Fall. This procedure has its importance, for it helps us to view the nature of man in direct relation to the grace of God in which human nature really consists and in which human nature possesses a high dignity. To think of man simply as he is would be to think of him "within the confines of human pollution".[1] This would lead us to think contemptuously of man, and would mean dishonour to the Creator as well as to His creation. We must take care to keep our thought of man close to our thought of God. "He who truly worships and honours God will be afraid to think slanderously of man."[2] But, in addition to this, when we come to think of man as he actually is, a fallen being, to do him justice and to do justice to the Creator, we must still think of man, even in his fallen condition, within the context of the grace from which he has fallen. How can we do that better than by looking to the grace in which he is renewed where we see again the grace from which he is fallen? Therefore, when Calvin approaches the facts of man's fallen and depraved nature, he refuses to enunciate a doctrine in abstraction from the new creation in Christ where man is placed in the light of his original truth which is still the truth about man, no matter how much he has perverted it and himself. That is the Word of grace by which he was made, and to which he is called to conform, toward which his life is desti-

---

[1] *Instit.* I. 1. 2. Cf. I. 15. 1: We must take care lest we attend only to the natural ills of man.
[2] *Comm. on James* 3 : 9.

nated. And so the *imago dei* in which and unto which man is created we see at last in Christ, who is identical with God's gracious action toward man. Here we see man more truly than anywhere else, because we have "a far richer and more powerful manifestation of divine grace in this second creation than in the first".[1] Inasmuch as man's original existence in the *imago dei* was rooted and maintained in grace, it is here, where grace restores man's existence to its proper ground, that we see man set out both in his true actuality now, and in relation to his final truth which will become actual in the resurrection. "As the animal nature which has precedency in us is in the image of Adam, so we shall be conformed to Christ in the heavenly nature; and this will be the completion of our restoration. For we now begin to bear the image of Christ, and are every day more and more transformed into it, but that image consists in spiritual regeneration. But then it will be fully restored both in body and in soul, and what is now begun will be perfected and accordingly we shall obtain in reality what as yet we only hope for."[2]

This means that, by starting from the fact of grace, Calvin forms his doctrine of man's present depravity only as a corollary of grace.[3] The revelation of the grace of God in Christ which results in a new creation carries with it a total judgment upon man as he is, including his mind and will — i.e., upon the natural man. The fact that man must receive in faith his salvation, his true life, his righteousness, and wisdom *from outside himself in Christ alone,* carries with it the inference that in himself man has been utterly deprived of the *imago dei* wherein his true nature consists. It is because faith must speak of salvation and forgiveness in total terms that it must also speak of sin and depravity in total terms. It is only within this context of grace, and only on the ground of this grace, that we have any right to make such a total judgment upon man as he is, but on this ground, that is, of a new creation, we must set aside the old man and all that pertains to him as having come under the total judgment of God manifested on the Cross.[4]

---

[1] *On Eph.* 4 : 24; see *Instit.* 1. 15. 4.

[2] *Comm. on* 1 *Cor.* 15 : 49.

[3] See especially *Comm. on John* 3 : 3 ff.; 3 : 17 ff.; *on Rom.* 6 : 21; Cf. *Instit.* 2 : 16 1-3; *Comm. on* 1 *John* 5 : 16.

[4] *Comm. on Gen.* 1 : 26; *on Isa.* 35 : 5; *on Hab.* 2 : 4; *on John* 3 : 6; 17 : 3; *on Acts* 15 : 9; *on Rom.* 1 : 18 f.; 12 : 2 f.; *on* 1 *Cor.* 1 : 30; 15 : 49; *on Eph.* 4 : 24; *on Col.* 2 : 3; 3 : 10; *Instit.* 1. 15. 4; 2. 1. 5 f., 9; 2. 3. 1, 6, 9; 2. 5. 19; 2. 12. 6; 3. 14. 5, etc.

This applies equally to the *imago dei*. On the one hand, it becomes apparent from the act of grace in Christ that the *imago dei* in the strict sense is Christ, and is not man's own possession.[1] It was indeed only by means of Christ, the real image of God, that Adam "approximated to the glory of his Maker".[2] And for this very reason we see that the *imago dei* is not just some one thing in man but refers to his total relation with God, and concerns the totality of his being. Our renewal in Christ makes it quite clear that the image of God has to do with "the entire excellence of human nature".[3] It is essential to man as God made him, and is constitutive of his whole person. No doubt it is entirely spiritual and can be mirrored therefore only in the light of intelligence, that is, of the heavenly intelligence,[4] but it does have outward tokens in man's rational existence which was created for this very purpose,[5] and through this spiritual knowledge by which man reflects the image of Christ and approximates to the glory of God, man's whole person (body and soul viewed as a unity) does receive a "true and substantial integrity".[6] In this way *imago dei* has to do with the whole man. It is not therefore external to him,[7] nor is it something super-added.[8] It is absolutely essential to true human nature. On the other hand, because it is only in Christ that man can have the rectitude and integrity which are constitutive of his true human nature and which concern his whole being, it is also apparent that fallen man possesses the *imago dei* no more than he possesses Christ, and that if we must speak of his relation to Christ in total terms we must also speak of his depravation of the image of God in total terms. Because grace implies a total judgment on man, it also implies a total judgment on his possession of the *imago dei*. It is an inescapable inference from the revelation of grace that Christ is our righteousness, and wisdom, and *imago dei*, that fallen man is quite bereft of the image of God.[9]

[1] *Instit.* 2. 2. 1, 4; 1. 15. 4; 2. 1. 6; 4. 17. 2.
[2] *Instit.* 2. 12. 6; see *Comm. on Col.* 3 : 19; *on Eph.* 4 : 24; *on John* 1 : 4.
[3] *Instit.* 1. 15. 4.
[4] *Instit.* 1. 15. 4; see *Comm. on Acts* 17 : 28. Calvin does say that "the mind of man is His true image" (17 : 22), but clearly this does not mean anything different from the idea that the *imago dei* is essentially rational (see *Comm. on Jer.* 5 : 23).
[5] *Instit.* 2. 1. 5; *Comm. on* 1 *Cor.* 15 : 45.
[6] *Instit.* 1. 15. 4.
[7] *Instit.* 1. 15. 4.
[8] Calvin does hold however that the image of God is a supernatural gift, as we have already noted (see *Comm. on John* 3 : 6). To the believer the image of God is imputed, and is possessed by faith. One day he will be fully clothed with it (*Comm. on* 2 *Cor.* 5 : 3).
[9] *Serm. on Eph.* 2 : 1 f.; *Comm. on Gen.* 3 : 1.

He is therefore alienated from himself,[1] and is totally corrupted or perverted.[2] If there is anything left of the image of God in him it is a "fearful deformity".[3]

There can be no doubt, therefore, in the mind of Calvin, that from the point of view of salvation in Christ faith must speak of fallen man in total terms.[4] By the single word of our Lord that we must be born again, he says, "our whole nature is condemned".[5] "In our nature there is nothing but perversity."[6] "Our whole nature is so vitiated that we can do nothing but sin."[7] "The soul of man is totally perverted and corrupted."[8] Even the natural virtues and the natural goodness of men must be regarded as "wholly iniquity".[9] Calvin can even say of fallen men: "Their proper nourishment is sin and there is not so much as one drop of goodness to be found in them, and, to be short, as the body receives its sustenance from meat and drink, so also men have no other substance in them than sin: all is corrupted."[10] "There is

---

[1] *Comm. on Gen.* 3 : 1.

[2] *Serm. on Eph.* 2 : 1 f.; 4 : 17 f.; *Serm. on Gal.* 5 : 19-23. Nowhere in all his commentaries or sermons is Calvin so clear and outspoken as in these *Sermons on Galatians* and *Ephesians* on the totality of human corruption.

[3] *Instit.* I. 15. 4; cf. 2. 2. 1; *Serm. on Job* 14 : 13. Cf. also *Institutio* (1536) 28: *Verum ubi in peccatum lapsus est, hæc imago et similitudo Dei inducta et obliterata est, hoc est, omnia divina gratia bona perdidit, quibus in viam vitæ deduci poterat. Præterea longe a Deo divisus est, et prorsus alienus factus. Unde consectarium est, omni sapientia, iustitia, virtute, vita exutum et spoliatum, quas nisi in Deo haberi non posse, iam ante dictum est. Quare nihil illi reliquum fuit nisi ignorantia, iniquitas, impotentia, mors, et iudicium: hi nempe sunt fructus peccati.*

[4] For a typical statement see the *Catechisme*, 1537, C.R. 22, 36: "*Lhomme fut premierement forme a limage et semblance de Dieu, affin quen ses ornemens desquelz il avoit este noblement vestu de Dieu il eust en admiration laucteur diceulx, et par telle recognoissance quil estoyt convenable il lhonorast. Mais parce que sestant confie dune si grande excellence de sa nature, ayant oublie dont elle estoit venue et subsistoit, il sest esforce de seslever hors du Seigneur, il a este necessaire quil feust despouille de tous les dons de Dieu desquelz follement il senorgueillissoyt, affin que estant desnue et despourveu de toute gloire il cogneust Dieu, lequel estant enrichy de ses largesses il avoit ose contempner. Par quoy nous tous qui avons nostre origine de la semence de Adam, ceste semblance de Dieu estant en nous esfacee, nous nayssons chair de chair. Car combien que soyons composez dune ame et dun corps, toutesfois nous ne sentons rien que la chair: tellement que en quelconque partie de lhomme que nous tournions les yeulx il nest possible de rien voir qui ne soit impur profane et abominable a Dieu. Car la prudence de lhomme, aveuglee et enveloppee dinfinis erreurs, tousiours contrarie a la sapience de Dieu: la volunte maulvaise et pleyne daffections corrumpues ne hait rien plus que la iustice dicelluy: les forces impuissantes a toutes bonnes oeuvres tendent furieusement a iniquite.*"

Cf. also *Instit.* 2. 1. 9; 2. 3. 1 f.; 2. 5. 9, 10; 3. 3. 23; 3. 14. 1; 4. 15. 10; *Comm. on Gen.* 3 : 1-6; *on Isa.* 35 : 5; *on Ezek.* 18 : 21; *Serm. on Matt.* 26 : 36 f.; *Comm. on Matt.* 13 : 24 f.; *on John* 3 : 6; *on Rom.* 7 : 14, etc.

[5] *Comm. on John* 3 : 6; see *Instit.* 2. 1. 9.

[6] *Serm. on Eph.* 2 : 1 f.

[7] *Dedication to the Catholic Epistles*; also *Comm. on Rom.* 6 : 6.

[8] *Serm. on Eph.* 2 : 1 f. Cf. *Instit.* 2. 2. 1: "The dominion of sin has complete possession of the soul."

[9] *Serm. on Eph.* 2 : 3 f.; *on Gal.* 1 : 8-9.

[10] *Serm. on Job* 15 : 11 f.

more worth in all the vermin of the world than there is in man, for he is a creature in whom the image of God has been effaced."[1] Again, speaking of man after the fall, Calvin says: "And truly, it was a sad and horrible spectacle that he in whom recently the image of God was shining should lie hidden under fetid skins to cover his own disgrace, and that there should be more comeliness in a dead animal than in a living man."[2] "It is true that our Lord created us after His own image and likeness, but that was *wholly defaced and wiped out* in us by the sin of Adam: we are accursed, we are by nature shut out from all hope of life."[3]

There is no doubt that the student of Calvin is faced with a difficult problem here, for in spite of taking this total view of man's corruption, Calvin can still admit that *something remains in fallen man*.[4] Salvation is indivisible, and righteousness is indivisible;[5] from which it ought to follow that corruption is indivisible, but Calvin says that there is still *a portion of the image of God* in fallen man.[6] He can also speak of the image of God as "sullied and *all but* effaced by the transgression of Adam".[7] Or again: "Were any one to say that the image of God in human nature has been blotted out by the sin of Adam; we must indeed confess that it has been miserably deformed, but in such a way that some of its lineaments still appear. Righteousness and rectitude, and the freedom of choosing what is good, have been lost; but many excellent endowments, by which we excel the brutes, still remain."[8] How are we to understand these apparently contradictory statements?

Calvin makes it quite clear that *spiritually*, fallen man is dead —

---

[1] *Serm. on Job* 2 : 1 f.: "*Quand donc l'homme sera considéré en soy et en sa nature, que pourra-on dire? Voilà une creature maudite de Dieu, laquelle est digne d'estre reiettee du rang commun de toutes autres creatures, des vers, des poux, des puces, et des vermines: car il y a plus de valeur en toutes les vermines du monde, qu'il n'y a pas en l'homme: car c'est une creature où l'image de Dieu est effacee où le bien qu'il y avoit mis est corrumpu, il n'y a que peché, tellement que nous sommes au diable, et non seulment il nou gouverne, mais il nous a en sa possession, il est nostre prince.*"

[2] *Comm. on Gen.* 3 : 22. See also *Serm. on Deut.* 28 : 46 f.

[3] *Serm. on Deut.* 24 : 19 f.

[4] *Comm. on Gen.* 9 : 6; *on Ps.* 8 : 7 f.; *on John* 1 : 5; *on James* 3 : 10. Cf. *on Heb.* 6 : 6; *Instit.* 2. 1. 11; 2. 2. 12-16; 2. 3. 3; 3. 4. 12, etc.

[5] *Comm. on Hab.* 2 : 4.

[6] *Comm. on Ps.* 8 : 5; *Instit.* 2. 2. 17; *Serm. on Job* 14 : 13 f.

[7] *Instit.* 3. 3. 9: *Uno ergo verbo paenitentiam interpretor, regenerationem, cuius non alius est scopus nisi ut imago Dei quæ per Adæ transgressionem fœdata, et* tantum non obliterata *fuerat, in nobis reformetur.* Cf. *Comm. on Gen.* 3 : 1; *on Ezek.* 16 : 10-13.

[8] *Comm. on James* 3 : 9. It would appear that, psychologically speaking, elements of the image remain: that is, so far as man is still a *rational* and a *social* animal, as distinguished from a *mere* animal.

not sick, but dead, so that "there is not a drop of life in him".[1] That is the certain conclusion of faith and regeneration in Christ. "If there be no approach to God, but by faith, we are forced to conclude that unbelief keeps us in a state of death."[2] "Our ordinary life as men is nothing more than an empty image of life, not only because it quickly passes but also because, while we live, our souls not keeping close to God are dead."[3] "The condition of the soul thus corrupted and depraved differs little from death, and tends altogether to death."[4] "It is a condition of wretched and shameful destitution",[5] in which man is "interwoven with death".[6] In this state, man must be thought of as cut off from the Kingdom of God and bereft of the image of God's grace.[7]

It is important to notice, however, that Calvin makes a clear distinction between the natural and the spiritual. He agrees with the statement, for example, that at the fall man is deprived of spiritual gifts and corrupted in his natural gifts. He is "despoiled of the gifts of the Holy Spirit" — that is, of the spiritual image of God.[8] That means that he has lost his glory.[9] By being deprived of his spiritual or supernatural gifts is meant that man is deprived of "the light of faith and righteousness which would have been sufficient for the attainment of heavenly life and everlasting felicity. When he withdrew his allegiance to God, man was deprived of the spiritual gifts by which he had been raised to the hope of eternal salvation. Hence it follows that he is now in exile from the Kingdom of God, so that all things which pertain to the blessed life of the soul are extinguished in him until he recover them by the grace of regeneration. Among these are faith, love to God, charity towards our neighbour, the study of righteousness and holiness. All these when restored to us by Christ are to be regarded as *adventitious and above nature*. If so, we infer that they

---

[1] *Serm. on Eph.* 2 : 1 f.; 2 : 3 f.
[2] *Comm. on John* 17 : 3; cf. *Instit.* 2. 1. 6. f.   [3] *Comm. on Eph.* 4 : 18.
[4] *Comm. on Ps.* 19 : 7 f.; *Comm. on Rom.* 6 : 12.
[5] *Comm. on Ps.* 8 : 5; cf. *Instit.* 2. 2. 1, where Calvin calls this condition of man "miserable destitution", and also *Comm. on Ps.* 9 : 19, where Calvin discusses the Hebrew word for *man* as meaning *miserable*.
[6] *Instit.* 1. 17. 10; *Comm. on Eph.* 2 : 1: *Nam quum spiritualis mors nihil aliud sit, quam alienatio animæ a Deo, omnes mortui nascimur, et mortui vivimus, donec efficiamur vitæ Christi participes. Instit.* 4. 16. 17: *In Adam nihil quam mori possumus.*
[7] *Serm. on Job* 14 : 1 f.; cf. 19 : 26.
[8] *Comm. on Gen.* 3 : 6; *Instit.* 2. 1. 5. Cf. *Brief Confession of Faith* (Eng. tr. by Beveridge, p. 131): "I confess that in original sin are included blindness of mind and perverseness of heart, so that we are utterly spoiled and destitute of those things which relate to eternal life, and even all natural gifts in us are tainted and depraved."
[9] *Comm. on Gen.* 3 : 22; *on 2 Pet.* 1 : 3; *on Rom.* 3 : 23.

were previously *abolished*. On the other hand, soundness of mind and integrity of heart were, at the same time, withdrawn, and it is this which constitutes the corruption of natural gifts. For although there is still some residue of intelligence and judgment as well as will, we cannot call a mind sound and entire which is both weak and immersed in darkness. And as to the will, its depravity is but too well known. Therefore, since reason by which man discerns between good and evil, and by which he understands and judges, is a natural gift, it could not be entirely destroyed; but, being partly weakened and partly corrupted, a shapeless ruin is all that remains. In this sense it is said (John 1 : 5) that 'the light shineth in darkness, and the darkness comprehendeth it not': these words clearly expressing both points, viz., that in the perverted and degenerated nature of man there are still some sparks that show that he is a rational animal, and differs from the brutes inasmuch as he is endued with intelligence, and yet that this light is so smothered by clouds of darkness that it cannot shine forth to any good effect. In like manner, the will, because inseparable from the nature of man, did not perish but was so enslaved by depraved lusts as to be incapable of one righteous desire."[1] Calvin also makes it clear that man was punished not only "by a withdrawal of the ornaments with which he was arrayed, viz., wisdom, virtue, justice, truth, and holiness", but also "by the substitution in their place of dire pests, blindness, impotence, vanity, impurity, and unrighteousness".[2] In other words the fall of man did not entail merely a *defectio boni* but entailed a *positive element* in its corruption.

Here Calvin is anxious to combat the teaching of Rome that, when man was deprived of supernatural gifts at the fall it did not really make any difference to his nature as man, and that while his natural gifts were corrupted, that was held to mean only in the sensual part of man's nature so that reason remained entire and the will was scarcely impaired.[3] Against this, Calvin insists that when man was deprived of the spiritual image, that entailed the corruption of his whole nature,[4] of mind and all,[5] so that there was nothing in the heart of man but perversity. Perversity took

[1] *Instit.* 2. 2. 12.   [2] *Instit.* 2. 1. 5.
[3] *Instit.* 2. 2. 4; see especially *Serm. on Eph.* 2 : 3 f.; and 4 : 17 f.; *Comm. on Ezek.* 11 : 19, 20.
[4] *Serm. on Eph.* 2 : 1 f.; 4 : 17 f.
[5] *Ibid.; Comm. on Gen.* 8 : 21; 3 : 1; *on Ezek.* 18 : 20; *on Rom.* 2 : 28; *on Eph.* 4 : 19; *on* 1 *Cor.* 10 : 24; *on Rom.* 7 : 14 f.

over from rectitude and integrity the character and mastery of the whole person of man. "We are so utterly mastered under the power of sin that our whole mind, heart, and all our actions bend towards sin."[1] Man has fallen from nature to de-nature,[2] and not simply been wounded in nature, as we see from the fact that we become wholly new in Christ, and receive a new nature.[3] We can draw no half-way line here, and speak of some "intermediate nature",[4] for "the Word of God leaves no half-life to man. He has utterly perished."[5] "Man revolted from His Maker, became entirely changed, and so degenerate, that the image of God in which he had been formed was obliterated."[6] "Since the time that Adam was spoiled of the image of God, Scripture saw nothing to remain in the heart of man besides perversity (or frowardness)."[7] Therefore it is not so much a *reparation* that man needs but an entirely *new creation* by which the old or whatever is left of it is *destroyed*.[8]

This language leaves us in little doubt about Calvin's thought, but at the same time it is apparent that he is somewhat sensitive about it lest he should be misunderstood. Our natural gifts, he says, "cannot be polluted in themselves in so far as they proceed from God; but they have ceased to be pure to polluted man, lest he should by their means obtain any praise".[9] We must not "despise the gifts", for that is "to insult the Giver".[10] Calvin seems to have in mind here the doctrine of evil as privation of being, a doctrine which prevailed among the Schoolmen and which prevented them from regarding the sin of man in the totality given to it by the act and judgment of grace. At any rate it seems clear that while Calvin thinks of our natural gifts as being totally corrupted, they are not deprived of being.[11] That is evident when he thinks of the conversion of man in which he gains a new nature, but in such a way that while it is "wholly of God", "everything essential to our original nature remains".[12]

[1] *Comm. on Rom.* 7 : 14.
[2] *Comm. on Gen.* 8 : 21, where Calvin says "men degenerated from their proper nature" and that "the order of the creation was subverted".
[3] *Instit.* 2. 3. 6-9; cf. 2. 1. 9; 2. 5. 19. See also *on Jer.* 2 : 21; *on Eph.* 2 : 3.
[4] *Instit.* 2. 3. 1; cf. 2. 5. 19; 2. 1. 9; 2. 3. 6-9.
[5] *Instit.* 2. 5. 19.   [6] *Comm. on Gen.* 3 : 1; see 3 : 6.
[7] *Comm. on Rom.* 7 : 14.   [8] *Instit.* 2. 3. 6; 2. 5. 15.
[9] *Instit.* 2. 2. 16.   See also *Comm. on Lev.* 16 : 16.
[10] *Instit.* 2. 2. 15.
[11] *Comm. on Eph.* 2 : 1: *Nam infidelitas non extinguit omnem sensum, nec voluntatem, nec alias animæ facultates.*
[12] *Instit.* 2. 3. 6.

And yet he can say in almost the same breath that by this new creation "everything of our common nature is destroyed".[1] It is plain therefore that Calvin does not think of sin as involving any ontological break with God, for that would mean that man would be wholly annihilated.[2] Thus he says in a sermon: "Ye see how God is estranged and separated from us: and what is the cause of it? Our sins, saith the prophet Isaiah. For God dwells in us by His power. How have we our being, our moving and our life? How have we any continuance at all but by reason of the fact that God's power is spread throughout all things? And yet for all that we cease not to be separated from Him through our sins and iniquities."[3] And again, commenting on the sentence already cited to the effect that fallen men have no other substance in them than sin, for all is corruption: "Not that the very substance (as men term it) of our bodies and of our souls is an evil thing: for we are God's workmanship. But in this case we speak grossly to express that all that is ever in us is shaped in sin. Truly our bodies in their own being are the good creatures of God, and so likewise our souls; but all that is in them is perverted. For whereas God created our souls good, they are infected with evil, and there is not one drop of goodness in them which is not stained and utterly corrupted. Thus ye see what in effect is shown us here: that there is a great difference between weakness and corruption."[4] . . . There is no doubt that Calvin thinks of total corruption and total destruction primarily in a spiritual sense, and as compatible with the fact that God still keeps us in existence, even when we are sinners, with natural gifts from His hand.[5]

The words that Calvin constantly uses to describe this state in fallen man are *perversity, depravity,* and *corruption.* These do not mean that man is reduced to nothing by sin, but that as an existing man he is wholly sinful. He *moves and has his being* in God, even as a sinner, but sin has thoroughly perverted that relation without breaking it off — only God could do that — so that he cannot be said to *live* in God in the proper sense of the term. Because this fundamental relation with God is perverted, the whole nature is depraved, and all parts of him are corrupted. That is to say, *total corruption* and *total depravity,* in the spiritual sense in which Calvin uses these expressions, mean *total perversion* or the total loss of rectitude and integrity. Fallen man is actually *turned away* in being

---

[1] *Instit.* 2. 3. 6.
[2] *Instit.* 2. 2. 16; *Comm. on Acts* 17 : 27.
[3] *Serm. on Job* 9 : 29 f.
[4] *Serm. on Job* 15 : 11 f.
[5] *Instit.* 2. 2. 17.

and act *from the divine rectitude or order*, and that is his complete alienation or death.[1] And so Calvin can define "original sin as a hereditary corruption and depravity of our nature extending to all parts of the soul",[2] and can even say that "the whole nature is, as it were, a seed-bed of sin" in which "perversity never ceases".[3] Therefore all that is and remains man is perverted — which applies equally to the *imago dei*, for whatever remains of that is now nothing but a "horrible deformity".[4] "True it is when we come into this world we bring some remnant of God's image wherein Adam was created: howbeit the same image is as disfigured as we are full of unrighteousness, and there is nothing but blindness and ignorance in our minds."[5]

It is difficult to see how there can be any ultimate reconciliation between Calvin's doctrine of total perversity and his doctrine of a remnant of the *imago dei*, though the very fact that he can give them both in the same breath seems to indicate that he had no difficulty in reconciling them. That there is an ultimate inconsistency seems demanded by Calvin's denial that there is any *seed of election* or any *germ of righteousness* in fallen man.[6] In other words, both the doctrine of election as Calvin holds it and the doctrine of justification by faith alone seem to imply that there is *no remnant of the imago dei*. In regard to election, Calvin holds, as we shall see, that God does not forgo His original intention in regard to the creation of man in His own image, and therefore man's destiny in the image remains in spite of the fact that in himself he is totally depraved — but that again is hardly consistent with the doctrine that some men are expressly predestined to damnation. In regard to justification by faith alone the issue seems clearer, for if *imago dei* means a resemblance to God in righteousness and holiness, then justification by faith alone says that there is not a shred or a germ of that left. Men have nothing in their being or in works that can glorify God, that is, that can image His glory. Therefore it is only by faith that we can glorify God.[7] What reflection of God's glory does that still leave to fallen man?[8] If one is forced to speak about a remnant of the image of God,

---

[1] *Comm. on John* 11 : 25; cf. 17 : 6: *maxime ab ipso alieni sunt.*
[2] *Instit.* 2. 1. 8; cf. *Comm. on Eph.* 2 : 3.
[3] *Ibid.; Instit.* 4. 15. 10: "There whole nature is, as it were, a seed of sin."
[4] *Instit.* 1. 15. 4. "Miserable ruin" is another favourite expression (1. 15. 1).
[5] *Serm. on Job* 14 : 13 f.   [6] *Instit.* 3. 24. 10, 11.   [7] *Instit.* 3. 18. 4.
[8] *Comm. on Rom.* 3 : 23: "Man is altogether spoiled of all glory, and partial righteousness (*partialis iustitia*) is a fable."

surely it can no longer image God's glory. The image in fallen man therefore can no longer be used in relation to the glory of God — it does dishonour to God. That is why Calvin insists again and again that man must be reduced to nothing in his own estimation, for as long as he thinks of there being anything left in himself, any shred of glory, he robs God of His glory and praise.[1] There is a sense, however, in which Calvin can speak of an *external image* of righteousness, or a *lifeless image*, or an *outward semblance*.[2] There is no true righteousness or virtue here, and therefore nothing that really images the glory of God. "When we remember that the object at which righteousness always aims is the service of God, whatever is of a different tendency deservedly forfeits the name. Hence as they have no regard to the end which the divine wisdom prescribes, although from the performance the act seems good, yet *from the perverse motive it is sin*."[3] At the same time, because the *providence* of God continues to maintain order in the world, God keeps alive the distinction between justice and injustice among men, and even visits those who cultivate virtue with temporal blessings. "Not that that external image of virtue in the least degree merits His favour, but He is pleased thus to show how much He delights in true righteousness, since He does not leave even the outward semblance of it to go unrewarded. Hence it follows that those virtues or rather images of virtues of whatever kind are divine gifts, since there is nothing in any degree praiseworthy which proceeds not from Him."[4] That seems to be the sense in which Calvin holds to a doctrine of the remnant of the image of God. It is actually maintained by God by the distinction between good and evil engraved on the minds of men, and confirmed by providence; but, in spite of that, it can bear no real relation to the glory of God, and no true relation to the renewed image of God in man. The act of God's grace in Christ, and especially in the death of Christ on behalf of

---

[1] *Instit.* 3. 18. 1 f. It is against the glory of God (see below).

[2] *Instit.* 3. 14. 2. Cf. also *Comm. on Matt.* 13 : 12: "The reprobate are endued with eminent gifts, and appear to resemble the children of God: but there is nothing of real value about them: for their mind is destitute of piety and has only the glitter of an empty show. Matthew is therefore justified in saying that they have *nothing*, for what they have is of no value in the sight of God, and has no permanency within." See further *on Mark* 10 : 21; *on* 1 *John* 5 : 10, 11; *on James* 2: 14-18.

[3] *Instit.* 3. 14. 3.

[4] *Instit.* 3. 14. 2. He says also: "Whatever excellent endowments appear in unbelievers are divine gifts", although in the previous paragraph he has just said: "When men are judged by their natural endowments, not an iota of good will be found."

men, has convinced Calvin that in response to that total act man must yield a total sacrifice even in the realm of the very virtues maintained in him by the Spirit of God. It is not a denial of the existence of natural goodness but a repudiation of it in face of the death of Christ and justification by grace alone. Calvin's final position then is clear: If justification by faith alone means that the sinner is clothed with a righteousness not his own,[1] clothed with Christ Himself the very image of God, then either he has not a shred of an image in himself, or, if he has, he must set it aside altogether and put on Christ alone.[2]

The implications of the destruction of the *imago dei* in the natural man by grace will be discussed later, but at this point there are several elements in Calvin's thought that need to be pointed out.

(a) When Calvin uses quantitative terms such as *portion* or *remnant* it is quite clear that his mind is for the moment running on psychological rather than on theological lines, and he is thinking of our natural gifts which, though they have been corrupted, still remain in man, for they are part of the groundwork of his creation.[3] "God does not forsake the work of His hands; men still have *the marks of the Spirit*, without the Spirit of regeneration."[4] "I readily acknowledge that in the soul of man there remains some remnant of life, for understanding, and judgment, and will, and all our senses are *so many parts of life*. But as there is *no part* which rises to the desire of the heavenly life, we need not wonder if the *whole man*, so far as related to the Kingdom of God, is accounted *dead*. And this death Paul explains more fully when he says, that we are alienated from the pure and sound reason of the understanding, that we are enemies to God, and opposed to righteousness, in every affection of our heart; that we wander in darkness like blind persons, and are given up to wicked lusts. If a nature so corrupted has no power to desire righteousness, it follows that the life of God is extinguished in us."[5] There is no doubt here that the *remnant* refers to the natural gifts, while spiritually the *imago dei* is wholly defaced.[6] This seems to be substantiated from

---

[1] See *Comm. on Rom.* 8 : 3.   [2] See below.   [3] *Instit.* 2. 2. 12-16.
[4] *Comm. on Ps.* 138 : 8. It is to be remembered that Calvin often defines the *imago dei* as the *Spirit of regeneration*—see above. In regard to this spiritual image, therefore, Calvin says: "Et cela se trouvera-il entre les hommes prophanes? voire entre ceux qui sont les plus honorez? Il est certain que non." *Serm. on Eph.* 2 : 1-5.
[5] *Comm. on John* 5 : 25.
[6] See above *on Instit.* 2. 2. 12.

the following passage as well. "Through the offence of Adam we are so alienated from God that all our powers are corrupted and faulty. By the powers of the soul, I mean the understanding, reason, will, and judgment, all these things are utterly perverted by Adam's turning away from God. And for proof thereof, the reason and wisdom which the first man had, were not in himself, saving in that he was fashioned after God's image, and therefore as soon as he was separated from his Creator, who is the fountain of all goodness, he could not but be deprived of all the graces that God had at first bestowed upon him. You see then how Adam did so banish himself from the Kingdom of God, that instead of the *spiritual riches* with which he was at first endowed, there is nothing in him now but all manner of wretchedness. For the heritage which we have from him is to be altogether sequestered from God's grace. It is true there do still remain certain imprints of them, to the intent that we should not be like the brute beasts, I mean even *by nature*. Although pagans are not reformed by the Spirit of God, yet they are not as oxen, asses, or dogs. Therefore we still bear some mark of the image of God which was imprinted in the first man, although we have corrupted that altogether. For although we can judge between good and evil,[1] still it is not able to lead us to perfection of true doctrine, neither is it able to make us know our God, to honour Him sincerely as we ought; but whereas we have a certain seed of knowledge that there is a God, we are dazed in our thoughts and forge vain dotages to ourselves. Thence come all the idolatries that ever were in the world. For although men understand very well that there is a certain divine majesty which ought to be honoured, yet they are not able to attain to it, but beguile themselves with certain imaginations, notwithstanding the light that is in them, whereby they show that because of sin they are bereft of all good understanding so as not to be able to set one foot forward to go in the right way. To be short, all the understanding and reason which we have serves but to make us the more inexcusable, for we cannot plead ignorance. Now then we perceive that there is no understanding in men that they should know God, though He has opened Himself to them. Therefore St. Paul says that the natural man is not able to understand the things which belong to the Spirit. He says not that men are so

---

[1] Sometimes Calvin denies that the Fall left man with any discretion; see *Serm. on Eph.* 4 : 20-23.

froward that they *will not* understand, but that *they cannot at all*: the power of ability for it is not in us. . . . As the will is froward in us, even so is our spirit enwrapped in great ignorance so that God must enlighten us by a special grace or else we shall never judge of His Word or Works as becomes us. Until God give us ears and eyes, and a spirit of heart, we cannot but go clean contrary to His will."[1]

It would seem from this that the power of judging between good and evil is regarded as a natural gift of reason,[2] but, in fallen man, at any rate, it bears no relation to spiritual things. Man has become quite carnal and earthly. "The corruption of our nature causes us to show forth nothing worthy of our original. So God, in complaining that man is become flesh or carnal as the brute beasts, *leaves nothing to him but what is earthly.* . . . Furthermore the nature of men is called corporeal, because being deprived of grace, it is only a deceivable shadow or image."[3] Spiritually, then, the image of God has been *wholly defaced*, but, naturally, one may still see "some remains of the liberality which God displayed towards man",[4] and "the lineaments of the image appear".[5] Man was made a rational creature with a mind and will in order to reflect the image of God, and though he no longer knows God, and is utterly deprived of God's glory in rectitude and righteousness and love, the *mirror* remains, though grievously impaired, and we may see God's workmanship in it, especially in his creation as a rational and conscious creature, and in that sense it reflects God's image. *But all creatures reflect God's image in this sense.* At the same time it is only the eye of faith that sees this image of God's glory.

(*b*) More important however is the fact that God has not let go His original intention in regard to man. "Should anyone object that this divine image has been obliterated, the solution is easy. First there still exists some remnant of it, so that man is possessed of no small dignity; and, secondly, the Celestial Creator Himself, however corrupted man may be, still keeps in view the end of his original creation; and according to His example, we ought to consider for what end He created men, and what excellence He has bestowed upon them above the rest of living

---

[1] *Serm. on Deut.* 29 : 1 f.   [2] *Instit.* 2. 2. 12.
[3] *Comm. on Rom.* 6 : 12; cf. *on Rom.* 7 : 24.
[4] *Comm. on Ps.* 8 : 7 f.
[5] *Comm. on John* 3 : 10; cf. *on Acts* 17 : 28.

G

beings."[1] It was an act of sheer grace that He created man to reflect His glory, and man's image rests first of all and fundamentally in that objective act of grace in which God condescends as a loving Father to behold us as His workmanship, even though we have fallen and do despite to His grace. No doubt even in God's judgments upon man He is working out a "clean contrary end" to our destruction.[2] In this sense all men are in the image of God inasmuch as God's gracious purpose remains and cannot be set aside. God does not take pleasure in "defacing His own glory which appears and shines in men", but when men blot out the image of God in themselves God does destroy the unrighteous and the wicked.[3] Thus although God wills that all men be saved, He resists the proud, and "dislikes men when they are so perverted and turned away from the righteousness and soundness which He put into them".[4] Even here we see that "God always acknowledges His workmanhip in men, although He always utterly dislikes their sin which does not proceed from Him, and cannot be fathered upon Him".[5] And so although we are God's creatures He disowns us in our sin, does not acknowledge His image in us,[6] and will not recognize us as His children until the image of God has been created anew in us through Christ.[7] We are detestable and abominable to God so long as we are thus perverted.[8] The important fact here is that Calvin thinks

---

[1] *Comm. on Gen.* 9 : 6: *Si quis obiiciat imaginem illam deletam esse: solutio facilis est, manere adhuc aliquid residuum, ut præstet non parva dignitate homo. Deinde ipsum cælestem fictorem, utcunque corruptus sit homo, finem tamen prima creationis habere ante oculos: cuius exemplo reputare nos docet quorsum homines condiderit et qua excellentia eos dignatus sit præ animantibus reliquis.* See also *Comm. on Isa.* 45 : 18.

[2] *Serm. on Job* 2 : 1 f.   [3] *Serm. on Job* 10 : 7 f.

[4] *Ibid.*   [5] *Ibid.*

[6] *Comm. on Ezek.* 16 : 10-13; cf. *on Matt.* 15 : 26, where Calvin says that from being in the image of God men have become bastards and are by nature dogs.

[7] *Serm. on Eph* 4 : 23 f.: ". . . *Nous somme retranchez et abolis du nombre des creatures de Dieu. Et aussi ce n'est point sans cause que Dieu prononce ceste sentence tant horrible, qu'il se repent d'avoir fait l'homme: car en cela il desadvoue la corruption qui est en nous, et puis le peché. Non pas que Dieu ait quelque passion humaine mais c'est pour monstrer que nous luy sommes detestables, iusques à ce que son image soit reparee en nous. . . . Nous ne pouvons pas estre recognus de Dieu pour ses enfans, iusques à ce que son image soit reparee en nous: ce qui se fait par ceste creation nouvelle.*"

[8] *Comm. on* 1 *Pet.* 1 : 21; *Serm. on Job* 15 : 11 f. This never means in the thought of Calvin that God's love has been removed from us, for this is the reaction of His *love*.

Cf. *Comm. on Ezek.* 18 : 1 f.: "True, indeed, we are abominable in God's sight, through being corrupted by original sin, but inasmuch as we are men, we must be dear to God, and our salvation must be precious in His sight." And also *Serm. on Deut.* 10 : 1 f.: "We are creatures shaped after the image of God, but to the utmost of our power we have defaced God's image in us, and we are so marred and corrupted by original sin, that God disclaims us, and yet, for all that, He vouchsafes to gather us to Himself."

of God's disavowal of man as the action of divine grace resisting in man the sinful motion that defaces the divine glory in him. The image of God in man is perverted when man does dishonour to God's glory, but this image-turned-into-dishonour has objective basis in God's repudiation of it, in "God's dislike" of man, and in His judgment on him. Fallen men are both *children of disobedience* and *vessels of wrath.* "As believers are recognized to be sons of God by bearing His image, so the wicked are properly regarded as the children of Satan, from *having degenerated into his image.*"[1] Therefore we must think of the *imago dei* in man, not as wiped out absolutely, inasmuch as God's gracious purpose of creation remains, but as remaining even in the very wrath of God, and in such a way that the image has become demonic or has been turned into its opposite,[2] that is, is become a dishonour to God. Man remains the creature of God, with the marks of God's workmanship on him, and with the divinely given endowments of body and soul, but all these are now perverted into a dishonour-able form, so that even the gifts of God minister to man's confusion. "Seeing we are so corrupted in Adam as we are, it is certain that we ought to be doubly ashamed. And why? For we were created after the image of God. And what manner of image is it now? It is a disfigured one. We are so defaced that the mark which God has put into us to be glorified thereby is turned into His dishonour, and all the gracious gifts that were bestowed on us, become as many records to make us guilty before God, because we defile them, and so long as we continue in our nature, we do but abuse the benefits which we have received, and apply them unto evil. And so you see that always our confusion increases by all the gifts which God has bestowed upon us."[3] "The gifts which we receive from God's hand ought to be invitations to

---

[1] *Instit.* 1. 14. 18. Cf. also *Comm. on John* 8 : 44; *on Rom.* 9 : 22; *on 2 Cor.* 4 : 4; *on Eph.* 2 :2; *on 1 John* 3 : 8; *Instit.* 2. 16. 3. Cf. *Comm. on Matt.* 12 : 43: "This is the *glory of our nature,* that the devil has his seat within us, and inhabits the body and the soul."

[2] Cf. *Comm. on Rom.* 5 : 14: "Even in things most contrary there appears some similitude !"

[3] *Serm. on Job* 33 : 1 f.: "*Estans corrompus en Adam (comme nous sommes) il est certain que nous devons estre doublement confus. Et pourquoy? Nous avons esté creez à l'image de Dieu: et ceste image-la quelle est elle? Elle est disfiguree: nous sommes tellement pervertis, que la marque que Dieu avoit mise en nous pour y estre glorifié, est tournee en son opprobre: et toutes les graces qui nous estoyent conferees, nous sont autant de temoignages pour nous rendre coulpable devant Dieu: d'autant que nous les polluons, et que l'homme demeurant en son naturel ne fera qu'abuser des biens qu'il a receus, et les appliquera à tout mal. Et ainsi voila touiours nostre confusion qui s'augmente par tous les dons que Dieu nous aura communiquez.*"

gratitude: but we are puffed up by pride and luxury, so that we profane God's gifts, in which His glory ought to shine forth. . . . God therefore, as it were, transfigures Himself, so as to reprove His own gifts, conferred for the purpose of our glorying only in Him."[1] This "transfiguring Himself" on the part of God by which He turns from love to wrath, from mercy to judgment, is the objective basis of the "fearful deformity" of the image of God as it is turned into its opposite, entailing total perversion of all gifts. Man is so perverted and alienated in his perversity that every natural movement he makes is towards destruction. Therefore even by the *exercise of his natural gifts*, which are meant to image the glory of God, he is helped on the way to perdition. "For that men live and breathe and are endued with sense and understanding and will, all this tends to their destruction, for there is no part or faculty of the soul that is not corrupted and turned aside from rectitude."[2] That then is true of the *imago dei* in so far as it refers to the *mirror* itself in man, i.e., to his natural gifts, but in so far as it refers to man's *true life and nature*, to God's original intention for him, which God will not forgo, we must think of the *imago dei* as remaining *not in man*, so much as *over man*, in that *God's Word of grace still holds*, though in himself man is *nothing* because by his rebellion he has cut himself off from the image of God, and defaced it from His life.[3] On the one hand therefore we must hold firmly to this: "God remains pure, although all the world be unholy, and consequently *whatever God has appointed changes not its nature through the sins of men*."[4] But, on the other hand, "*We must think of ourselves as nothing*. It is true that God has still left some marks in us whereby it may be perceived that He has exalted us in worthiness and excellence above the brute beasts, *inasmuch as it was His will to create us after His own image*. If we have respect to the thing that God *did put* into us, the same ought still to be esteemed, though for all that *in respect of our own persons we are nothing*."[5] The important fact in all this, as far as the present discussion is concerned, is that in

---

[1] *Comm. on Ezek.* 16 : 15. Cf. *on Luke* 16 : 15: "Not that God rejects those virtues, the approbation of which He has engraven on the hearts of men; but that God detests whatever men are disposed of their own accord to applaud." See also *on Luke* 18 : 9-14, and *Instit.* 2. 1. 11.

[2] *Comm. on John* 11 : 25. See also *on Rom.* 2 : 5.

[3] Calvin does say, however, that the reprobate may have for a while a faint reflection of the image when they hear the Word of God. *Comm. on Heb.* 6 : 6; *Instit.* 3. 2. 12; 3. 24. 8.

[4] *Comm. on Lev.* 16 : 16.   [5] *Serm. on Gal.* 5 : 2 f.

regard to fallen man the image performs a function opposite to
that which it is intended to do. Just as Calvin thinks of the Word
of God in its own nature as a savour of life, but as a savour of
death to the unbelieving,[1] so the *imago dei is turned into its opposite*.
It is now a judgment of disgrace upon man, rather than an
honour.[2] "The whole human race having been undone in the
person of Adam, the excellence and dignity of our origin, is so far
from availing us, that *it rather turns to our greater disgrace*, until God,
who does not acknowledge man when defiled and corrupted by
sin as His own work, appear as a Redeemer in the person of His
only begotten Son."[3]

(c) There are, however, other passages in his works in which
Calvin links on what remains of the original creation of man in
the image of God to a *spark of knowledge* or a *portion of light* or a
seed of religion still lurking in the soul.[4] This we shall discuss more
fully later, but here it will be in place to point out that Calvin's
thought, though at first apparently self-contradictory, is fairly
consistent and clear. He indicates that the natural man does have
a dim sort of awareness of God, but that *from the very start it is
perverted*,[5] so that it is really nothing but the fountainhead of all
his superstition and irreligion.[6] "In this corrupted and degenerate
nature *light* has been turned into *darkness*. And yet the *light* of the
understanding is not wholly extinguished, for amidst the thick
darkness of the human mind, some remaining sparks of the
brightness still shine. . . . Although by that small measure of
light which still remains in us, the Son of God has always invited
men to Himself, yet this was attended by no advantage, because
seeing they did not see. For since man lost the favour of God, his

---

[1] *Comm. on* 2 *Cor.* 2 : 15, 16; *on Rom.* 1 : 16; 7 : 10 f. Cf. *Serm. on Deut.* 2 : 24 f.
"Whether God's Word brings life or death to men, it is always a good and sweet
savour before God. True it is that God's Word of itself is always the savour of life.
For what is it that God intends, if we consider His Word in its own nature? The
calling of men back, to the end that they may be saved. Yet for all that we see it as
an odour and savour of death inasmuch as the wicked are strangled and choked with
it, as soon as they but take the scent or smell of it. . . . And so we see that God's
Word brings the occasion of death to a great number of men."
[2] *Comm. on Rom.* 9 : 4: *Docet impios non posse ita contaminare bonas Dei dotes, quin
semper merito sint laudabiles ac suspiciendæ, quanquam illis ipsis, qui abutuntur,* nihil
inde accedit nisi maius probrum.
[3] *Instit.* 2. 6. 1. As man's supreme *ignominia* the *imago* can no longer image the
glory of God; rather is it a case of: *Deum maligne sua gloria fraudamus (ibid.)*. "Surely
this is the height of deformity" (*Comm. on Ezek.* 16 : 10-13).
[4] For example, see *Comm. on John* 1 : 5; *Serm. on Eph.* 1 : 17, 18.
[5] *Instit.* 1. 4. 1; 1. 5. 11 f., 14 f.; 1. 11. 8; 2. 2. 24; *Comm. on Rom.* 1 : 20; *on* 1 *Cor.*
1 : 21; *on Heb.* 11 : 3.
[6] *Comm. on Ps.* 97 : 7 f.; *on John* 3 : 6; *on Acts* 17 : 23.

mind is so completely overwhelmed by the thraldom of ignorance that any portion of *light* which remains is quenched and useless. This is daily proved by experience; for all who are not regenerated by the Spirit of God possess some reason, and this is undeniable proof that man was made not only to breathe, but to have understanding. But by that guidance of their reason they do not come to God, and do not even approach to Him, so that all their understanding is nothing else than mere vanity. Hence it follows that there is no hope of the salvation of men, unless God grant new aid; for though the Son of God shed His *light* upon them, they are so dull that they *do not comprehend* whence that *light* proceeds, but are carried away by foolish and wicked imaginations to absolute madness. The *light* which dwells in corrupt human nature consists chiefly of two parts: for, first all men naturally possess some seed of religion, and, secondly, the distinction between good and evil is engraven on their consciences. But what are the fruits that ultimately spring from it, except that religion degenerates into a thousand monsters of superstition, and conscience perverts every decision, so as to confound vice with virtue? In short, natural reason will never direct men to Christ."[1] "Consider who thou art, and do but enter into thyself, and be judge of thine own estate. There we shall find a bottomless gulf of sinfulness in us, and that we are enwrapped in such ignorance as is horrible to behold, which is, as it were, a darkness so thick that it utterly chokes and strangles us. And so far off are we from having eyes to perceive God, that we do not see the thing that is before our noses."[2] In our perverted nature, "we have such a corrupted reason that we cannot judge anything of God", so that "in comparison with the beasts there is more soundness in a horse or an ox than in a man".[3] Man's reason is turned into maliciousness instead of honouring God for the benefits received. "Our reason which we think ourselves to have is utter beastliness", and "all the light which we have by nature is turned into darkness".[4] Or again, as Calvin puts it elsewhere: "The light of the intelligence being extinct . . . the order being appointed by God has been so greatly disturbed, that God's own image has been transformed into flesh."[5] "Alienated from right reason, man is almost like the cattle of the field."[6]

[1] *Comm. on John* 1 : 5.
[3] *Serm. on Job* 35 : 8 f.
[5] *Comm. on Gen.* 6 : 3.

[2] *Serm. on Job* 13 : 11 f.
[4] *Ibid.*
[6] *Ibid.*

In spite of this, Calvin declares that in His mercy God has allowed us the power of judgment between good and evil by which we are distinguished from the beasts.[1] "For all that, there are very few that seek rightly to have a true judgment, inasmuch as they prefer to turn away and wander after their own fancy and become brutish in themselves."[2] True discretion consists in submitting ourselves to God wherever He manifests Himself,[3] but that is just what sin refuses to do, and so inevitably turns the light of nature into darkness.[4] Therefore Calvin never thinks of man's natural discretion as constituting a predisposition for faith.[5] Calvin has said in a passage cited above that "by the small measure of light which still remains in us, the Son of God has always invited men to Himself", but he hastens to add: "yet this was attended by no advantage, because seeing they did not see . . . so that any portion of light which remains is quenched or useless."[6] Over against God's grace, "we can do nothing beforehand, but rather still draw backward from Him".[7] We can make *no prejudgment* in coming to God,[8] for we inevitably pervert the truth, and deform the glory of God.[9] "God dwells in light unapproachable. God then cannot be known by us. The more a man will lift himself up, the further he will go from Him. So then men cannot of themselves approach unto God; but He will approach unto us, and we must conceive Him as He offers Himself by His Word, contenting ourselves with that which is contained there."[10]

Calvin gives us a clear exposition of his views on the darkness of fallen man in his comments upon the words of the Psalm: "For with Thee is the fountain of life, and in Thy light we shall see light."[11] "As the ungodly profane even the best of God's gifts by their wicked abuse of them . . . it were better for us to perish

[1] *Serm. on Job* 35 : 8 f.; *Comm. on Gen.* 2 : 9; *on John* 1 : 9; 3 : 6; *Instit.* 1. 3. 3; 1. 15. 3-5.
[2] *Serm. on Deut.* 4 : 3 f.
[3] Therefore, strictly speaking, all true discretion is grounded upon the Word of God. "It is by setting His Word before us that He gives us discretion and wisdom." (*Ibid.*)
[4] *Ibid.; Serm. on Job* 35 : 8 f.
[5] *Comm. on Rom.* 6 : 18.
[6] *Comm. on John* 1 : 5. See also *Serm. on Eph.* 4 : 17-19; *Comm. on Heb.* 1 : 16.
[7] *Serm. on Job* 33 : 26 f.
[8] *Comm. on Acts* 14 : 16; see 16 : 14; *on Eph.* 1 : 19; *on John* 1 : 5-8; 11 : 25; *Serm. on Deut.* 10 : 1 f.
[9] *Comm. on Acts* 17 : 24; *on Rom.* 1 : 25.
[10] *Serm. on Job* 22 : 12 f.; 10 : 16 f.
[11] *Comm. on Ps.* 36 : 9; cf. *on John* 1 : 5.

a hundred times of hunger than to be fed abundantly by the goodness of God. The ungodly do not acknowledge that it is in God they live and move and have their being, but rather imagine that they are sustained by their own power; and accordingly, David, on the contrary, here affirms from the experience of the godly, and, as it were, in their name, that the fountain of life is in God. By this he means that there is not a drop of life to be found without Him, or which flows not from His grace. The metaphor of *light*, in the last clause of the verse, is tacitly most emphatic, denoting that men are altogether destitute of light, except in so far as the Lord shines upon them. If this is true of the light of this life, how shall we be able to behold the light of the heavenly world, unless the Spirit of God enlighten us? For we must maintain that the measure of understanding with which men are by nature endued is such that *the light shineth in darkness, and the darkness comprehendeth it not* and that men are enlightened only by a supernatural gift. But it is the godly alone who perceive that they derive their light from God and that without it they would continue, as it were, buried and smothered in darkness." The following passage relates this to the *imago dei*: "We are destitute of the righteousness of God. Our true ornament was that we could have fashioned ourselves to all manner of right, and now we are spoiled of it. As then we had reason and understanding, so now we are become beastly, for the brightness that should shine in us is become darkness. Again, we are covered with reproach, and whereas the image of God should shine in us, now we have the marks of sin."[1] If we think of there being a relic of the image of God in man in terms of light or truth or knowledge we must think of that as essentially perverted into darkness, as truth turned into a lie, as a horrible deformity of the truth, so that it is utterly impossible for man to come to a knowledge of God through it. So deep is man's perversity that it actually converts the good gifts of God, whether in the form of natural endowments or in the form of the Law and the Gospel, against their own true nature to his own destruction.[2] It is precisely by this strange activity, in turning the truth into falsehood, in trying to use this knowledge for his own ends, in trying to appropriate to himself the glory of God, that man sins and corrupts himself.[3]

---

[1] *Serm. on Deut.* 28 : 46 f.
[2] *Comm. on Rom.* 7 : 10-13.
[3] *Comm. on Gen.* 2 : 9. See also *Instit.* 2. 2. 1; 2. 2. 10; *Comm. on Rom.* 1 : 21 f.

The more he presumes upon the relic of the *imago dei* within him, the deeper he gets into the abyss of darkness and corruption and death. If the light that is in him is darkness, how great is that darkness![1]

See *Comm. on Matt.* 6 : 22 f.; *on John* 1 : 5-9; 12 : 39.

Chapter Eight

TOTAL PERVERSITY (2)

Calvin's doctrine of total perversity must be interpreted in line with his doctrine of the dynamic relation of man to God. Total perversity thus means that man's personal being, grounded by grace in a continuous relation with the living God, has been perverted into an existence in which he is continually turned away from God, so that all that he does in the exercise of his God-given gifts is against God. In all this there is a strong element of wilful disobedience. Man cannot change or better himself; he can only move farther away in alienation from God. This perversity never ceases. It is within this context that Calvin thinks of the destruction of the image of God, which becomes so radically perverted that it is turned into its opposite, into dishonour. Man is fixed in this condition by the action of the Law, which includes the imago dei as the law of his being in the will of God. That gives objective depth to his perversity. However, because the Law comprehends within it the imago dei, because God's original intention in creating man in that image cannot be set aside by sin, we must regard all men as created unto this image, even though not a trace of the image is to be found in them. What is actually found is a contrary law inscribed on men's hearts, which fights against the Law of God, and the true law of man's being. This contrary law is in reality the imago dei turned into its opposite, so that fallen man now lives in a constant disclaimer of the image of God; instead of imaging the glory of God, he does God constant dishonour. This is particularly evident in the contradiction of the natural man to the grace of God.

A LARGE part of the difficulty in determining Calvin's views on the depravity of man is due to the fact that he lapses back again and again, at least in language, from a dynamic to a more static conception of man. But when we keep his essentially dynamic view of man before us and interpret his statements in that light they appear more consistent.[1] Thus the total corruption of fallen man, and the destruction of the image of God, really mean that man's existence as a person in a living orientation toward God has been *perverted* into an existence in which he is continually turned away from God.[2] That is to say, the corruption of his nature in the image of God is the corruption of the relation

---

[1] See, for example, *Comm. on Acts* 17 : 28.   [2] *Comm. on Eph.* 4 : 24.

between God and man's mind and will. Obedience has been displaced by disobedience, knowledge by confusion, though Calvin insists also that in this turning away from God there is a strong deliberate element, in which it can be said that "men spited God through a purposed malice".[1] Fallen man lives in deliberate and constant rebellion. There can be no neutrality here: either men are rebels or they are sons. There can be no *intermediate nature*.[2]

The use of the word *nature* in this connection is sometimes ambiguous, but Calvin usually succeeds in making himself quite clear. It is his view that while depravity is *against the order of nature* as God created it, it is now *natural* to man.[3] That is to say, "man is corrupted by natural viciousness, but not by one which proceeds from nature. In saying that it does not proceed from nature, we mean that it was rather an adventitious event which befell man, than a substantial property assigned to him from the beginning."[4] "There is a twofold nature: the one was produced by God, and the other is the corruption of it. This condemnation therefore which Paul mentions (that we are by nature children of wrath) does not proceed from God, but from a depraved nature: for we are not born such as Adam was at first created, we are not 'wholly a right seed, but are turned into a degenerate' (Jer. 2 : 21) offspring of a degenerate and sinful man."[5] Men either have a depraved nature, or in Christ they receive a new nature, and there is no half-way state between the two. And yet, at the same time, Calvin can say that "the nature of man is not wholly vicious", apparently referring to the *being* of man (as distinct from character) and meaning that though men are rebels against God and are therefore alienated from their original natures, and their own true natures, they still remain men, and are *not blocks,*[6] *nor are they like horses and dogs without intelligence and without discretion.*[7] Calvin refuses to agree to the Roman doctrine that fallen man retains human nature in its essential integrity, though he has lost the

[1] *Serm. on Job* 32 : 1 f.
[2] *Instit.* 2. 3. 1.
[3] *Instit.* 1. 11. 4. Cf. *Comm. on Rom.* 8 : 20.
[4] *Instit.* 2. 1. 11; cf. also 2. 2. 20.
[5] *Comm. on Eph.* 2 : 3. For a similar statement see *on John* 11 : 33.
[6] *Instit.* 2. 2. 20; cf. *Comm. on Ps.* 40 : 7.
[7] *Serm. on Eph.* 4 : 17-19. "Or ici on pourroit faire une question, si les hommes (ie di ceux qui sont delaissez de Dieu) estoyent là sans intelligence et sans discretion, qu'on en verriot les exemples. Il est bien certain qu'ils ne sont pas semblables ni a des chevaux, ni à des chiens: mais notons que tout l'intelligence et discretion qui est en nous, et tout le jugement qui nous pouvons avoir, ne tend à autre fin que de nous rendre inexcusables."

supernatural grace and the ornaments which that brings. He insists that while fallen man remains human his essential *integrity* is lost, so that natural intelligence and judgment do not and cannot serve to lead him back into the positive relation with God in which he finds his true nature—but God uses this intelligent nature of fallen man and his power of discretion in good and evil to make him conscious of culpability before God.[1] However, inasmuch as his whole nature is essentially perverted, his mind and will included, as is seen in the deliberateness of sin, he cannot change himself, for his whole life and being are now bound up with a contradiction to the grace and will of God. All men enter this perverted relation at birth, so that they are *misframed by nature*.[2] "As spiritual death is nothing else than alienation of the soul from God, we are all born as dead men, and we live as dead men, until we be made partakers of the life of Christ."[3]

It is significant to see what an important part this notion of perversity plays in Calvin's thought. He thinks of the whole order of creation as having been perverted as a consequence of the fall of man, a perversion which is stamped and made constant by the curse of God.[4] Everything that takes its origin within this perversion is against God and partakes of perversity. And because Calvin thinks in terms of a dynamic relation between God and creation even when it has fallen, he says that this perversity is active and *never ceases*.[5] That is why every movement in the fallen world is perverse, and *off the course* from the very start.[6] At the very root there is a basic perversion which characterizes everything that goes down to that root.[7] It is plain therefore that man is utterly unable of himself to restore the world or his own nature to its original integrity, for he cannot get outside of this radical perversion even if he would. He has lost all rectitude, that is, the divine order in creation, and is governed by a perverted order.[8] He can only move in the direction of evil and

[1] *Ibid.*: "*Voilà donc comme il est demeuré quelque intelligence aux hommes: mais ce n'est pas pour les conduire au chemin de salut, c'est seulement pour les rendre tant plus coulpables devant Dieu.*"

[2] *Serm. on Job* 14 : 1 f.

[3] *Comm. on Eph.* 2 : 1.

[4] *Instit.* 2. 1. 5; *Comm. on Ps.* 19 : 8; *on Jer.* 2 : 23; *on Gen.* 3 : 6; *on Heb.* 11 : 6.

[5] *Instit.* 2. 1. 8; 4. 15. 11.

[6] *Instit.* 3. 14. 4; 3. 21. 2, etc.

[7] *Serm. on Job* 15 : 11 f. Calvin says of fallen man that his very nourishment is nothing but sin.

[8] *Comm. on Gen.* 1 : 26; 2 : 16; *on Ps.* 8 : 6 f.; *on Eph.* 1 : 10; *on Col.* 3 : 10; *Instit.* 1. 15. 7.

confusion.[1] Far from being able to "tend toward a right end",[2] man "tends altogether to death",[3] "always downward".[4] As such he is "lost and drowned in spiritual destruction".[5] It is within this context that Calvin thinks of the destruction of the *imago dei*. It is destroyed in the sense that it has been radically perverted, or turned into its opposite, and into dishonour. "Since the time that Adam was spoiled of the image of God Scripture sees nothing to remain in the heart of man besides perversity."[6] The truth of God has been turned into a lie,[7] and God's glory stained.[8] As such man is alienated from God and from himself and from the world.

In this state, man would utterly waste away were it not for the mercy of God. On the one hand, Calvin thinks of God as having judged man for his sins, but that very act of judgment has the effect of fixing man in his being as a man under God's judgment, and therefore maintains him in existence even if it be existence under judgment.[9] The worst thing that could befall man would be for God to let him utterly alone. God does not do that. He holds on to man even in judgment, and so the divine Law becomes a veritable bond of human existence, even though man is constantly fighting against it. On the other hand, Calvin thinks of God as suspending His judgment, or as suspending His full judgment, on man's sin, else man would be utterly annihilated. Therefore, he argues, "we must consider that notwithstanding the corruption of our nature there is some room for divine grace, such grace as, without purifying it, may lay it under internal constraint. For did the Lord let every mind loose to revel in its lusts, doubtless there is a not a man who would not show that his nature is capable of all the crimes with which Paul charges it."[10] "Had not God so spared us, our revolt would have carried along with it the entire destruction of nature."[11] And so our human nature is "preserved from being broken up by certain sacred bonds".[12] Among these Calvin thinks undoubtedly of the *imago*

<hr>

[1] *Instit.* 2. 3. 5; *Comm. on Ps.* 119 : 105. [2] *Comm. on Gen.* 8: 21.
[3] *Comm. on Ps.* 8 : 21; *on Gen.* 2 : 16.
[4] *Comm. on Acts* 17 : 23; *on Gen.* 2 : 2; *on Rom.* 11 : 36; *Serm. on Job* 33 : 1 f.
[5] *Instit.* 1. 15. 8. [6] *Comm. on Rom.* 7 : 15. [7] *Serm. on Job* 15 : 17 f.
[8] *Comm. on Rom.* 1 : 25; *Instit.* 2. 1. 4; 1. 11. 1.
[9] *Instit.* 3. 6. 1; cf. *Comm. on Gen.* 6 : 3; *Serm. on Job* 15 : 23: "God sends fearfulness upon the wicked, and torments them and disappoints them, and *turns all things clean contrary to their intent*, because they lift themselves up against Him." See also *Comm. on Rom.* 7 : 13.
[10] *Instit.* 2. 3. 3.
[11] *Instit.* 2. 2. 17; see also *Comm. on Gen.* 8 : 21. [12] *Comm. on Ps.* 8 : 5.

dei, but not as something inherent in man. Rather does he think of it as God's intention for man or His persistent will to regard man as His workmanship and which He refuses to destroy without due cause, any more than He will deface His own glory. "This tie is sacred and inviolable, and no man's depravity can abolish it."[1] Because this *imago dei* hangs over every man,[2] Calvin insists that we must treat all men as brothers, having respect not to their persons as such, but to the image of God in and unto which they are made. "The image of God ought to be particularly regarded as a sacred bond of union; and for that very reason no distinction is to be made between friend and foe, nor can the wickedness of men set aside the right of nature."[3] By *right of nature* Calvin clearly means the *law of man's origin* which is still manifested in the claim of the divine Law which as such *comprehends the imago dei*.[4] "The Celestial Creator Himself, however corrupted man may be, still keeps in view the end of His original creation; and, according to His example, we ought to consider for what end He created men, and what excellence He has bestowed upon them above the rest of living beings."[5] Therefore although the image of God in man has been obliterated, "there still exists some remnant of it so that man is possessed of no small dignity."[6] "Wherefore if we would not violate the image of God we must hold the person of man sacred."[7] "We are not to look to what men *in themselves* deserve, but to attend to the image of God, which exists in all, and to which we owe all honour and love. . . . Say that you are bound to him by no ties of duty. The Lord has substituted him as it were in His own place, that in him you may recognize the many great obligations under which the Lord has laid you to Himself. Say that he is unworthy of your least exertion on his account; but the image of God, by which he is recommended to you, is worthy of yourself and all your exertions. . . . In this way only we attain to what is not to say difficult, but altogether against nature, to love those that hate us, render good for evil, and blessing for cursing, remembering that we are not to reflect on the wickedness of men, but to look

---

[1] *The Catechism of the Church at Geneva* (Eng. tr. by Beveridge), p. 68.
[2] *Instit.* 3. 6. 1.
[3] *Comm. on Gal.* 5 : 14. But cf. *on Heb.* 2 : 5, where it means man's right to exercise law in the world, an inferior dominion which depends on the higher (2 : 8).
[4] Cf. *Instit.* 3. 6. 1.
[5] *Comm. on Gen.* 9 : 6.　　　　　　　　　　[6] *Comm. on Gen.* 9 : 6.
[7] *Instit.* 2. 8. 40; see *Serm. on Job* 16 : 1 f.; *on Deut.* 2 : 8 f.; 4 : 39 f.; 5 : 13 f.; 12 : 19 f., etc.

on the image of God in them, an image, which covering and obliterating their faults, should by its beauty and dignity allure us to love and embrace them."[1] Here Calvin has been speaking largely of the Christian's duty, but it is quite clear that he applies this to all men as well.[2] They may not be able to perceive the image of God, but they have a natural inclination to cherish their own flesh, and in thus cherishing human nature they are restrained from destruction.[3] In this way the *imago dei* may still be a bond of unity because, and in spite of the fact that "the order appointed by God has been so greatly disturbed that His own image has been transformed into flesh".[4] And this has its divine counterpart, for "God gives the name of flesh as a mark of ignominy to men, whom He nevertheless had formed in His own image".[5]

This position of Calvin may be made clear by pointing out that while he believed that corresponding to the written Law there was an "internal law which is in a manner written and stamped on every heart",[6] yet he says too that man is so depraved and perverted that he "is continually opposed" to God, and is characterized by "infirmity and nervelessness for good, by impotence and unrighteousness."[7] But actually when we look at the human heart from the point of view of grace we see that men "have engraven on them a *contrary law*, for perverse passions rule within, which lead us to rebellion . . . and our will is carried away by a sort of insane impulse to resist God."[8] Calvin maintains that all good order in the world comes from God, and all virtue wherever it is to be found, and all skill and wisdom are imparted by God. "Not a particle of light or wisdom or justice or power or rectitude or genuine truth will be found anywhere which does not flow from Him, and of which He is not the cause."[9] In a real sense therefore God is present to all men, even the sinful,[10] and so far as men are good they have a kind of *imago dei*, but it is *lifeless*,[11] for they are

---

[1] *Instit.* 3. 7. 6.
[2] *Comm. on Gen.* 37 : 27; *on Isa.* 58 : 7; *on Gal.* 5 : 14.   [3] *Ibid.*
[4] *Comm. on Gen.* 6 : 3; cf. *on Rom.* 6 : 12; 7 : 24.   [5] *Ibid.*
[6] *Instit.* 2. 8. 1. Thus a "sense of deity is indelibly engraven on the human heart" (1. 3. 3), but this goes back to a primitive Word given by God and handed on before the written Word and Law were given.
[7] *Instit.* 2. 8. 1.
[8] *Comm. on Heb.* 8 : 10. Cf. *on Rom.* 7 : 15-21. The inveterate enmity of man to God, his constant malediction, and will to war against God, is the emphasis again and again in the *Sermons on Galations* 5 and *on Ephesians* 2 and 3.
[9] *Instit.* 1. 2. 1; see *Comm. on John* 1 : 5.
[10] *Instit.* 2. 2. 1; *Comm. on Acts* 17 : 27.   [11] *Instit.* 3. 14. 2.

quite off the course of divine rectitude.[1] Calvin's point, however, is that when viewed from the angle of God's gracious action in Christ, by whom we are renewed in God's image, we see that these good gifts of God have but ministered to our confusion, and as such they must come under the total judgment of grace.[2] They have all become *flesh* so that "the whole man is naturally flesh, until by the grace of regeneration he begins to be spiritual".[3] Calvin thinks of man always as a unity, and insists therefore on judgments of totality in regard to man. He is spiritual or carnal; there is no neutral state. He is either off the mark, and in death, or he is in Christ and alive. No other course was open to Calvin with his essentially dynamic view of creation and man's being. Sin and evil are not thought of atomistically, but as the motion of active and unceasing perversity in which not only is the soul of man "vitiated in every part, and alienated from right reason",[4] but it cannot move or begin to move except "in the direction of evil".[5] He can only go wrong,[6] and his reason fails at every step.[7]

Calvin admits, as we have already had cause to notice in passing, that when the reprobate hear the Word of God *in some sort* it is engraven on their hearts,[8] or at least some rays of God's grace *glimmer* there for a while,[9] so that they are without excuse,[10] but inasmuch as they will not hear in their perversity, God does not let it so penetrate their hearts as to be engraven there by His Spirit.[11] Therefore He refuses to reveal His Word further to them, and He allows it to vanish away. Indeed He delivers them over to a reprobate mind. Because of their self-will and persistent opposition to His grace God deliberately blinds them lest they should understand and be converted.[12] The voice of God only hardens them in their sinful state.[13]

The fundamental thought behind Calvin's position is that the

---

[1] *Instit.* 3. 14. 4. 　　　　　[2] *Comm. on Rom.* 6 : 21; 7 : 18.
[3] *Comm. on Gen.* 6 : 3; cf. on *Rom.* 6 : 12; 7 : 24.
[4] *Comm. on Gen.* 6 : 3.
[5] *Instit.* 2. 3. 5; *Serm. on Job* 33 : 1 f.
[6] *Comm. on Ps.* 119 : 105. It is in this sense only that Calvin thinks of the *necessitas peccandi.*
[7] *Comm. on Matt.* 6 : 22; *Instit.* 1. 2. 3.　　　[8] *Comm. on Heb.* 6 : 5.
[9] *Instit.* 3. 2. 12. This Calvin calls a *temporary faith; Instit.* 3. 2. 10, 11; 3. 24. 8; 4. 17. 33; *Comm. on Ps.* 106 : 12; on *Mark* 4 : 7; on *Luke* 17 : 13; on *Matt.* 13 : 20.
[10] There is also a faint natural knowledge of sin: "a cold and semi-dead knowledge of sin which is inherent in the minds of men" (*Comm. on Gen.* 3 : 7).
[11] *Serm. on Job* 33 : 14 f.
[12] *Ibid.* See *Comm. on Isa.* 6 : 10; on *Matt.* 12 : 3-14, 15; on *Mark* 4 : 12; on *Rom.* 1 : 18; on 1 *Cor.* 2 : 10; on *John* 9 : 39; *Serm. on Job* 17 : 1 f.
[13] *Comm. on Eph.* 4 : 18; on *Isa.* 6 : 10, etc.

fallen nature of man consists in a motion over against God, and of opposition to God's grace, even in the act of being maintained in existence by Him.[1] And so *man lives in a constant disclaimer of the image of God, disgracing it, dishonouring it, defacing it*.[2] That is matched by God's opposition to man's sin, and His disavowal of man as His child until the image has been renewed in him. The life of fallen man, in spite of the mercy of God, is a contrary motion to grace, and in that contrary motion the whole of his life with all his natural gifts and his natural goodness is caught up and given a false antithetical rectitude which is perversity or depravity.[3] Sin is not just a negative action which defects from the Law or defects from the *imago dei*. It is a positive contradiction or malediction and maintains itself in an active opposition. Hence sin does not destroy the image of God, but perverts the whole.[4] Sin partakes of man's positive relation to God and is a complete perversion of it—that is why it must be regarded as total. Calvin does not speak of a half-destroyed image of God in man, though when he is tempted into language that looks like that, he adds always that even the remnant is wholly perverted, but that we have already discussed. Actually a partly destroyed image of God is a confusion due to pictorial language. Calvin is quite clear about his basic position. He is ready to agree with Augustine that grace does not destroy man's will, for example, but repairs it; "repairs it", however, means to change it entirely.[5] "The Word of God", he says, "leaves no half-life to man, but teaches that, in regard to life and happiness, he is utterly perished. Paul when he speaks of our redemption says not that the dead are cured (*Eph.* 2 : 5, 30; 5, 14), but that those who were dead are raised up. He does not call upon half-dead men to receive the illumination of Christ, but upon those who are asleep and buried. In the same way, our Lord Himself says: 'The hour is coming and now is when the dead shall hear the voice of the Son of God' (John 5 : 25). . . . True! man has a mind capable of understanding, though incapable of attaining to heavenly and spiritual wisdom; he has some discernment of what is honourable; he has some sense of

---

[1] *Instit.* 2. 3. 1; 2. 7. 7; 2. 8. 1; 2. 16. 3; 3. 14. 15; *Comm. on Rom.* 7 : 15; 8 : 20; *on 2 Cor.* 10 : 4.
[2] *Serm. on Job* 31 : 9 f.; *on Eph.* 4 : 23-26; cf. *Instit.* 3. 13. 1 f.; 3. 20. 41.
[3] *Serm. on Job* 35 : 8 f. For a full statement, see *on Job* 15 : 11 f.
[4] *Instit.* 1. 15. 1; 2. 1. 9.
[5] *Instit.* 2. 5. 15. Cf. *Serm. on Eph.* 4 : 17 f.: "*Il faut que Dieu nous reforme, non pas à demi, mais du tout.*"

H

divinity, though he cannot reach the true knowledge of God. But to what do these amount? They certainly do not refute the doctrine of Augustine—a doctrine confirmed by the common suffrage even of the Schoolmen, that after the fall the free gifts on which salvation depends were withdrawn, and natural gifts corrupted and defiled. Let it stand, therefore, as an indubitable truth which no engines can shake that the mind of man is so entirely alienated from the righteousness of God that he cannot conceive, desire, or design anything but what is wicked, distorted, foul, impure, and iniquitous; that his heart is so thoroughly envenomed by sin that it can breathe out nothing but corruption and rottenness; that if some men occasionally make a show of goodness, their mind is ever interwoven with hypocrisy and deceit, their soul inwardly bound with the fetters of wickedness."[1]

When we narrow all this down again we see that Calvin thinks of the fundamental motion in perversity as the ingratitude which presumes that the *imago dei* belongs to himself, when it is grounded only in the grace of God.[2] That was the root of Adam's sin, in wanting to make the image of God a matter of his own being.[3] "Man is not to be denied anything that is truly his own", says Calvin, but "he was created in the image of God—the Scripture thereby intimating that the blessings in which his true happiness consisted were *not his own*, but derived by divine communication".[4] Man's sin consisted in an act of ingratitude which by investing himself with more than he possessed, trying to add God's glory to himself, only added sacrilege to his ruin, thrusting him down from the highest glory to the extreme ignominy.[5] And so he was stripped of all glory.[6] Thus "man cannot arrogate to himself one particle beyond his due, without losing himself in vain confidence, and by transferring divine honour to himself, becoming guilty of the greatest impiety. And assuredly whenever our minds are seized with a longing to possess a somewhat of our own which may reside in us rather than in God, we may rest assured that the thought is suggested by no other counsellor than he who enticed our first parents to aspire to be like gods, knowing good and evil."[7] This is a constant note of Calvin's thought that man disclaims the image and defaces it from himself by usurping the same image and all that it implies as though it belonged to him.[8]

[1] *Instit.* 2. 5. 19.   [2] *Comm. on 2 Pet.* 1 : 3.   [3] *Comm. on Gen.* 3 : 6.
[4] *Instit.* 2. 2. 1.   [5] *Ibid.*   [6] *Ibid.*   [7] *Instit.* 2. 2. 10.
[8] *Serm. on Job* 9 : 29 f.; 5 : 20 f.; 28 : 10 f.; 10 : 2 f.; 3 : 1 f.; *Instit.* 1. 15. 3; 1. 2. 2;
1. 5. 4; 2. 2. 15, 18; 2. 3. 5, 10; *Comm. on Gen.* 2 : 9; 1 *John* 1 : 9; *on 2 Pet.* 1 : 3.

But that is the essential motion of sin, unthankful arrogance and self-glorification, which runs directly contrary to the very motion of the grace of God in which the image of God is rooted and grounded. For man to continue in his fallen nature is itself rebellion and enmity to grace.[1] No longer is the image of God a heritage to man.[2] Fallen man cannot beget men in the similitude of God, for he has lost that similitude. He can only beget men in his own image.[3]

In order to worship God aright, that is, in accordance with the motion of grace, man must learn to serve God *against his own nature*,[4] "acknowledging that he lives not by his own power but by the kindness of God alone, and that his life is not an intrinsic good, but proceeds from God alone. He cannot otherwise retain it than by acknowledging that it was received of God."[5] This means that Calvin defines the life-motion of man made in the image of God as the motion of faith, while the contrary motion of unthankfulness and rebellion he speaks of as incredulity and unbelief. "God does not manifest Himself to men otherwise than through the Word, so neither is His majesty maintained, nor does His worship remain secure among us any longer than while we obey His Word. Therefore unbelief is the root of defection; just as faith alone unites us to God."[6] Hence knowledge of God is possible only if the inverted motion of the soul in mind and will is re-inverted by an acknowledgment of grace such that it is dragged out of its self-assertion or concupiscence, out of its self-imprisonment and blindness, in order to find life and being only as deposited in the Word. The radical inversion of all human wisdom and understanding that this entails indicates how deep-going and total is the perversion of sin. A complete conversion of man's relation with God is required.

[1] *Serm. on Job* 10 : 16 f. Man has turned himself into an idol. *Serm. on Job* 5 : 20 f. Cf. *Instit.* I. II. 8.
[2] *Serm. on Job* 33 : 1 f.; 39 : 8 f.
[3] *Comm. on Rom.* 5 : 12. Therefore if believers have the *imago dei* it can only be by *imputation.* That is to say, it is an eschatological heritage in the Kingdom of God.
[4] *Serm. on Job* 10 : 16 f.; 37 : 1 f.; see also *Comm. on Rom.* 7 : 9 ff.
[5] *Comm. on Gen.* 2 : 9.
[6] *Comm. on Gen.* 3 : 6; *Instit.* 2. 2. 4; 2. 2. 12.

Chapter Nine

THE SIN OF MIND

Sin is properly of the mind, which is evident from the New Testament teaching about the renewing of the mind. As a natural gift, the reason is not totally destroyed, though it is seriously impaired, and totally perverted. The total perversion of the mind or the reason means that the whole inclination of the mind is in the direction of alienation from God. The reason has therefore lost its original rectitude, and is indeed alienated from right reason, until it is renewed by the Spirit through the Word. Calvin's view of reason is functional, not substantival. Reason cannot be regarded as a static gift from God, but is maintained in being by God's Spirit in the creatio continua *even in sinful men. Though God maintains the reason in being in the sinner, He does not choose to reveal Himself to the sinner in his perversity or his self-will, i.e., as long as man holds down the truth in unrighteousness. The understanding of man and his misunderstanding are thought of continuously over against the Grace and Will of God in such a way that the supreme factor is always in God's Will and Word. Two facts must be emphasized: (a) The reason was created in order to know God, and therefore its right exercise must be within the confines of grace. (b) As a matter of fact, the reason has been perverted, and therefore is now at variance with itself. A lawless element is in control which Calvin calls* concupiscence or the element of proud self-will *which is at enmity to God. Every action of the perverted reason partakes of this self-will or perversity, and every action is against the Truth of God. Calvin does, however, draw a distinction between the heavenly intelligence, in which the reason is directed above itself toward God, and the earthly intelligence, in which the reason is directed beneath it to inferior objects. In regard to the former, men are blinder than moles in their natural state, and have no spiritual discernment. In regard to the latter, there is an admirable display of ability and light, though even this has been impaired by sin. However, because of the total perversity in which man is engulfed, even these admirable gifts of God are made to minister to his confusion and greater darkness.*

WE have now reached a point where we must view in more detail Calvin's teaching about the human reason, and its relation to sin. It follows from the fact that Calvin thinks of man as a unity that he passes the same judgment upon the mind of

THE SIN OF MIND

man as he does upon his whole person, viz., total perversion.
The mind is indeed one of the natural gifts which were corrupted
at the fall of man when God removed His supernatural gifts
from him,[1] but mind has a total relation to the person of man who
is essentially a rational being. It is for that reason that when the
natural gift of reason is corrupted human nature becomes
degenerate.[2] There can be no evading of the fact, therefore, that
"sin is properly of the mind".[3] But Calvin only takes up this
position as a theological inference from grace: it is in no sense
a stricture upon rational nature as such. He starts off therefore
from such a word as that of St. Paul: "Be ye renewed in the
spirit of your mind", and draws out its implication on the sin of
the mind.[4] "Be renewed, not only with respect to the inferior
appetites or desires, which are manifestly sinful, but with respect
also to that part of the soul which is reckoned most noble and
excellent. And here again Paul brings forward to view that
Queen which philosophers are accustomed almost to adore.
There is an implied contrast between *the spirit of our mind* and the
divine and heavenly Spirit, who produces in us another and a
new mind. How much there is in us that is sound or uncorrupted
may be easily gathered from this passage, which enjoins us to
correct chiefly the reason or *mind*, in which we are apt to imagine
that there is nothing but what is virtuous and deserves com-
mendation."[5] Calvin makes a similar comment on the parallel
word of St. Paul in the Epistle to the Romans: "Note here what
kind of renewing is required of us, namely, not of the flesh only, as
the Sorbonnites who take this word for the inferior part of the
Soul, but of the mind, which is the most excellent part of us, and
to which the philosophers ascribe the principality. For they call

---

[1] *Instit.* 2. 2. 4, 12, 15.
[2] Calvin even equates *homo* with degenerate human nature. Cf. *Comm. on Rom.*
12 : 2: *Nam quum totus mundus in maligno sit positus, nos exuere convenit quicquid habemus
hominis, si volumus Christum vere induere.*
[3] *Comm. on Rom.* 2 : 1: *Peccatum proprie animi est.* For Calvin, *animus* includes *mens*
and *voluntas.*
[4] See also *Comm. on Ezek.* 11 : 19, 20.
[5] *Comm. on Eph. 4 : 23: Renovemini, non tantum quod ad inferiores appetitus aut con-
cupiscentias, quæ palam sunt vitiosæ, sed etiam quod ad partem illam animæ, quæ nobilissima
et præstantissima habetur. Hic enim rursus ponit reginam illam, quæ propemodum adoratur
a philosophis: et spiritum mentis nostræ divino ac cælesti tacite opponit, qui aliam in nobis
ac novam mentem generat. Unde colligere promptum est, quid sit in nobis sanum aut incor-
ruptum, quum rationem aut mentem potissimum corrigi præcipiat, in qua nihil videtur esse
præter virtutem et laudis materiam.* See *Serm. on Eph.* 2 : 23-26. Calvin argues similarly
from the light of the Gospel to the blindness and darkness of the mind (see *Comm.
on John* 8 : 12).

it *hegemonikon*, that is, the prince or principal spirit, and reason is feigned to be a very wise queen. Howbeit, Paul throws her out of her throne, and so brings her to nothing, while he teaches that we must be renewed in mind; for however we flatter ourselves, yet that sentence of Christ is true, that man must be born again who will enter into the Kingdom of God, seeing, both in mind and heart, we are altogether devoid of the righteousness of God."[1] There can be no escaping the judgments of faith in regard to the mind. "We are so utterly mastered under the power of sin, that our whole mind, heart, and all our actions, bend towards sin."[2] When a man sins he sins "with all the inclination of his mind", "with the whole consent and agreement of mind".[3] "Abominable impiety has seized upon the very citadel of his mind, and pride penetrated to his inmost heart."[4] And this pride is to a large extent the "judgment of the flesh" by which man has "overweening confidence in his own intelligence and integrity".[5]

How far does this "depravity of the human mind"[6] mean the destruction of intelligence and reason? Calvin's views here are consistent with his general doctrine of corruption so that he does not think of corruption as affecting the being of the mind in itself, for the mind is still maintained in being by the direct action of God. As a natural gift it is not removed but perverted. "By his revolt man lost the *light* of the understanding, yet he still sees and understands, so that what he *naturally* possesses from the grace of the Son of God is not entirely destroyed."[7] "In the perverted and degenerate nature of man there are still some sparks which show that he is a rational animal, and differs from the brutes, inasmuch as he is endued with intelligence, and yet this light is so smothered by clouds of darkness that it cannot shine forth to any good effect."[8] "Although there is still some residue of intelligence and judgment as well as will, we cannot call a mind sound and entire which is both weak and immersed in darkness... Therefore, since reason, by which man discerns between good and evil, and by which he understands and judges, is a natural gift, it could not be

[1] *Comm. on Rom.* 12 : 2.
[2] *Comm. on Rom.* 7 : 14. Cf. *on Gen.* 8 : 21: "Let men therefore acknowledge that inasmuch as they are born of Adam, they are depraved creatures, and therefore can conceive only sinful thoughts, until they become the new workmanship of Christ, and are formed by His Spirit to a new life."
[3] *Comm. on Rom.* 7 : 15.   [4] *Instit.* 2. 1. 9.   [5] *Instit.* 2. 1. 3.
[6] *Instit.* 1. 2. 2; *Comm. on Isa.* 40 : 17.
[7] *Comm. on John* 1 : 5; *on Ezek.* 11 : 19, 20.
[8] *Instit.* 2. 2. 12; *Comm. on Ps.* 36 : 9.

entirely destroyed, but being partly weakened and partly corrupted, a shapeless ruin is all that remains."[1] This expression *shapeless ruin* is typical of Calvin, for he thinks of the true shape of the reason as coming from the Truth and Word of God, so that a reason alienated from God's Truth is inevitably shapeless and ruined,[2] and in contradiction to itself.[3] Another way of saying the same thing is to say that reason has lost all *rectitude*. "If there is need of a new spirit and a new heart, it follows that the soul of man is not only injured in each part, but so corrupt that its depravity may be called death and destruction, *as far as rectitude is concerned*."[4]

Calvin has a great respect for man's natural gifts, especially for the wonderful gift of intelligence by which we are made almost supernatural creatures like the angels, and are able by reason to transcend ourselves and nature in an astonishing fashion,[5] but, he goes on to say, "lest any one should imagine a man to be very happy merely because, with reference to the elements of this world, he has been endued with great talents for the investigation of truth, we ought to add, that the whole power of the intellect thus bestowed is in the sight of God fleeting and vain whenever it is not based on a solid foundation of truth".[6] Our natural gifts of mind are "not polluted in themselves in so far as they proceed from God, but they have ceased to be pure to polluted man".[7] Calvin's favourite expression for the corruption of man's reason is that he has been *alienated in mind* from God.[8] Men have been "alienated from God in the whole of their mental system".[9] Quite frequently Calvin speaks of unbelievers as mad and insane.

[1] *Instit.* 2. 2. 12.

[2] *Instit.* 2. 8. 1: *Ingenium nostrum . . . pravum et contortum.* Cf. *Instit.* 2. 8. 35. Again and again he speaks of the reason of natural man as an *abyss of horrible confusion* (see below).

[3] *Instit.* 1. 15. 6; cf. *Comm. on Gen.* 3 : 1.

[4] *Comm. on Ezek.* 11 : 19, 20. "We have put off that integrity of nature which God had conferred on us at the beginning." Cf. *on Ezek.* 18 : 20, where Calvin says that God has taken away the *spirit of rectitude* from the reprobate.

[5] *Instit.* 1. 5. 2; *Serm. on Job* 10 : 7 f.; *Comm. on* 1 *Cor.* 1 : 20.

[6] *Instit.* 2. 2. 16.

[7] *Ibid.* Cf. *Comm. on Matt.* 11 : 25; and *Serm. on Eph.* 4 : 23-26: "*Vray est que nostre raison en soy sera tousiours louable: mais nous sommes tellement depravez par le peché d'Adam, que nous ne sçaurions concevoir une seule bonne pensee qui ne soit tortue et pleine de malice et rebellion a l'encontre de Dieu.*"

[8] *Comm. on* 1 *Cor.* 1 : 21. The expression is *mente alienatus.* See *on Col.* 1 : 21; *on John* 5 : 25; *Instit.* 2. 5. 19; *The True Method of giving Peace to Christendom and of Reforming the Church,* Calvin's *Tracts* (Eng. tr.), Vol. 3, p. 242 Cf. *Comm. on Eph.* 1 : 10; 2 : 1; *on Jer.* 31 : 19.

[9] *Comm. on Col.* 1 : 21: *Penitus et toto mentis sensu abalienatos fuisse a Deo.*

At the same time it is quite clear that he is not referring to mental lunacy, but to spiritual perversity in the mind which masters it as it revolts from the Word of God.[1] The mind has been made to reflect the glory of God, and therefore when it is not employed and directed toward the glory of God the whole order of nature is overthrown. "Whereupon it follows that those cogitations are absurd and far from reason, yea, they are mad, whatsoever they be, that tend to the diminishing of His glory."[2] But this means that man is "alienated from *right reason*".[3] It is to this *right reason*, or *right mind*, that a man is renewed in faith,[4] that is to say, not merely to "that reasonable part of the soul which the philosophers make so much of, but that which is illuminated with the Spirit of God to understand and will aright".[5] There is a sense in which all reason is given by the Spirit of God, but it is only in faith that a man receives that illumination of the Spirit through which his perverted reason is restored to truth and sanity.[6]

This becomes clearer when we realize that Calvin never thinks of reason as substance, but adopts a functional or dynamic view of man's mental nature, which is quite in accord with his general view of creation and providence. Because God made us reasonable creatures in order to reflect His image and glory, reason is reasonable when it exercises this its true function.[7] Apart from this function it cannot really be said to be anything but vicious, for if it is not performing its true function it is performing a perverse one, for God has not made us to be idle.[8]

A fundamental factor in Calvin's thought here is that we have our reason only as a gift from God, and only in His continuing favour.[9] God continues His favour to us in this way even though we have fallen from His grace, and been deprived of His supernatural gifts.[10] Indeed, all the skill and wisdom of man comes from God, for "He fills and moves and invigorates all things by

---

[1] *Comm. on Eph.* 4 : 18, 19; *on Gen.* 2 : 3; 3 : 5, 6; *Instit.* 2. 3. 1; *on Job.* 14 : 5 f.
[2] *Comm. on Rom.* 11 : 36.
[3] *Comm. on Gen.* 6 : 3. Cf. 2 : 16. It is the obedient who are truly rational.
[4] *Comm. on Jer.* 31 : 19.
[5] *Comm. on Rom.* 7 : 25. Calvin does not therefore think of Aristotle as insane, but as extinguishing the light (*on Ps.* 108 : 43).
[6] *Comm. on 1 Cor.* 2 : 14, where Calvin can say on the one hand: "It is from the Spirit of God that we have the feeble spark of reason which we all enjoy"; but on the other hand: "All mankind are by nature destitute of the Spirit of God", and, "The soul belongs to nature, but the spirit is of supernatural communication."
[7] *Comm. on Acts* 17 : 27.
[8] *Serm. on Job* 29 : 18 f.; 34 : 16 f.; 34 : 33 f.; 35 : 8 f.; 37 : 14 f.; *Instit.* 1. 14. 2; 2. 1. 8.
[9] *Serm. on Job* 11 : 7 f.; *Instit.* 2. 2. 15; 2. 4. 7.   [10] *Instit.* 2. 2. 15.

virtue of His Spirit, and that according to the peculiar nature which each class of beings has received by the law of creation. But if the Lord has been pleased to assist us by the work and ministry of the ungodly in physics, dialectics, mathematics, and other similar sciences, let us avail ourselves of it lest by neglecting the gifts of God spontaneously offered to us, we be justly punished for our sloth."[1] Calvin even says that "men's minds are entirely under the control of God".[2] "Your mind depends more on the agency of God than the freedom of your own choice."[3] When we know God it is not as if "our minds were illuminated in a single day, so as to see of ourselves",[4] but our knowing of God is only while He gives Himself to be known,[5] and known in the manner in which He reveals Himself to our minds.[6] When we do not know Him, it is not simply because we have revolted from Him, but also because He has blinded us lest we should know Him in our *perverse disposition*.[7] That is to say, God refuses to commit Himself in full revelation to men as long as they are bent on *holding down the truth in unrighteousness*. "He disappoints them since they do not come to Him with sincere hearts and desires, for they wish to transform God into their own nature and character, and they bend not themselves to His service nor submit to His Word."[8] Of this perverse activity in fallen man Calvin says: "There was none who would not bring the majesty of God under his capacity, and make God such a one as he could conceive in his own sense. This temerity is not learned in schools but is innate in us".[9] To this perverted activity God has given men over as a punishment. Man has undoubtedly perverted himself, but God gives him over to a reprobate mind when he persists in perversity, and even in the revelation of His Gospel, which is a savour of life unto life and death unto death, He hardens them in

---

[1] *Instit.* 2. 2. 16.

[2] *Instit.* 2. 2. 17.

[3] *Instit.* 2. 4. 7. This does not mean determinism, for Calvin excludes *coaction*, *Instit.* 2. 3. 5 f.; 2. 5. 1; *Comm. on Rom.* 7 : 14.

[4] *Instit.* 2. 2. 25. Cf. *Comm. on Matt.* 16 : 14: The human mind is so weak that "even out of true principles it coins errors".

[5] *Serm. on Job* 2 : 1 f.; *Comm. on Col.* 1 : 9 f.

[6] *Comm. on Gen.* 2 : 6; 3 : 6-22; *Serm. on Job* 1 : 1: "It must be in such a way as He has uttered Himself."

[7] *Comm. on Eph.* 4 : 19. See especially *on Ezek.* 20 : 1, 2: God will not be inquired of men when they neglect His Word because they are still *perverse in their disposition*. See also *on Matt.* 13 : 2-13.

[8] *Comm. on Jer.* 37 : 9, 10.

[9] *Comm. on Rom.* 1 : 22. Paul's argument in the first chapter of the Epistle to the Romans is one that Calvin reproduces again and again in various forms.

their perversity.[1] That is also the revelation of His wrath. Thus the understanding and the misunderstanding of man are thought of continuously over against the grace and will of God and in such a way that the supreme factor is always God's Will and Word.

This is clearly expounded in an argument which Calvin developed while preaching on the eleventh chapter of *Job*.[2] "All the wit which we have is God's gift besides our nature." A child is not born in the world with any wisdom of its own, nor any understanding that has its roots, as some philosophers have supposed, in the roots of the memory, as if it was necessary to have "a sense enclosed in us beforehand". When he is born into the world a man has less reason and understanding than a brute beast.[3] "And how is it that we have the spirit of understanding when we come to full age? God must give it to us. And so you see why it is said that 'the empty man shall be endued with heart'; for in Scripture this word *heart* means *understanding*. Let us mark then how it is shown here that when we have wit or reason, that comes not of our own nature, neither do we possess it as though it grew up with us, but it behoves us to know that it is an excellent benefit which God has bestowed on us.[4] Seeing then we have it at His hand, what unthankfulness it is of us to abuse it against Him? Therefore let us acknowledge His benefit in giving us wisdom and discretion when we come to age, to know both Him and ourselves, and to honour Him." Calvin is deliberately avoiding a substantival view of reason, such as prevailed among the Schoolmen ever since Boethius, but insists instead on a conception of reason as having its being only in immediate relation to the continuous activity of God's grace. The general argument in the same sermon, which this genetic account of reason was designed to support, is even more instructive. There he declares that because men have no understanding except as God gives it, they have no right "to value themselves by their own reason after any ordinary manner", for "there is none but He alone competent to know". Reason must rest in God there-

---

[1] *Comm. on 2 Cor.* 2 : 15 f.; *on Acts* 27 : 26; *on Matt.* 13 : 13 f.; 15 : 13; 16 : 19; 18 : 15; *on Mark* 4 : 12.

[2] *Serm. on Job* 11 : 7 f.

[3] For the development of evil in the child, see *Comm. on Ezek.* 18 : 20, where Calvin says that "even before the child is born its mental intelligence is buried in darkness, and its will perverse and rebellious against God".

[4] Cf. *Serm. on Deut.* 16 : 18: "Wisdom does not grow out of men's brains, it is the gift of God."

fore and find its authority in God's knowledge.[1] When we suppose that we have any wisdom, and imagine that we may "climb high", then "God withdraws Himself from us that we may vanish away in our own imaginations". Our knowing depends entirely on our being known by God, and therefore man must learn to subject himself and his reason to God's knowing of him, and find his true knowledge and understanding in humility.[2] Calvin ends up the sermon with a prayer to God "to grant us the grace to apply all our wits and endeavour to consider what we are, to wit, wretched, vain, and unprofitable creatures, unable to do anything of ourselves, so that He must furnish and strengthen us, or else we must utterly quail. And that such knowledge of our own weakness and feebleness may provoke us to return with greater desire to the grace which our good God offered us, seeking nothing but to be filled with the same to the end that we may honour and magnify Him in all respects, until He has brought us unto the perfection whereunto we are called, without swerving one way or another, for fear of turning out of the right way of salvation."

Calvin is emphatic upon two points. On one hand, he holds that man was created a rational being in order to exercise the motion of his reason toward God, and in such a motion that it depends on God from step to step, and finding thus its true felicity, might *conserve itself as enclosed within the grace and Word of God*.[3] On the other hand, Calvin is equally emphatic upon the fact that that motion of reason has been perverted, so that now *reason is at variance with itself*,[4] and "its whole procedure proves how unfit it is to seek the truth and find it".[5] Indeed the depravity of man's nature must be described as a "most forward bias of the mind" such that man "cannot move and act except in the direction of evil".[6] This perverse motion in the mind Calvin calls *concupiscence*,[7] which is given an essentially spiritual inter- pretation. He speaks of concupiscence as comprising "the violent lawless movements which war with the order of God", and as "a perpetual disorder and excess apparent in all our actions", and as

<hr/>

[1] See also *Comm. on* I Cor. 2 : 5, 15; 4 : 4; *on* 2 Pet. I : 3; *Serm. on Eph.* 4 : 17 f.; *Instit.* I. 6. 3, etc.
[2] See *Comm. on Gal.* 4 : 9; *on Mal.* 3 : 15: "Faith alone humbles us."
[3] *Instit.* I. 14. 1; 2. 12. 5.
[4] *Instit.* I. 15. 6.
[5] *Instit.* 2. 2. 12.
[6] *Instit.* 2. 3. 5.
[7] *Instit.* 2. 1. 8; 3. 3. 11, 12, etc. Calvin also speaks of the "wantonness and prurience of the human mind" (2. 12. 5).

"inordinate desire".[1] This is the "perversity in us" that "never ceases".[2] This perversity is not just a habit, but the present "nature" of fallen man, for the "order of creation was subverted", and men "have degenerated from their proper nature".[3] As soon as men "are of age to begin to form thoughts, they have *radical corruption of mind*".[4] The perversity of this motion can be described as "contempt of God, pride, self-love, ambition, hypocrisy, and fraud".[5] It cannot but be that all men's "thoughts are contaminated with such vices; they cannot tend towards a right end".[6] Thus "reason is turned into maliciousness instead of honouring God for the benefits received".[7]

There is not the slightest doubt in Calvin's mind, therefore, about the fact that reason "cannot judge anything of God",[8] nor can the "wise men of the world frame themselves to the Gospel".[9] From the start the perverted mind by its very action inverts the truth, and cannot take any step whatever in the right direction.[10] The more man contrives methods of approaching God, the more he alienates himself.[11] "All the soundness of judgment which is given to men is corrupted and perverted, so that not even one spark of light continues to dwell in them."[12] All action on the part of the perverted reason is the action of self-will, but no self-willed movement can reach God, for it always meets with the divine judgment and is accordingly inflicted with blindness. It meets that aspect of the divine Majesty whereby God repels men and separates them from Himself, hardening them in their sin and defection and error. It is impossible to reach God except by His will, and in the way in which He reveals Himself. He has circumscribed men's minds by His grace,[13] so that they not only owe their origin to grace, and depend on grace from moment to moment, but cannot have any true motion

---

[1] *Instit.* 3. 3. 12. This means that *concupiscentia* is diametrically opposed to the *imago dei* which reflects the *order of God* in creation. It is through this *unorderly dealing* that the creation is perverted, and God's glory diminished. Cf. *Comm. on Rom.* 11 : 36; and *on Isa.* 48 : 16, where Calvin speaks of "the wicked exercise of our understanding which always contrives in what way it shall rob God of the praise which is His due".
[2] *Instit.* 2. 1. 8.   [3] *Comm. on Gen.* 8 : 21.   [4] *Ibid.*
[5] *Ibid.* Cf. *Serm. on Job* 33 : 1 f.   [6] *Comm. on Gen.* 8 : 21.
[7] *Serm. on Job* 35 : 8 f.   [8] *Ibid.*   [9] *Serm. on Job* 17 : 10 f.
[10] *Instit.* 1. 4. 1; 1. 5. 11 f., 14 f.; 1. 11. 8; 2. 2. 24; *Comm. on Rom.* 1 : 20; *on* 1 *Cor.* 1. 21; *on Heb.* 11 : 3; cf. *on Matt.* 6 : 22: "I confess indeed that men naturally possess reason to distinguish between vices and virtues; but I say that it is so corrupted by sin that it fails at every step."
[11] *Comm. on* 1 *Tim.* 2 : 5.
[12] *Comm. on Matt.* 6 : 22; cf. *on Isa.* 40 : 14.   [13] *Ibid.*

except in accordance with grace, and within these "barriers". To transgress these gracious bounds is presumption and sin, and can only end in destruction. Thus our first parents *died* when they "erred in not regulating the measure of their knowledge by the will of God".[1] Being "incredulous at His Word . . . they began like fascinated persons to lose reason and judgment", until their "mind was smitten with blindness and infected with innumerable errors".[2] Because of this *perverse procedure* "all the studies in which men think they attain the highest wisdom" must be pronounced "vain and frivolous".[3]

Calvin makes a distinction, however, between the intelligence as directed toward "inferior objects", and as directed toward "superior objects".[4] It is a distinction between "one kind of intelligence of earthly things, and another of heavenly things". "By earthly things", he says, "I mean those which are related not to God and His Kingdom, to true righteousness and future blessedness, but have some connection with the present life, and are in a manner confined within its boundaries. By heavenly things, I mean the pure knowledge of God, the method of true righteousness, and the mysteries of the heavenly Kingdom. To the former belong matters of policy and economy, all mechanical arts and liberal studies. To the latter belong the knowledge of God and His will, and the means of framing the life in accordance with them."[5] In regard to the intelligence of earthly things, there is "an admirable display of light", so that "the human mind, however much fallen and perverted from its original integrity, is still adorned and invested with admirable gifts from its Creator. If we reflect that the Spirit of God is the only fountain of truth, we will be careful, as we would avoid offering insult to Him, not to reject or contemn truth wherever it appears. In despising the gifts we insult the Giver."[6] But, as we have already had occasion to note, Calvin goes on to say that "the whole power of the intellect thus bestowed is, in the sight of God,

---

[1] Cf. *Comm. on* 1 *Tim.* 6 : 16: "The light of God is unapproachable, if anyone will endeavour to approach Him in his own strength." See also *Serm. ad loc.* "Hence if anyone desires to ascend to the clouds and to inquire what God will answer, he departs from Him, although he pretends to approach Him. Hence this moderation is to be observed, that our faith may acquiesce in the authority of the one God, and not be carried hither and thither by the will of men." *Comm. on Ezek.* 20 : 1.

[2] *Comm. on Gen.* 3 : 6; 6 : 3; *on Eph.* 4 : 19; *on Jonah* 1 : 5: *Ingenium hominis officina est omnium errorum.*

[3] *Instit.* 2. 2. 12.   [4] *Instit.* 2. 2. 13.   [5] *Ibid.*
[6] *Instit.* 2. 2. 15.

fleeting and vain whenever it is not based on a solid foundation of truth".[1] It is only by the mercy of God that these natural gifts were not "carried along with the entire destruction of nature".[2] They are maintained by God's mercy in fallen man, though "they have ceased to be pure to polluted man, lest he should by their means obtain any praise".[3] "We must now explain what the power of human reason is in regard to the Kingdom of God and spiritual discernment which consists chiefly of three things: the knowledge of God, the knowledge of His paternal favour toward us, which constitutes our salvation, and the method of regulating our conduct in accordance with the divine Law. With regard to the former two, but more properly the second, men otherwise the most ingenious are *blinder than moles*.[4] I deny not, indeed, that in the writings of philosophers we meet occasionally with shrewd and apposite remarks on the nature of God, though they invariably savour somewhat of a giddy imagination. As observed above, the Lord has bestowed on them some slight perception of His Godhead, that they might not plead ignorance as an excuse for their impiety, and has at times instigated them to deliver some truths, the confession of which should be their condemnation. Still, though seeing, they saw not. Their discernment was not such as to direct them to the truth, far less to enable them to attain it, but resembled that of the bewildered traveller, who sees the flash of lightning glance far and wide for a moment, and then vanish into the darkness of the night, before he can advance a single step. So far is such assistance from enabling him to find the right path."[5]

Calvin makes it quite clear then that in natural knowledge there is a "small flame or rather spark" of divine light, but "not such that it enables man to comprehend God".[6] The element of truth is inevitably turned into the darkness of a lie by the perversity of the mind,[7] in which he is a rebel against God's grace; but "without

---

[1] *Instit.* 2. 2. 16.   [2] *Instit.* 2. 2. 17.   [3] *Instit.* 2. 2. 16.

[4] Cf. *Confession de la Foy* (1537) C.R. 22, 88: "*Puis que lhomme est naturellement (ainsi comme dit a este) despourveu et desnue en soy de toute lumiere de Dieu et de toute justice, nous recongnoissons quen soymesmes il ne peult attendre que lire et la malediction de Dieu, et pourtant quil doibt chercher autre part quen soy le moyen de son salut.*"

[5] *Instit.* 2. 2. 18.

[6] *Instit.* 2. 2. 19; *Comm. on John* 1 : 5; *Serm. on Eph.* 1 : 17, 18.

[7] *Comm. on Rom.* 1 : 25; *on Acts* 17 : 24; *Serm. on Job* 15 : 17 f., where Calvin speaks of "truth turned upside down and converted into falsehood". Cf. also *The Secret Providence of God*, Art. 13, 14: "Reason, by its own power of sight, can do nothing but turn the truth into a lie, and adulterate whatever of light and understanding true religion and faith possess."

this divine favour", says Calvin, "the mind of man must ever remain a mere chaos of confusion".[1] Or as he says in a passage already cited, "there is not a more horrible confusion than man's reason when it cannot subject itself to the Word of God".[2] "All the light which we have by nature is turned into darkness . . . Reason is turned into maliciousness instead of honouring God for the benefits received."[3]

[1] *Instit.* 2. 2. 18.   [2] *Serm. on Job* 37 : 14 f.
[3] *Serm. on Job* 35 : 8 f.; *Comm. on Matt.* 6 : 23.

Chapter Ten
THE MIND'S KNOWLEDGE OF GOD

The knowledge of God is an operation of grace beyond the natural capacity of the human mind. We must go outside of ourselves and not measure God by the acuteness of our intellects, or try to subject His Truth to our capacity. This means that God must let Himself down to the measure of our understanding, and temper His revelation to our knowing, at the same time as He raises our minds up to know Him through the power of the Spirit and the Word. How the human mind knows God is ultimately a mystery of the Spirit, who creates in man the capacity to receive the Word with understanding, and forms the mind to know God. The Spirit does not appeal to any secret or special capacity in the natural man. When men try to know God by themselves, they inevitably act contrary to the will of God to reveal Himself, and cannot come at the Truth. Although knowing God and being in the image of God are closely interrelated, it is impossible to seize upon the image and use it as a means of knowing God, for the image is always only a reflex of the glory of God, and a reflex of His Word. We must therefore keep our minds within the bounds of the Word, and not indulge in speculative imagination. All knowledge of God, apart from His revelation, is a vast abyss that swallows up our thoughts in the thickest darkness. God is Himself the Author of all our knowledge of Him, while His Word is both the standard and the warrant of its Truth. All correct knowledge of God, therefore, flows from obedience. Faith is the obedience of the mind toward God, and is grounded upon a double relation to the Word and to the Spirit. Calvin's emphasis upon the Word means that all our knowledge of God is essentially analogical, i.e., through a revelation which accommodates itself to the humble capacity of the human mind, giving us a knowledge of God through comparison with things which we know. But in all this God alone is the supreme authority, and He alone testifies of Himself through the Word—hence also the emphasis upon the Holy Spirit. This means that we must not choose the analogies for our knowledge of God, but must keep close to the Word in its accommodating activity. The relation between God and the analogical element is not ontological but essentially sacramental. In comparison with God these elements are nothing, but though they must be apt symbols in themselves they only become vehicles of the Truth through the Spirit. The whole emphasis is upon the revelation which supervenes upon these human or worldly analogies

*and uses them in the accommodating activity of the Word and in the
sacramental operation of the Spirit. In our fallen world of perversity
this necessarily entails the radical inversion of our natural analogies and
conceptions (objectively through the Cross, subjectively in* metanoia).
*There is no reasoning from the mind or being of man which can raise man
up to God, but in every instance knowledge of God is gained through the
acknowledgment of a revelation. This is the act of faith, but faith con-
tains at its heart a confession that God is not like man, though it attains to
a knowledge which forms man in the image of God.*

"GOD puts a perpetual distinction between the human mind
and the revelation of His Spirit."[1] How then does the
human mind know God? To that question Calvin gives a clear
answer. It is only by an act of God's grace beyond the natural
capacity of the human mind. In order to know God it is necessary
for us to go beyond our own judgments, since God's Truth is
"too transcendent for us to estimate".[2] We cannot "know God
by the acuteness of our own intellect",[3] for "with all his acuteness, man is as stupid of obtaining by himself a knowledge of
the mysteries of God as an ass is qualified for understanding
musical harmonies".[4] It is a constant theme of Calvin that the
"natural perspicacity is of no avail for understanding spiritual
wisdom".[5] Therefore "we must go outside of ourselves and not
measure God by the capacity of our minds",[6] or try to "subject
His will to our standard".[7] "This knowledge is so much
superior that the human mind must far surpass and go beyond
itself in order to reach it. Nor even when it has reached it does it
comprehend what it feels, but persuaded of what it comprehends
not, it understands more from mere certainty of persuasion than
it could discern of any human matter by its own capacity."[8] Or
again: "No man can approach unto God without being raised
above himself, and above the world."[9] If we are unable to know

---

[1] *Comm. on Ezek.* 13 : 2.   [2] *Comm. on Ezek.* 13 : 1-3. Cf. *on Rom.* 7 : 14.
[3] *Comm. on Eph.* 3 : 19: *Meminerimus ergo, fidei certitudinem esse scientiam, sed quæ
Spiritus Sancti magisterio, non ingenii nostri acumine discitur.*
[4] *Comm. on* 1 *Cor.* 1 : 20.
[5] *Comm. on Rom.* 1 : 20; cf. *on* 2 *Pet.* 1 : 3; *on John* 1 : 9; *Instit.* 1. 13. 21; 3. 2. 14;
Comm. on 1 *Tim.* 6 : 16; *Serm. on Job* 34 : 33 f.
[6] *Comm. on Acts* 17 : 23.
[7] *Serm. on Job* 8 : 1 f.: "Il ne faut pas qu'il nous soit subiet, et que nous le vueillons
assubiettir à nostre mesure." Cf. *Comm. on Acts* 17 : 30: "To bring God within bounds
is a most unseemly thing, and contrary to nature herself."
[8] *Instit.* 3. 2. 14.
[9] *Comm. on Eph.* 3 : 19; *on Heb.* 6 : 4; *Instit.* 3. 23. 4. Cf. 1. 14. 3: "We must raise
our minds higher than our eyes can penetrate." Also see 3. 2. 41.

God without rising above our understanding, this does not mean that we are to take leave of our senses,[1] but that God must "let Himself down to the measure of our understanding".[2] Speaking of the Old Testament believers, Calvin says: "God did not appear as He really is, but as far as He can be seen by mortal men. . . . For God is infinite, and when the heaven of heavens cannot contain Him, how can our minds apprehend Him? But although God has never appeared in His immeasurable glory, and has never manifested Himself as He really exists, yet we must nevertheless hold that He has so appeared as to leave no doubt in the minds of His servants as to their knowing that they have seen God. . . . At the same time, God never gave the Fathers a sight of Himself except according to their capacity. He always had respect to their faculties".[3] What must we do then? "We must lift up our minds higher than our natural understanding mounts. But shall a man ever attain unto God, if he judge according to his own fancy, and fleshly reason? No. But we shall rather darken His glory. So then, if we would glorify God, let us learn to reach out our knowledge far and wide. And how? For a man shall never reach out his knowledge as he ought to do, to speak of God, except that he know that His majesty is higher than his understanding, and therefore that He must come down to us, and lift us up to Him. Thus we must humble ourselves with all reverence to the end that God may lift us up to Him, and shew Himself to us and make us partakers of the doctrine to which we would otherwise never attain."[4] That is, for Calvin, the essential movement of true knowledge. We must on our part "employ ourselves in it to the uttermost, and strain ourselves above all our forces",[5] but "God tempers His revelation to our knowing",[6] having in Christ "accommodated Himself to our capacity, lest our minds should be swallowed up by the immensity of His glory".[7] And further-

---

[1] *Comm. on Heb.* 11 : 27.

[2] *Comm. on Deut.* 29 : 29; *on Exod.* 33 : 20. At the same time, "it is necessary that God's Word should correspond with the nature of its Author" (*on Jer.* 36 : 29, 30). Cf. also *Serm. on Deut.* 30 : 15 f.: "There is a likeness and conformity between God and His Word." Therefore the Word does not lose its transcendent nature. "Though it resounds on the earth, enters our ears, and settles in our hearts, yet it still retains its celestial nature, for it descends to us in such a manner that it is not subject to the changes of the world." *Comm. on Ps.* 119 : 92. "The Word of God stands firm in its own eternity" (119 : 96). See also *Instit.* 4. 14. 3.

[3] *Comm. on Ezek.* 1 : 28.   [4] *Serm. on Job* 13 : 1 f.   [5] *Ibid.*

[6] *Comm. on Exod.* 33 : 19.

[7] *Instit.* 2. 6. 4. Cf. *Comm. on Isa.* 25 : 9; *on Matt.* 13 : 34. Calvin's favourite expression in this connection is *accommodate to our capacity*.

more, by His. Spirit "God applies to our capacity whatever He testifies of Himself".[1] "For as men are made known by their countenance and speech, so God utters His voice to us by the voice of the prophets, and in the sacraments takes as it were a visible form from which He may be known by us according to our feeble capacity."[2] "While God withholds us from a complete knowledge of Himself (for that incomprehensible brightness would bring us to nothing), nevertheless He manifests Himself as far as it is expedient; nay, attempering the amount of light to our humble capacity. He assumes the face that we are able to bear."[3] At the same time, Calvin makes it quite clear that, in this act of revelation by accommodating Himself to our capacity, God still holds Himself apart, and only gives Himself in such a way that we do not make Him our *underling*. That is the importance, he says, of the Old Testament insistence that it is only through His voice that God gives Himself to be known: that is, in such a way that we may know Him without subduing Him to the will of our own minds, but must rather be *imprisoned* to His voice, and be content to be taught by Him.[4]

It must be admitted that how the human mind ultimately knows God is a mystery of His Spirit, which He works in an "incomprehensible fashion".[5] "As· we cannot come to Christ unless drawn by the Spirit, so when we are drawn, we are exalted both in mind and spirit far above our understanding. For the soul when illumined by Him *receives as it were a new eye enabling it to contemplate heavenly mysteries*, by the splendour of which it was previously dazzled. And thus, indeed, it is only when the human intellect is irradiated by the light of the Holy Spirit that it begins to have a taste of those things which pertain to the Kingdom of God. Previously it was too stupid and senseless to have any relish for them."[6] How far we are from being able to know God of ourselves is evident from the fact that even when we see the very image of God in Christ "so plainly exhibited, we have not eyes to perceive it".[7] "What? Did not Christ descend into the

---

[1] *Comm. on Rom.* 1 : 19.   [2] *Comm. on John* 5 : 37.
[3] *Comm. on Exod.* 33 : 20. See especially *Serm. on* 1 *Tim.* 1 : 17-19. Cf. *on Ezek.* 18 : 32: "Because we cannot ascend to that height, it is needful for God to *conform Himself to our ignorance*, and to descend to us in some way since we cannot ascend to Him." Also *on Ezek.* 1 : 13, 25, 28.
[4] *Serm. on Deut.* 4 : 10 f.   The whole sermon is on this subject.
[5] *Serm. on Job* 32 : 4 f.
[6] *Instit.* 3. 2. 34; cf. *Serm. on* 2 *Tim.* 2 : 3 f.; *on Eph.* 1 : 17 f.
[7] *Instit.* 2. 2. 20.

world that He might make the will of His Father manifest to men, and did He not faithfully perform the office? True, He did: but nothing is accomplished by His preaching unless the inner Teacher, the Spirit, *open the way into our minds*.[1] Only those therefore come to Him who have heard and learned of the Father. And in what is the method of this hearing and learning? *It is when the Spirit, with a wondrous and special energy, forms the ear to hear and the mind to understand.*"[2] "The faculty of seeing and hearing is naturally implanted in the eye and ear, whereas *Christ acts in our minds above the measure of nature by special grace.*"[3] This means that the Word of God does not appeal to anything, such as a *secret analogy of being*, or a *remnant of the imago dei*, or an *inner ear already in man*, but brings with it the power by which it is apprehended.[4] "We must perceive with the ear before we receive in the heart. And they philosophize with more subtlety than truth who say, that *the interior hearing precedes*, inasmuch as the ears are struck by the sound in vain, unless the heart is already docile. For although God prepares His elect for hearing, and gives them ears for that purpose, yet His teaching does not penetrate into their minds before it has been received in the ear."[5] "God indeed works efficiently by His own Words, but we must hold that this efficacy is not contained in the Words themselves, but proceeds from the secret instinct of the Spirit. This work of the Spirit then is joined with the Word of God. But a distinction is made, that we may know that the external Word is of no avail by itself, unless animated by the power of the Spirit. . . . All power of

[1] Cf. *Comm. on John* 12 : 42: *Eo magis admiranda Spiritus Dei virtus fuit, qua eo penetravit, quo nullus accessus patebat.*

[2] *Instit.* 2. 2. 20, 21.

[3] *Instit.* 4. 14. 9: *Audiendi videndique facultas naturaliter auribus et oculis indita est: Christus autem præter naturæ modum speciali gratia idem in animis nostris agit.*

[4] Cf. *Comm. on John* 14 : 1: "The Son of God, who is Jesus Christ, holds out Himself as the object to which our faith ought to be directed and by means of which it will easily find that on which it can rest; for He is the Immanuel *who answers within*, as soon as we seek Him by faith." Also 18 : 37: "When Christ says that they are of the truth, He does not mean that they naturally know the truth, but that they are directed by the Spirit of God."

[5] *Comm. on Ezek.* 3 : 10, 11. See also *on John* 6 : 44, 45: "Men are not fitted for believing until they have been drawn . . . The grace by which they are drawn is efficacious." "The willingness with which men follow God is what they already have from Himself, who has formed their hearts to obey Him"—that is, as Calvin says, in the same passage, through the Word and the Spirit, so that they have a new understanding and a new perception. "All that remains for us therefore is that everyone commit himself to the guidance of the Spirit, that He may inscribe in our hearts what otherwise would never have even entered into our ears" (*on John* 6 : 60).

action, then, resides in the Spirit Himself, and thus all praise ought to be referred entirely to God alone. We hold therefore that, when God speaks, He adds the efficacy of the Spirit, since His Word without it would be fruitless; and yet the Word is effectual, because the instrument ought to be united with the Author of the act. . . . Hence we conclude that it is not in our power to obey what God commands, unless this power proceeds from Him."[1] "It is true indeed that the Word of God is like a lamp, but it shines in darkness and amidst the blind, until the inward light is given by the Lord, to whom it belongs peculiarly to enlighten the blind. And hence it is evident how great is the corruption of our nature, since the light of life exhibited to us in the heavenly oracles is of no avail to us. Now if we do not perceive by the understanding what is right, how would the will be sufficient for yielding obedience? We ought therefore to acknowledge that we come short in every respect, so that the heavenly doctrine proves to be useful and efficacious to us only so far as the Spirit both *forms our minds to understand it, and our hearts to submit to its yoke;* and, therefore, that in order to our being properly qualified to become His disciples, we must lay aside all confidence in our own abilities, and seek light from heaven; and abandoning the foolish opinion of free-will, must give ourselves up to be governed by God. Nor is it without reason that Paul bids men become fools, that they may be wise unto God, for no darkness is more dangerous for quenching the light of the Spirit than reliance on our own sagacity."[2] "Nothing is more certain than this doctrine, that the Lord *calls those things which are not* (Rom. 4 : 17); *raises the dead* (Luke 7 : 22); *unites Himself to those who were strangers to Him* (Eph. 2 : 12); *makes hearts of flesh out of hearts of stone* (Ezek. 36 : 26); *manifests Himself to those who do not seek Him* (Isa. 65 : 1; Rom. 10 : 20)."[3] "There is no man who anticipates the Lord, but we are all without exception delivered from the bottomless pit of death by His free mercy, when there is no knowledge of Him, no desire of worshipping Him, to conclude,

---

[1] *Comm. on Ezek.* 2 : 2. Cf. *Serm. on Deut.* 1 : 42 f.: "God's power is after a fashion enclosed in His Word that it may be received as it deserves and as every man submits himself to it." And *on Deut.* 31 : 22 f.

[2] *Comm. on Luke* 24 : 45. Cf. *on Ps.* 119 : 105; 146 : 8; *on* 1 *Cor.* 3 : 18.

[3] *Comm. on John* 16 : 27. The Word of God does not even presuppose addressibility: "*Quand il est question de la vie celeste, il n'y a nulle adresse en nous*" (*Serm. on Eph.* 1 : 15-18). "*Il nous donne sne veuë nouvelle, laquelle nous n'avions pas, car nous avons les yeux plus que crevez, iusques à ce qu'il les illumine par son Sainct Esprit . . . Il faut donc que Dieu nous donne de nouveaux yeux*" (*Ibid*).

no sense of His truth."[1] "Away now with those who idly say that men are prepared for receiving the grace of God *by the motion of nature*. They might as well say that the dead walk."[2] "No, it is of God's working in men's hearts, who makes a preparation there by the grace of the Holy Spirit. For by nature we have no ability but to go clean contrary to God's will."[3] "They are not capable of grace, whoever abide in the flesh. By the course of nature we rush headlong into death, because we conceive nothing of ourselves but what is deadly."[4] "The preparation of the heart in man and the answer of the tongue are from the Lord."[5] "From some unknown depth of the judgments of God which we cannot scrutinize, all our ability proceeds. I see that I am able; but how able I see not. This far only I see, that it is of God."[6]

That is the essential movement in the human mind when it knows God, but when men try to assume this movement into their own hands,[7] thus usurping in self-exaltation and ingratitude[8] what is God's, they oppose God's grace and are unable to come to the truth, if only because God refuses to reveal Himself to self-will.[9] "The rule of God's will is the only light of truth."[10] Although God has made us in His own image, He reveals Himself to us only by accommodating Himself to our capacity, but when we seize upon the image of God or what we imagine to be the image of God and try to use it in order to climb up to knowledge of God, thus "putting God under such rule as we can conceive in our own understanding",[11] we invert the essential movement of knowing God, and pervert the image of God into its opposite.[12] "And this was the original source of idolatry that

---

[1] *Comm. on Rom.* 10 : 20: *Siquidem nemo est qui Dominum præveniat, sed omnes sine exceptione, gratuita eius clementia e profundissima mortis abysso eripimur: ubi nulla eius cognitio, nullum colendi eius studium, nullus denique veritatis eius sensus.*

[2] *Comm. on John* 11 : 25: *Eant nunc qui naturæ motu præparari homines garriunt ad recipiendam Dei gratiam, perinde est acsi dicerent, mortuos ambulare.* Cf. 5 : 25: *Primo admonet Christus nos omnes esse mortuos antequam nos ipse vivificet. Atque hinc patet quid tota hominis natura ad salutem comparandam valeat.*

[3] *Serm. on Deut.* 10 : 1 f. Calvin repudiates the idea of connatural grace. "They imagine that a universal grace has been given to them, as if it had been implanted by nature." *Comm. on John* 15 : 1 f.; cf. on *John* 18 : 37; on *Rom.* 8 : 6-9, 28.

[4] *Comm on Rom.* 8 : 6.   [5] *Prov.* 16 : 1, cited in *Instit.* 1. 16. 6.

[5] *Instit.* 3. 2. 35. "There is no power but that which is grounded on the Word of God" (*Serm. on Deut.* 31 : 22 f.).

[7] *Serm. on Job* 5 : 20 f.

[8] *Serm. on Job* 10 : 7 f. Cf. *Comm. on 2 Pet.* 1 : 3; on *Gen.* 2 : 9; *Instit.* 2. 2. 1; 2. 2. 10.

[9] *Serm. on Job* 34 : 29 f.; on 33 : 14 f.; *Comm. on Eph.* 4 : 19; on *Col.* 2 : 23; *Instit.* 3. 12. 5-8.

[10] *Comm. on Rom.* 2 : 8: *Regula divinæ voluntatis sola veritatis lux est.*

[11] *Serm. on Job* 23 : 1 f.; 8 : 1 f.

[12] *Serm. on Job* 33 : 1 f.; 5 : 20 f.; 9 : 29 f.; 28 : 10 f.; *Comm. on Gen.* 3 : 6; *Instit.* 2. 2.10.

men supposed they could not otherwise possess God unless by subjecting Him to their own imagination. Nothing however can be more preposterous; for, since the minds of men and all their senses sink far below the loftiness of God, when they try to bring Him down to the measure of their own weak capacity, they travesty Him. In a word, whatever man's reason conceives of Him is mere falsehood; nevertheless this depraved longing can hardly be repressed, so fiercely does it burst out."[1]

Knowing God and being in the image of God are so reciprocally interwoven that if a man tries to know God out of his own *imago dei* he really makes himself equal to God, because it means that he is in the *imago dei* of himself.[2] "Man is in no danger of taking too much from himself provided he learns that whatever he wants is to be recovered in God. But he cannot arrogate to himself one particle beyond his due without losing himself in vain confidence, and by transferring divine honour to himself, becoming guilty of the greatest impiety."[3] But it is the constant sin of man that "the human mind, stuffed as it is with presumptuous rashness, dares to imagine a god suited to its own capacity",[4] instead of acknowledging that it is in the image of God only on the ground that God graciously wills to behold man with His fatherly eye, and to set His mark on him as a child in His own image. Calvin does not say so in as many words, but it is very clear that he holds it to be a fact that the being of man in the image of God is not logically or noetically reversible.[5] Indeed, to invert it thus is the essential motion of self-will to which God is always opposed and which He judges with blindness. God proportions Himself to our apprehension,[6] and we may know

---

[1] *Comm. on Exod.* 32 : 1; cf. *on Deut.* 4 : 15; and *Serm. ad loc.*

[2] *Comm. on Gen.* 3 : 6; *on Exod.* 32 : 1; *Serm. on Job* 5 : 20 f.; 9 : 29 f.; *Comm. on Isa.* 6 : 5; 29 : 16; 31 : 3.

[3] *Instit.* 2. 2. 10: *Non enim periculum est ne sibi nimium adimat homo, dummodo recuperandum in Deo discat quod sibi deest. At sibi ne tantillum quidem sumere ultra ius suum potest, quin et inani confidentia se perdat et divinum honorem ad se traducens, immanis sacrilegii reus fiat. Et sane quoties hæc libido mentem nostram incessit, ut aliquid nostrum habere expetamus, quod in nobis scilicet potius quam in Deo resideat, cogitationem hanc non ab alio consiliario sciamus nobis suggeri, quam qui primos parentes induxit ut diis esse similes vellent, scientes bonum et malum.* See also *Instit.* 2. 2. 1; *Serm. on Gal.* 5 : 2 f.

[4] *Instit.* 1. 11. 8: Calvin says "the human mind is a perpetual forge of idols", for "the flesh is always restless until it has obtained some figment like itself with which it may vainly solace itself as a representation of God".

[5] Though the order of nature is bound to the grace of God, it is an error "to bind the grace of God to the accustomed order of nature. . . . What He freely confers upon us is entirely the result of His own will. . . . Lest any one should glory in the flesh He designedly illustrates His own free mercy in choosing those who had no worthiness of their own." *Comm. on Gen.* 48 : 17.

[6] *Serm. on 1 Tim.* 1 : 17-19: "He declares Himself in portion and measure."

Him only as we follow that movement of grace in obedience and in gratitude.[1] *We cannot fix Him,* and so adore Him[2]—that would be sheer impiety. We worship God only in an image of *His* choosing.[3] "All that the Father had, He deposited with His only begotten Son, in order that He might manifest Himself in Him, and thus by the communication of blessings express the true image of His glory. The invisible Father is to be sought nowhere but in this image."[4] "Christ is the living image of the Father, and in Him are laid up all the treasures of wisdom and knowledge. As soon, then, as we turn aside from Him, we cannot do anything else but wander in error."[5] Therefore Calvin will have nothing to do with faith as an *imaginative speculation,* for only by the particular image of God in Christ can we know Him.[6] "Hence all knowledge of God without Christ is a vast abyss which immediately swallows up all our thoughts."[7] "We cannot believe in God except through Christ, in whom God in a manner makes Himself little, that He may accommodate Himself to our apprehension."[8]

This means that we must think of God as the Author of our knowledge of Him.[9] He must be the supreme and only Subject of our knowing and our judging. "Authority belongs exclusively to Him."[10] He is His own standard, and it is His Word which makes the real judgment in our knowing Him, and not our own discernment.[11] His Word and His Truth are essentially self-authenticating. "God guides and governs us by His own pure Truth. Our faith rests not on men, nor on any mortal creature, but the living God is the Author and *He will be the warrant of it.*"[12]

---

[1] *Comm. on* 1 *Pet.* 1 : 22; *Instit.* 3. 2. 6.

[2] *Instit.* 1. 11. 9. Rather must faith be "wholly fixed in the beholding of Christ", *Comm. on Acts* 20 : 21.

[3] *Instit.* 1. 11. 9; *Comm. on John* 8 : 12; 14 : 6; *on Luke* 10 : 22; *on Acts* 7 : 44; 20 : 21; 26 : 17 f.; *on* 1 *Cor.* 2 : 2; *on* 2 *Cor.* 4 : 6; *on* 1 *Pet.* 1 : 21.

[4] *Instit.* 3. 2. 1; *Comm. on John* 5 : 22; 6 : 27; *Serm. on* 1 *Tim.* 1 : 17-19; 6 : 15-16.

[5] *Comm. on John* 3 : 23.

[6] *Comm. on* 1 *Pet.* 1 : 21; cf. *Comm. on Micah* 4 : 1, 2: "The Truth of God is not speculative." See also *Serm. on* 1 *Tim.* 1 : 17-19.

[7] *Comm. on* 1 *Pet.* 1 : 21.

[8] *Ibid.* Cf. *Comm. on John* 11 : 41; and 14 : 1: "Faith will never reach heaven unless it submit to Christ, who appears to be a low and contemptible God, and it will never be firm if it does not seek a foundation in the weakness of Christ." It is to this *imago* that we must conform in our knowledge of God, if we would be restored to the *imago dei* (*Serm. on Deut.* 28 : 2 f.).

[9] *Comm. on* 2 *Pet.* 1 : 3. "Hence the effectual cause of faith is not the perspicacity of our mind but the calling of God."

[10] *Comm. on* 1 *Cor.* 4 : 3 f.; *Serm. on Luke* 2 : 9 f.; *Instit.* 3. 12. 2: "It is by God's judgment that the decision must be given."

[11] *Comm. on* 1 *Cor.* 2 : 15. [12] *Serm. on Deut.* 1 : 1 f. Cf. *Instit.* 1. 7. 4.

"God's Word is so authenticated that men must know it to be the Word of God, and submit themselves to it."[1] "We must go to the Word where the character of God drawn from His works is described accurately and to life; these works being estimated *not by our depraved judgment, but by the standard of eternal Truth.*"[2] In other words, when we try to know God, we must yield ourselves and our knowing to God, so that it is He who takes control, and our part is to respond to His initiative, and His movement, *correspondent to His Word*[3] which alone can serve as a thread to guide us through the inextricable labyrinth.[4] "The first step in true knowledge is taken when we reverently embrace the testimony which God has been pleased to give in the Word of Himself. For not only does faith, full and perfect faith, but *all correct knowledge of God, originate in obedience.*"[5] "Our minds should always be included within the bounds of the Word, and not wander from the true God, if we would desire to retain Him. We must continue within the limits of the Word, and not turn away on either one side or the other, since numberless fallacies of the devil will meet us immediately, unless the Word holds us in strict obedience."[6] "The obedience of faith is the commencement of right understanding, or rather because faith itself is truly the eye of the understanding. But immediately afterwards knowledge (*notitia*) is added, which distinguishes faith from erroneous and false opinions. Knowledge (*cognitio*) is connected with faith, because we are certain and fully convinced of the Truth of God, not in the same manner as human sciences are apprehended, but when the Spirit seals it in our hearts."[7] "Faith cannot flow from a merely experimental knowledge of events, but must draw its origin from the Word of God. . . . It acquiesces in the simple Word, and does not in the least depend on carnal sense or on human reason. Faith has its own sight but one which does not confine its view to the world and to earthly objects. For this reason faith is called a *demonstration of things invisible and not seen,* and Paul contrasts

---

[1] *Serm. on Deut.* 4 : 32 f. See *Comm. on 1 John* 2 : 27.
[2] *Instit.* 1. 6. 3: Cf. *Catechisme* (1537—C.R. 22. 35): "*Il fault doncq venir a la parolle ou Dieu nous est tres bien descript par ses oeuvres, pourtant que icelles œuvres y sont estimes non pas selon la perversite de nostre iugement mais par la reigle de leternelle verite.*"
[3] *Serm. on Deut.* 9 : 20.   [4] *Instit.* 1. 6. 3.
[5] *Instit.* 1. 6. 2.   [6] *Comm. on Dan.* 6 : 25 f.
[7] *Comm. on John* 6 : 69: *Rectæ intelligentiæ initium est fidei obedientia, imo fides ipsa vere mentis oculus est. Verum continuo post notitia subiicitur, quæ fidem ab erroneis falsisque opinionibus discernit. At fidei annexa est cognitio, quia nobis certo et indubie constat Dei veritas: non qualiter apprehenduntur humanæ scientiæ, sed dum eam cordibus nostris Spiritus obsignat.*

it with *sight*, meaning that it does not rest satisfied with looking at
the condition of present objects, and does not cast its eye in all
directions to those things which are visible in the world, but
depends on the mouth of God, and relying on His Word rises
above the whole world, so as to fix its anchor in heaven. It
amounts to this, that faith is not of a right kind, unless it be
founded on the Word of God alone, and rise to the invisible
kingdom of God, so as to go beyond all human apprehension."[1]
"Faith is a miracle of God whereby He makes Himself to be seen
by us, although He is hidden from us, and we can by no means
come nigh to Him."[2]

This means that the relation which obtains in faith between the
words or symbols which it uses and the reality which they are
intended to convey is not just a logical relation, but a profounder
relation of personal *intercourse* or *communication* or even *incorporation*
with Christ the Word.[3] Behind the *verbal analogical* relation there
is a sacramental relation *through the Spirit*, and these are inseparable
from one another. Faith is essentially grounded upon this double
relation,[4] in such a way that its *hypostasis* lies in the Word and
beyond the word, so that through faith "we transcend the reach
of the intellect and raise our eye above all worldly objects".[5]
Calvin admits that the *manner* of this is *hidden from us*[6]—it is the
secret operation of the Spirit, though we are given definite visible
signs, in the sacraments particularly, which become to faith the
visible pledges of the secret sealing of the Spirit, that is, the
transcendent *ratification* to faith, without which it would have
neither *notitia* nor *cognitio*.[7] It is because faith rests on this double
basis that the parabolic teaching of Christ could not be understood
on its purely parabolic or analogical level — that is as *simple
knowledge*.[8] On that level it actually hardened and blinded men, at
least those who refused to commit themselves to Christ in faith,
but to those who did believe there was given a new understanding

[1] *Comm. on John* 20 : 29. Cf. on *Rom.* 4 : 18: "Surely there is no greater enemy of
faith than to tie our minds to our eyes."
[2] *Serm. on* 1 *Tim.* 1 : 17-19.
[3] See *Comm. on Luke* 11 : 27; on *John* 6 : 35, etc.; also *Instit.* 3. 2. 1-43, especially 24 ff.
[4] *Comm. on John* 15 : 27; 16 : 25.   [5] *Instit.* 1. 2. 41.
[6] *Comm. on John* 3 : 7, 8; *Instit.* 4. 17. 31, where Calvin speaks of *arcana operatio*,
arcana vis, incomprehensibilis virtus, etc. Cf. on *John* 14 : 20: "We *cannot by indolent
speculation know* what is the sacred and mystical union between us and Him, and
between Him and the Father; but the only way of knowing it is, when He diffuses
life in us by the secret efficacy of the Spirit, and this is the *experimentum fidei*." See
also *Instit.* 4. 17. 1, 7.
[7] This is the burden of Calvin's *Commentary on John*.
[8] See especially *Comm. on Matt.* 13 : 11 ff.; *Instit.* 4. 17. 5.

which transcended the analogical level and penetrated the mysteries of the Kingdom.[1] That is the level of *real* (true and substantial) *communication*.[2]

It is not difficult to understand why Calvin expresses dubiety about employing analogies from the world in our knowledge of God, for it is only as these analogies are under the control of the Word, and are used by the Spirit as vehicles of a Truth that is essentially self-authenticating, that they have their value in our knowledge. We must guard against going "a step beyond the confines of God's Word".[3] "He Himself alone, with legitimate authority, testifies of Himself to us by the Word."[4] "He alone is a fit witness to Himself who is known only by Himself."[5] "He alone can give the sign, and bear witness to Himself."[6] The signs which God gives us are essentially sacramental, but that does not mean that anything which we imagine to be appropriate can be turned into a sign, a real vehicle of knowledge. And so, when speaking of Christ and the distinctions of the Trinity, Calvin says: "I am not sure whether it is expedient to borrow analogies from human affairs to express the nature of this distinction. The ancient Fathers sometimes do so, but they at the same time admit that what they bring forward as analogous is very widely different."[7] In his *Commentary on the Epistle to the Hebrews*, Calvin adds: "We must allow that there is a degree of impropriety in the language when what is borrowed from created things is transferred to the hidden majesty of God. But still the things which are evident to our senses are fitly applied to God, and for this end that we may know what is to be found in Christ and what benefits He brings us."[8] That is always the thought involved in any use of *analogy* or *comparison* in the mind of Calvin. It is the Word of God supervening upon wordly *analogies* or *comparisons* which accommodates itself to our minds in the act of revelation,[9]

[1] Cf. *Comm. on John* 6 : 63: *Fateor quidem in cælestibus mysteriis totam humani ingenii vim evanescere ac deficere.* And *Instit.* 4. 17. 15: "In the mysteries of faith we do not consult common apprehension."
[2] *Instit.* 4. 17. 5-12, 19.
[3] *Instit.* 1. 13. 21; 3. 21. 2. Cf. 2. 12. 5; *Comm. on Isa.* 8 : 20; 29 : 16; 40 : 18.
[4] *Instit.* 4. 19. 2: *Solus ergo ipse est qui de se nobis per verbum suum testificatur legitima autoritate.* See *Comm. on* 1 *John* 2 : 27.
[5] *Instit.* 1. 13. 21. This is a citation from Hilary.   [7] *Instit.* 1. 13. 18.
[6] *Instit.* 4. 18. 19.
[8] *Comm. on Heb.* 1 : 3. Cf. also *Comm. on Micah* 5 : 7, 8; *on Amos* 3 : 3-8.
[9] Cf. *Comm. on Dan.* 7 : 27, where Calvin thinks of the Word accommodating itself to the *dullness* of men to enable them to perceive the analogy between things earthly and visible and the *spiritual blessedness* which our minds *cannot naturally comprehend.* See also *on John* 6 : 35.

though in the actual analogy the thing brought into comparison with God is *nothing*.[1] And unless it is recognized as nothing, we cannot apprehend the truth. We must always understand this therefore as an act by which "the Holy Spirit would rather speak childishly than unintelligibly to the humble and unlearned".[2] "For thus the Lord often prattles with us and borrows comparisons from matters that are familiar to us, when He speaks of His majesty, that our ignorant and limited minds may better understand His greatness and excellence. Away then with all gross conceptions of God, for His greatness far exceeds all creatures, so that heaven and earth and sea and all that they contain, however vast may be their extent, *yet in comparison with Him are nothing.*"[3] That applies also to the very highest endowments of man, such as his spirit. And so in a neighbouring passage Calvin writes: "*Spirit* here denotes reason, judgment, or understanding; for He borrows a comparison from the nature of men that He may more fully accommodate Himself to them. And I do not think that this ought to be understood as denoting the essential Spirit of God."[4] Calvin makes it quite clear therefore that the only knowledge of God possible is analogical knowledge. "For God cannot reveal Himself to us in any other way than by a comparison with things which we know."[5] But He is equally emphatic upon this: that we have no right to engage in these comparisons ourselves, or frame any image of Him according to our own choosing or by our naked imagination.[6] "In order, therefore, to know God we must not frame a likeness of Him according to our own fancy, but we must betake ourselves to the Word in which His lively image is exhibited to us. Satisfied with that communication, let us not attempt anything else of our own."[7] "The highest injury is done to God not only by comparing His majesty with things of no value, but even by not placing Him far above all the angels and everything else that is reckoned divine."[8] "On this account the

[1] See *Instit.* 4. 14. 12.

[2] *Comm. on Ps.* 136 : 7. The reference in this instance is to astronomy. Here Calvin thinks of God's Word as using ordinary language in order to convey the truth, even though in itself it may be analogically and scientifically wrong. "The Holy Spirit had no intention to teach astronomy", adds Calvin.

[3] *Comm. on Isa.* 40 : 12; cf. *on John* 3 : 12: "God prattles to us in Scripture in a rough and ready style."

[4] *Comm. on Isa.* 40 : 13.   [5] *Comm. on Isa.* 40 : 18.

[6] By naked imagination Calvin refers to the fancy of the mind that is not bound to the Word and the Spirit. "God is not known by a naked imagination, since He reveals Himself to us by His Spirit." *Comm. on* 1 *John* 2 : 4.

[7] *Comm. on Isa.* 40 : 18; see also *on Acts* 7 : 44; *Instit.* 4. 17. 21.

[8] *Comm. on Isa.* 40 : 18.

Lord repeats, as it were in indignation, 'To whom will ye liken Me?'; as if He had said, 'Will ye rob Me of My Majesty by your comparisons?' For although men have various thoughts of God, and transform Him according to their fancy, yet He continues to be like Himself, for He does not change His nature on account of the inventions of men."[1]

Calvin's thought may be clearly and truly expressed by saying that while knowledge of God must be analogical, entailing comparisons from things which we know, yet the relation between God and that to which He is brought into comparison is *not ontological* but *sacramental:* that is to say, it is a relation which has its validity through the Word and the Spirit, which use the visible or the analogical elements in order to convey the Truth,[2] but in such a way as to make it clear that these are symbols which are made to point beyond themselves and that in themselves they are seen to be *nothing in comparison with God.*[3] They are purely accommodations of the Word and by the Word in order "to raise up our thoughts by degrees" to that which "cannot be comprehended by human minds" except in this way.[4] Their sole efficacy, therefore, and all their true substance are lodged in the Word.[5] At the same time, Calvin insists that the signs used must be analogical, that is, they must have some *aptitude* or *affinity* or *appropriate representation* or *similarity,* though in themselves apart from the Word and the Spirit, all this analogical character is nothing at all.[6] Nevertheless "the meaning would have no congruity unless the truth which is there figured had a living image in the external sign".[7] Otherwise "where is the analogy or similitude to conduct us from the visible to the invisible?"[8] On the other hand, Calvin is equally emphatic upon the point that signs and images of this sort bear *no likeness to*

---

[1] *Comm. on Isa.* 40 : 25.

[2] *Instit.* 4. 14. 5: *Siquidem vir fidelis, dum oculis sacramenta obversantur, non in illo carnali spectaculo hæret; sed illis quos indicavi analogiæ gradibus ad sublimia mysteria quæ in sacramentis latent pia consideratione assurgit.* Also *Instit.* 4. 17. 3.

[3] *Comm. on Isa.* 40 : 17; *Instit.* 4. 14. 12; 4. 19. 7.

[4] *Comm. on Jer.* 31 : 12. Cf. *on John* 4 : 24: *Porro quia ad eius altitudinem conscendere non licet, meminerimus petendam esse ex eius verbo regulam, qua dirigamur.*

[5] Cf. *Instit.* 4. 19. 7: *In sacramentis divinitus traditis duo spectanda esse: substantiam rei corporeæ quæ nobis proponitur, et formam quæ illi a verbo Dei impressa est, in qua tota vis iacet.*

[6] *Instit.* 4. 17. 3, 10, 21, etc. Other expressions Calvin uses are *resemblance, conformity, appropriate figure,* etc.

[7] *Instit.* 4. 17. 14. Calvin insists that the doctrine of transubstantiation is a denial of analogy, and makes an absurdity of any real knowledge in the sacrament. It is a form of the docetic heresy. The same criticism applies to Calvin's form of the doctrine of predestination.

[8] *Ibid.*

the being of God, and for that very reason they may lead us upward instead of dragging God downward. "There is no proportion nor likeness between God and His creatures. Therefore we must seek God in such wise as He has vouchsafed to utter Himself to us",[1] for "there is a likeness and conformity between God and His Word".[2] It is this likeness and conformity which really gives substance to the appropriate symbols and makes them into real analogies: that is, through the Word and the Spirit alone. "The true way to seek God in the manner in which He has revealed Himself is that *after we once know Him,* we do also consider that He stoops to our rudeness, and yet cease not to seek Him by moving up higher, and by conceiving the things spiritually which the sacraments show us. It is true that by them God comes down to us, but that is not to hold us still down below, but to make us fly up to Him. It is quite as if He should reach down His hand to us and say, come to Me, and worship Me spiritually. Wherefore let us learn to seek God above us and not to tie Him to our carnal and mundane understanding."[3]

The main emphasis is always laid by Calvin on the *Word of God,* whether in the sacraments themselves or in those other signs and analogies which are used in our knowledge of God. "Words are nothing else than signs",[4] so that this sacramental relation is as much the concern of all the words we use in relation to God as it is with the specially appointed symbols of the sacraments. Unless God's Word, made efficacious through the Spirit, is dominant, all human symbols are nothing but dumb idols. There is nothing more perverse in our knowledge of God or in worship than a dumb sacrament or an idol. "God is not present with us by an idol but by His Word and by the power of the Spirit; and although He holds out to us in the sacraments an image both of His grace and of spiritual blessings, yet this is done by no other intention than to lead us upward to Himself."[5] And speaking again of such sensible symbols Calvin says: "Unless doctrine *precede* them to be a connecting link between God and man, they will be empty and elusive signs, however honourable may be the encomiums

---

[1] *Serm. on Deut.* 4 : 15 .
[2] *Serm. on Deut.* 30 : 15 f. This is because "He alone can give the sign and bear witness to Himself" (*Instit.* 4. 18. 19).
[3] *Serm. on Deut.* 4 : 15.
[4] *Instit.* 4. 14. 26: *Nihil aliud sunt verba quam signa.* This is really Augustinian.
[5] *Comm. on Isa.* 40 : 20. *Instit.* 4. 15. 14: "Nor does He feed our eyes with bare show; He leads to the actual object, and effectually performs what He figures." See especially *Instit.* 4. 14. 4 ff.

passed upon them. But inasmuch as mutual consent is required in all compacts, so when God invites His people to receive grace, He stipulates that they should give Him the obedience of faith, so as to answer *Amen*. Thus nothing can be more preposterous than the invention of dumb sacraments."[1]

In every true comparison, the Word must be pre-eminent, but in every true comparison in which the Word is pre-eminent, there is necessarily entailed an *inverse comparison* in which man and the world are made as nothing, in order that God may be all in all.[2] Unless there is this inverse comparison, the analogies or signs only succeed in dragging God downward without lifting us upward. Therefore we must so use them that we transcend them, that we mount up by seeing that in themselves they are nothing. This is the constant emphasis of Calvin, and in fact he will allow no comparison nor analogy where this does not hold: we know God only *in the inverse proportion of our poverty to His grace and glory*.[3] This method of knowing God is all the more necessary because of the self-assertion of sin in the mind. "The depravity of the human mind is such that it obscures the divine Majesty, and places above it those things which ought to have been subject to God. And therefore when we come to that contest we may boldly declare that everything that is compared with God is worthless."[4] "It is a very hard thing to forsake our own reason, so as not to be wise in our own conceits or to behave ourselves after our own liking, but to admit that there is nothing but vanity and untruth in us, and to learn to humble ourselves. That is contrary to our nature, for we have a fond belief that we are wise of ourselves. God, on the contrary, will have us bereft of in-turned understanding and self-grounded reason, and to give ourselves over to be

[1] *Comm. on Exod.* 24 : 5. "It must be added that the Word which gives life to the sacraments is not an obscure whisper . . . but it is a clear and distinct voice which is addressed to men and avails to beget faith in them." Cf. *on Exod.* 33 : 19: "Let it be observed that although a vision was exhibited to his eyes, the main point was in the voice, because true acquaintance with God is more by the ears than by the eyes." See *Instit.* 4. 14. 39.

[2] Cf. *Serm. on Eph.* 2 : 8-10 : "When we receive by faith the grace that is offered in the Gospel, we thereby confess that we have need of Christ, because there is nothing but perdition in ourselves. And when Paul says *by faith* he shews that if comparison is made between God and man, we must come as it were stark naked, and there must be nothing in us but shame and abasement, until God has received us with mercy. . . . God is not glorified as He ought to be, nor is it possible for us to glory in Him, till all that we ever think we have of our own nature is cast down and done away."

[3] *Instit.* 2. 2. 10 f.; 3. 12. 6-8; 1. 1. 1: *Ex nostra tenuitate melius apparet illa, quæ in Deo residet bonorum infinitas.* See also *Comm. on* 1 *Cor.* 3 : 20; 2 *Cor.* 1 : 9; *Instit.* 2. 2. 1.

[4] *Comm. on Isa.* 40 : 17.

governed by His Spirit."[1] The only way in which we can rise to God is to be "reduced to nothing"[2] in ourselves, and be "brought to nothing in our own estimation".[3] To try to rise by ourselves and from ourselves would be as ridiculous as to elevate ourselves by leaping, for we must immediately fall back upon the earth.[4] True elevation takes place when a "man sees nothing in himself which can raise his spirits so that he possesses nothing on which he can proudly plume himself".[5] This does not mean that man is nothing absolutely,[6] for, as we have already seen, he insists that God has made man to be something, but is an assertion that must be made in comparison with God, though only in such a comparison.[7] "It ought to be observed that this is spoken *comparatively*, in order to inform us that if there be in us anything excellent, it is not our own, but is held by us at the will of another. We know that God has adorned the human race with gifts that ought not to be despised. We know also that some excel others; but as the greater part of men neglect God, and flatter themselves beyond measure; and, as irreligious men go so far as to think that they are more than gods, Isaiah wisely separates men from God, which the Holy Spirit also does in many parts of Scripture: for, when we look at them in themselves, we perceive more fully the frail, fading, and transitory nature of our condition. Accordingly as soon as men make the smallest claim for themselves, they ought to have an opportunity of perceiving their vanity, that they may acknowledge themselves to be nothing. . . . Lastly we are brought back to God, the Author of every blessing, that we may not suppose that anything excellent is to be found but in Him, for He has not received what is due to Him, until the world has been stripped of all wisdom and strength and righteousness, and, in a word, of all praise."[8] By this comparative abasement man is actually elevated to the mercy and glory of God.[9] If he has been reduced to nothing, is nothing, then let us

---

Serm. on Deut. 4 : 19 f.

[2] *Instit.* 3. 2. 25; 2. 1. 3; *Comm. on* 1 *Cor.* 1 : 31; *on Dan.* 4 : 34, 35.

[3] *Comm. on* 1 *Cor.* 1 : 31. [4] *Comm. on Isa.* 40 : 22. [5] *Instit.* 2. 1. 3.

[6] *Instit.* 2. 2. 1: "Man is not to be denied anything that is truly his own, but he is deprived of everything like false boasting. If man had no title to glory in himself when by the kindness of his Maker he was distinguished by the noblest ornaments, how much ought he to be humbled now, when his ingratitude has thrust him down from the highest glory to extreme ignominy?"

[7] *Comm. on Isa.* 40 : 17; 31 : 3. [8] *Comm. on Isa.* 2 : 22; *Instit.* 3. 18. 3.

[9] *Instit.* 3. 18. 5: "Scripture humbles us more, and at the same time elevates us." Cf. *Comm. on Ezek.* 2 : 2: "God never prostrates His people so as to leave them lying upon the earth, but continually raises them up afterwards."

remember that "something of him still lurks in the heart of God".·
"For we are nothing but in God, and in order that we may begin
to be something in Him, we must first be convinced, and made
thoroughly to know, that we are vanity. Therefore does the Lord
breathe upon us that we may know that of ourselves we are
nothing."[2]

This elevation by abasement, or inverse comparison, is only
possible because it is grounded upon the action of God's mercy in
the death of Christ. That is to say, behind the motion of "faith,
which places all things in Christ, and nothing in ourselves",
there is a soteriological motion.[3] "This is *the wondrous exchange*
made by His boundless goodness. Having become with us the
Son of Man, He has made us with Himself sons of God. By His
own descent to the earth He has prepared our ascent to heaven.
Having received our mortality, He has bestowed on us His
immortality. Having undertaken our weakness, He has made us
strong in His strength. Having submitted to our poverty, He has
transferred to us His riches. Having taken upon Himself the
burden of unrighteousness with which we were oppressed, He
has clothed us with righteousness."[4] "*Wherefore*, the best and
only worthiness which we can bring to God, is to offer Him our
vileness, and, if I may so speak, unworthiness, that His mercy
may make us worthy; to despond in ourselves, that we may be
consoled in Him; to humble ourselves, that we may be elevated
by Him; to accuse ourselves, that we may be justified by Him."[5]

The soteriological inversion wrought out on the Cross must
take place in the minds of men, and, as it were, be reduplicated
there so that they become conformable to Christ, if they would
know God.[6] It is only by this *mortification* that we are renewed *in
the image of Christ* and the life of the Spirit, and by partaking in
this analogy, that we can rise to the knowledge of God.[7] We
must come to the point, which we can reach only at the Cross,
where "God bestows His grace upon us that we may know that
we are nothing, that we stand only in the mercy of God".[8]
When we have reached that point, we have risen indeed, but it is
only by "placing nothing in ourselves". "Since the Lord in
bringing assistance supplies us with what is lacking, the nature of

---

[1] *Instit.* 3. 2. 25.   [2] *Comm. on Isa.* 40 : 7.   [3] *Instit.* 4. 17. 42.
[4] *Instit.* 4. 17. 2.   [5] *Instit.* 4. 17. 42.
[6] *Serm. on Deut.* 28 : 2 f.; *Comm. on* 1 *Pet.* 4 : 1.
[7] *Comm. on Rom.* 6 : 7 f.; 6 : 11; 8 : 30.   [8] *Instit.* 2. 2. 11.

that assistance will immediately make manifest its converse, viz., our penury."[1] That is what Calvin sometimes calls an *argument from contraries*.[2] "What remains therefore now that man is stripped of all his glory, than to acknowledge the God for whose kindness he failed to be grateful, when he was loaded with the riches of His grace? Not having glorified Him by the acknowledgment of His blessings, now at least he ought to glorify Him by the confession of his poverty. In truth it is no less useful for us to renounce all the praise of wisdom and virtue than to aim at the glory of God. Those who invest us with more than we possess only add sacrilege to our ruin."[3] In such a comparison man does not make the motion of self-will, but of humility and obedience which is the motion corresponding to the essential motion of grace which is from God to man, an irreversible movement. Calvin is constantly quoting in this connection: "God resists the proud but gives grace to the humble."[4] "I call it not humility so long as we think there is anything residing in us."[5] Thus the knowledge of ourselves under the knowledge of God "principally consists in renouncing all ideas of our own strength, and divesting ourselves of all confidence in our righteousness, while on the other hand under a full consciousness of our wants, we learn true humility and self-abasement".[6] "This command to submit is very repugnant to the perversity of the human mind."[7] Therefore in order to know God the human reason must be "subdued to the obedience of faith".[8] Once however the reason attains its new orientation within faith and has the eyes of its understanding enlightened, it knows that the knowledge of God exceeds the natural capacity of man, and its glory transcends all his conceptions of it. "We never form adequate conceptions of the treasure revealed to us in the Gospel; or, if we do, we cannot persuade ourselves that it is

---

[1] *Instit.* 2. 3. 6.

[2] *Instit.* 3. 11. 13: *argumentum a contrariis* or *contrariorum comparatio.* This is really a form of the doctrine of justification by faith alone: "If we destroy the righteousness of God by establishing our own righteousness, then in order to obtain His righteousness, our own must be entirely abandoned." *Ibid.* Cf. also 3. 12. 2.

[3] *Instit.* 2. 2. 1.

[4] *Comm. on* 1 Pet. 5 : 5; *on* Jas. 4 : 6; *on* Ps. 138 : 6; *Instit.* 2. 2. 10; 3. 12. 5, etc.

[5] *Instit.* 3. 12. 6: *Non enim humilitatem voco, si quid nobis residuum esse putamus.* Cf. 3. 12. 5: *Fallitur enim, qui putat se huius fruenda esse capacem, nisi omnem prius animi altitudinem deiecerit.*

[6] *Instit.* 2. 8. 1: cf. *Comm. on* 1 Cor. 10 : 12 f.: "If there is a single drop of presumption in us we do despite to God's grace."

[7] *Instit.* 2. 8. 35. Cf. *Comm. on* Rom. 3 : 26: *Nihil homini difficilius, quam ut sibi omnia derogans, accepta Deo referat.*

[8] *Instit.* 1. 14. 2. Cf. *Comm. on* Rom. 11 : 19: "This answers to the nature of faith and is proper to it that it should beget in us a humbling of ourselves."

possible for us to do so, because *we perceive nothing in us that corresponds to it, but everything the reverse.*"[1] In other words, faith knows that *whatever small remnant of light was formerly possessed,*[2] it cannot in any way serve as a *predisposition*[3] for faith or as an analogical point of contact for the true knowledge of God. Far from there being anything in man to correspond to the Gospel there is only a *contrary law* which is antagonistic to it,[4] so that the only preparation a man can make is to deny himself and empty himself.[5]

This inverse comparison as the motion of the mind corresponding to the action of God's grace may be illustrated from Calvin's conception of human fatherhood. Man was made to be, in a sense, the *paterfamilias in mundo*, which is another way of expressing his dominion over the earth.[6] But all fatherhood on earth is designed by God to teach us "reverence, obedience, and gratitude", so that by learning reverent and thankful submission here, although it is repugnant to the perversity of the human mind, we might be led to our true subjection to God from whom all authority proceeds. Thus "the titles of Father, God, and Lord all meet in Him alone, and hence, whenever any one of them is mentioned, our mind should be impressed with the same feeling of reverence. Those, therefore, to whom He imparts such titles, He distinguishes by some small part of His refulgence, so as to entitle them to honour, each in his own place. In this way, we must consider that our earthly father possesses something of a divine nature, because there is some reason for his bearing a divine title, and that he who is our prince and ruler is admitted to some communion of honour with God."[7] Here the whole purport of Calvin's teaching is not that we should use human fatherhood in order to raise up our minds to apprehend God, but that we do

---

[1] *Comm. on Eph.* 1 : 19: *Nam aut nunquam satis digne reputamus, quantus sit thesaurus qui nobis proponitur in Evangelio: aut si id vere sentiamus, non possumus nobis persuadere, eius nos esse capaces: quia nihil in nobis cernimus quod respondeat, quin potius adversa omnia.* See also *on Ps.* 139 : 6.

[2] *Comm. on John* 9 : 39: *Exiguum illud nescio quid lucis quod illis erat residuum, which however is destroyed by the clear revelation of Christ.* See below.

[3] *Comm. on Acts* 14 : 16: see also 16 : 14. *Praeiudicium* is the word Calvin uses here. Preparation is only a hindrance (*Comm. on Ps.* 147 : 10): "Let man come in the preparation of his own strength, and with all the assistances that seem to him most prevalent, this will only issue in smoke and vanity; nay, in arrogating the very least to himself, this will only be a hindrance in the way of the mercy of God, by which alone we stand." Cf. 119 : 10; *on John* 11 : 25; *Serm. on Deut.* 10 : 1 f.; *Comm. on Gal.* 1 : 8-9; *on Eph.* 4 : 17-19.

[4] *Comm. on Heb.* 8 : 10: *contraria lex* which causes a *furiosus impetus ad repugnandum Deo.* Cf. *Serm. on Deut.* 4 : 10 f.; *Comm. on Rom.* 7 : 15, 21; 8 : 6 f.

[5] *See Instit.* 3. 7. 1 ff.; and 3. 8. 1 ff.

[6] *Comm. on Gen.* 1 : 28.   [7] *Instit.* 2. 8. 35.

God reverence only as we learn reverence, obedience, and gratitude through human fatherhood. That is to say, the analogy of
human fatherhood is used not to climb from man to God, but to
help us before God to bow in humble and obedient acknowledgment of His grace.

The same procedure may be illustrated from a passage where
Calvin discusses the divine providence in relation to predestination. "If there had been no predestination on God's part, there
had been no Deity, since He would have been forced into order
as if He were one of us: nay, *men are to a certain extent provident, as
often as God wills some sparks of His image to shine forth in them.* If,
therefore, the very smallest drop of foresight in men is laid hold
of, *what will it be in the fountain itself?*"[1] There is no doubt that
Calvin makes the analogical step here from human foresight to
the divine foresight in order to strengthen his argument, but at
the same time it is equally clear that this is possible only because
human foresight is essentially reflexive of the divine foresight,
and depends on the divine will from moment to moment. In
other words, an analogical argument is possible only within the
situation of faith created by the descent of God, or the accommodation of His Word to our ignorance. By ourselves and from
ourselves we are unable to make the step.[2] Therefore Calvin
adds to the above passage the words: "Because we cannot ascend
to that height, it is needful for God to conform Himself to our
ignorance, and to descend in some way to us since we cannot
ascend to Him."

This is the basic fact about all true knowledge of God: it is
essentially an acknowledgment, not an excogitation. It is the sin
of men that they will try to ground their knowledge of God upon
the exercise of their own imagination, upon analogies which the
human mind itself can manipulate, and so measure God by its
own capacity, but all this, says Calvin, only leads to a *feigned and
new God.*[3] Acknowledgment, on the other hand, is the act of
knowing in which men yield their minds to the imprint of the
divine Truth, and submit themselves to the accommodating

[1] *Comm. on Ezek.* 18 : 32: *Denique si nulla esset praedestinatio apud Deum, nulla esset
eius deitas, qua cogeretur in ordinem, ac si esset unusquispiam ex nobis: imo homines ali-
quatenus sunt providi, quoties scilicet vult Deus scintillas suae imaginis in illis micare. Si
ergo vel minima gutta providentia in hominibus deprehenditur, quid erit in ipso fonte?*
[2] Cf. *Comm. on Jas.* 1 : 16: "*We may not measure* the brightness of God by the
irradiation of the sun which appears to us."
[3] Cf. *Comm. on Rom.* 1 : 18 f.

activity of the Word. Instead of bringing God within the measure of their own minds, they admit that "there is a certain measure within which men ought to keep themselves, since *it is God who applies to our capacity whatever He testifies of Himself*".[1] "Therefore it is not for us to attribute anything to God, but it belongs to Him to utter Himself, and we must only receive what He reveals to us, and hold ourselves to it."[2]

We come back here to Calvin's teaching about the *imago dei*, that it is possessed only in thankful acknowledgment of the grace of the heavenly Father. The *imago dei* may be used analogically as the answer of man to the way in which God wills to reveal Himself,[3] in direct antithesis to the way of the flesh which "is always restless until it has obtained some figment like itself, with which it may vainly solace itself as a representation of God".[4] In other words, Calvin uses analogy not in the form of *analogia entis*,[5] but in the form of *analogia fidei*, that is in the form of an analogy which is subject to the Word of God.[6] It is always an accommodation on the part of the Word *to the grossness of our capacities*. "God is always like Himself, but with regard to the teaching of His Word, it is accommodated to our capacities."[7] It is impossible therefore to pass from the bare analogy itself to God, but *after we once know Him*,[8] and realize that the analogy is there because *God has stooped to our rudeness*,[9] then we may seek Him by passing beyond it. And that is possible only if these analogies are inscribed with the

[1] *Comm. on Rom.* 1 : 19; cf. 12 : 3: *Summa est, hanc rationalis nostri sacrificii partem esse, ubi se quisque mansueto ac docili spiritu regendum ac flectendum Deo præbet. Porro quum fidem humano iudicio opponens nos a placitis nostris cohibeat, mensuram simul consulto adiungit, ut se humiliter contineant fideles in suo quoque defectu.*
[2] *Serm. on Deut.* 4 : 15 f. Cf. *Comm. on Rom.* 10 : 14: *Neque enim est nostrum, qualem libuerit Deum fingere. Legitima ergo eius cognitio habenda est, qualis in eius verbo proponitur. Si quis vero Deum ex proprio sensu bonum concipiat, non erit certa nec solida fides, sed instabilis et fluxa imaginatio: proinde ad rectam Dei cognitionem verbum requiritur.* 10 : 17: *Quare facessant oportet omnia hominum commenta, ubi de fidei certitudine agitur.*
[3] *Instit.* 1. 4. 1.   [4] *Instit.* 1. 11. 8.
[5] Calvin would have condemned knowledge by *analogia entis* as "ambitious and perverse appetite for illicit knowledge"—*Comm. on Gen.* 3 : 22. It would be against the glory of God, cf. *Instit.* 3. 13. 1 f.; *Serm. on Job* 5 : 20 f.; 9 : 29 f.; 28 : 10 f.
[6] Of the *analogia fidei* in *Rom.* 12 : 3, 6, Calvin says that he prefers to think of it as "a peculiar gift of revelation that a man may rightly and learnedly play the part of an interpreter in opening the will of God"—see *Comm. ad loc.* According to this the sign must be subservient to the *Word; Instit.* 4. 16. 4, 5; 4. 17. 32.
[7] *Comm. on Jonah* 3 : 10.   [8] *Serm. on Deut.* 4 : 15 f.
[9] *Ibid.* Cf. *Comm. on* 1 *John* 3 : 2: *Deus nunc se nobis conspiciendum offert, non qualis est sed qualem modulus noster eum capit. . . . Quatenus autem renovatur in nobis Dei imago, oculos habemus ad Dei aspectum comparatos. Et nunc quidem Deus imaginem suam instaurare in nobis incipit: sed quantula ex parte? . . . Nec tamen tanta gloriæ erit perfectio in nobis, ut totum Deum aspectus noster comprehendat. Longa enim tunc quoque erit inter nos et ipsum proportionis distantia.*

Word of God and joined to the Spirit. There is no reasoning based *in the being of man* which can lead him to God. "The reason and wisdom which the first man had *were not in himself, but rather in that he was fashioned after the image of God* (i.e., were possessed reflexively), and therefore as soon as he was separated from his Creator, who is the fountain of all good, he could not but be deprived of all the graces which God had bestowed on him. . . . Therefore the natural man is not able to understand the things which belong to the Spirit; they cannot understand at all: the power or ability is not in us . . . so that God must enlighten us by a special grace or else we shall never judge of His Word or Works as becomes us."[1] However, because of *the inefficacy of His image* God has given us the assistance of *His Word* so that His Works "may be estimated not by our depraved judgment but by the standard of the eternal Truth. If we turn aside from it, however great the speed with which we move, we shall never reach the goal, because we are off the course."[2] Because man has been alienated from God in the whole of his mental system, because his being and mind have been perverted, every attempt to reach the truth is essentially a perverted attempt, and only alienates him all the more from God the Father.[3] On the one hand, Calvin says "that men are the generation of God, because by the excellency of nature they resemble some divine thing. This is what the Scripture teacheth, that we are created after the image and similitude of God."[4] But, on the other hand, Calvin says, "seeing that God far surpasses the capacity of our mind, whosoever attempts with his mind to comprehend Him, deforms and transfigures His glory with a wicked and false imagination".[5] Far from achieving what he wants in this way, man employs the seed of divinity deposited in human nature to suppress the name of God and put out the light intended to exhibit God clearly to

---

[1] *Serm. on Deut.* 29 : 1.

[2] *Instit.* 1. 6. 3. Cf. *Comm. on Ps.* 119 : 147: "It is only by having the Word of God continually before our eyes that we can bridle the wanton impetuosity of our corrupt nature."

[3] *Comm. on John* 16 : 9: "Men have nothing in them but what leads to sin."

[4] This does not mean, for Calvin, a similitude of *being*. It is only "by the *light* of reason, in righteousness and holiness, that men resemble their heavenly Father", *Comm. on Acts* 17 : 28. "All mortal men are called sons in general, because they draw near to God in mind and understanding; but because the image of God is almost blotted out in them so that there appear scarce any slender lines this name is by good right reserved for the faithful who have the Spirit of adoption given to them." Cf. *Instit.* 3. 18. 1.

[5] *Comm. on Acts* 17 : 29; on *Rom.* 1 : 21 f.

his mind.[1] "This is the first entrance into the true knowledge of God *if we go without ourselves, and do not measure Him by the capacity of our mind;* yea, if we imagine nothing of Him according to the understanding of our flesh, but place Him above the world and distinguish Him from creatures. From which sobriety the whole world was always far; because this wickedness is in men naturally to deform God's glory with their inventions. For, as they are carnal and earthly, they will have but one that shall be answerable to their nature. Secondly, after their boldness they fashion Him so that they may comprehend Him. By such inventions is the sincere and plain knowledge of God corrupt; yea, His Truth, as saith Paul, is turned into a lie. For whosoever does not ascend high above the world, he apprehends vain shadows and ghosts instead of God. Again, unless we are carried up into heaven with the wings of faith, we must vanish away in our own cogitations. . . . Men do always incline downwards, that they may apprehend God after a carnal manner; but God by the leading of His Word lifts them upward."[2] "If true religion is to beam upon us, our principle must be that *it is necessary to begin with heavenly teaching,* and that it is impossible for any man to attain even the minutest portion of right and sound doctrine without being a disciple of Scripture. Hence the first step in true knowledge is taken when we reverently embrace the testimony which God has been pleased to give of Himself therein. For not only does faith, full and perfect faith, but all correct knowledge of God, originate in obedience."[3]

At this point we must recall Calvin's conception of the *imago dei* discussed earlier. Properly speaking, that image can be seen only in Christ. He is the *imago dei* in *essence*,[4] but we who believe may have it by *communication* or by *imputation* or by *spiritual generation*.[5] In some sense there remain traces in fallen man, but the image is really invisible in him, and only begins to shine forth in the Christian.[6] But wherever the *imago dei* is to be found it is the *reflex of God's glory* through response to His grace. That is the way in which it was designed to shine forth in man. Strictly speaking, therefore, the *imago dei* exists only in faith and

[1] *Instit.* 1. 5. 4.   [2] *Comm. on Acts* 17 : 24.   [3] *Instit.* 1. 6. 2.
[4] Christ is the *imago dei* as *the essential Word of God*; we are in the image of God by *knowledge* of this Word. *Comm. on Col.* 3 : 10. Cf. *Instit.* 3. 2. 21.
[5] *Comm. on Gen.* 1 : 25; 6 : 3; *Instit.* 2. 2. 1, 20; 3. 6. 1; *Comm. on John* 17 : 3; on 2 *Cor.* 3 : 18; 5 : 3; on *Eph.* 4 : 24.
[6] *Instit.* 1. 15. 4; *Comm. on 2 Cor.* 3 : 18; on 1 *Cor.* 15 : 20. Cf. on *Eph.* 3 : 10. "Let us rest assured that the knowledge, whatever it may be, which we have acquired, is after all but a slender proportion." Cf. also on 1 *Cor.* 13 : 9-12.

will be revealed at the advent of Christ when He comes in His full glory.[1] If this is the case, how can we use the *imago dei* apart from faith to raise us up to a knowledge of God? And how can we use it independently of God's grace and revelation in order to prepare us for that revelation, if it is only a reflex of God's glorious grace? The very way to put out the light of God intended to exhibit God clearly to our minds is to appropriate as our own in this way what has been given to us from heaven.[2] Therefore, on Calvin's view, any attempt to build up a knowledge of God upon the examination of the *imago dei in man himself* would simply be a huge *petitio principii*. *Within faith* we know "that whatever God bestows upon us by Him belongs of right to Him in the highest degree; yea, He Himself is the living image of God, according to which we must be renewed, upon which depends our participation in the invaluable blessings here spoken of".[3] This means that we may use the *imago dei* as an analogy within faith, but *only within faith*, for "faith imports a knowledge of the Truth which excludes and shuts out whatever comes from men[4]." "*The ground of our faith consists in the acknowledgment and confession that God is not like men.*"[5] "There is no other way in which God is known but in the face of Jesus Christ, who is the bright and lively image of Him. . . . It is not every kind of knowledge which is described here, but *that knowledge which forms us anew into the image of God from faith to faith.*"[6] Moreover, Calvin says, whatever may be left of the image of God in the natural man is destroyed by the restoration of the image of God in us when we believe in Christ.[7] That means that the image of God which has been inverted by sin must be re-inverted. Because it is grace which strips a man of his perverted Adamic image, it is only stripped in the moment of the restoration of the true image in Christ.[8] In other words, we are restored to the true image of God only through conformity to the death and resurrection of Christ.[9] "Nothing is more opposed to spiritual wisdom than the wisdom of the flesh; nothing is more at variance with the grace of God than man's

---

[1] *Comm. on Col.* 3 : 3 f.; *on John* 3 : 7; *on* 1 *John* 3 : 1, 2; *on Rom.* 7 : 22.
[2] *Instit.* I. 5. 4.　　　　　　　　　　　　　　　　[3] *Comm. on Ps.* 8 : 6.
[4] *Serm. on Titus* 1 : 1 f. (1st Serm.). Cf. *on Deut.* 4 : 15 f.: "Let us understand that manifesting Himself by voice, God intended to bar all images."
[5] *Serm. on Titus* 1 : 1 f. (2nd Serm.).　　　　[6] *Comm. on John* 17 : 3.
[7] *Comm. on Rom.* 12 : 2; *on* 1 *Cor.* 5 : 51; *on* 2 *Cor.* 10 : 4; *on Col.* 3 : 10; *on* 1 *Pt* 1 : 13 f.; *on* 2 *Pet.* 1 : 3; *Instit.* 2. 1. 9; 2. 5. 19; 3. 2. 25; cf. *Comm. on Gen.* 1 : 26.
[8] *Comm. on* 1 *Cor.* 1 : 31; *on* 2 *Pet.* 1 : 3; *Instit.* 2. 2. 1; 3. 2. 25.
[9] See *Comm. on Phil.* 2 : 5 f.; 3 : 10; *Serm. on Deut.* 28 : 2 f.

natural ability, and so as to other things. Hence the only foundation of Christ's Kingdom is the abasement of men. . . . We
must give up our understanding, and renounce the wisdom of the
flesh, and thus present our minds empty to Christ, that He may
fill them."[1] Inasmuch, therefore, as only *by the grace of God in
Christ*, and *not by nature*, is the *imago dei* restored, so our knowledge of God which is bound up with this *imago dei* is gained by
grace alone, and not by nature.[2] And inasmuch as to put on the
new man after the image of God in Christ we must put off the
old man after the perverted image of Adam, so in order to know
God in Christ, we must put away all preconceived notions,[3] and
all natural knowledge proceeding from man independently of
faith in Jesus Christ. We must now turn to see how Calvin works
out this principle in his handling of natural theology.

[1] *Comm. on 2 Cor.* 10 : 4 f.
[2] *Comm. on John* 11 : 25; 15 : 1; 18 : 37; *Serm. on Titus* 1 : 15, 16; *on Gal.* 5 : 14 f.
[3] Cf. *Comm. on Matt.* 17 : 22: *Tantum valet praesumpta opinio, ut mentibus in luce
clarissima tenebras obducat.*

Chapter Eleven

NATURAL THEOLOGY (1)

There can be no doubt about the fact that the whole universe has been specially designed as a theatre to point man to God, so that in a manner God reveals Himself through the works of nature. Had Adam maintained his integrity, the genuine order of nature would have conducted him to a knowledge of God. As a matter of fact, however, men are unable to know God in this way. The order of creation has been so perverted, and the human mind is so blind, that even in the midst of light it can discern nothing. Though men are stone-blind so far as the knowledge of God is concerned, yet God has not left man in his sin without some sparks of light so that he is inexcusable through the conviction of his conscience. Because of perversity men are unable to use these sparks or mutilated principles of light to win a true knowledge of God. God allows men in their perversity sufficient light to see the distinction between good and evil, but they cannot find their way to God as long as they remain in their perversity. The light shines in the darkness, but man is so blind and so perverted in will that he is unable to trace that light to its source in God. They see sufficiently to know that it is their fault that they sin, but they are so imprisoned in the deception of this sin that they cannot extricate themselves. As man's perversity never ceases, any attempt to make use of this element of light only succeeds in turning it into the fountainhead of superstition and falsehood. In point of fact, sin is so deliberate that man even uses this natural light in order to suppress the name of God. Far from connecting itself up with this portion of light in the natural man, the light of the revelation of the Gospel actually destroys it and completely blinds the minds of men. This is an accidental result, for it is not the purpose of the Gospel to blind men but to bring light, yet this blindness is also an act of divine judgment upon those who rebel against the light. The strange fact is that it is the act of grace in Christ which blinds the wilfully blind, and it is the act of revelation that seals the darkness finally upon those who, when they meet the light, will not acknowledge it with gratitude and obedience. Basic to Calvin's whole position is the thought that God can be known and worshipped only as He gives Himself to be known and worshipped. Self-will is at the root of all blindness, and at the root of all natural theology which is nothing but a bottomless pit into which all light disappears.

154

IT has already been noted that in the teaching of Calvin the whole world has been specially designed and created as a theatre for the life of man so that he can best fulfil in it his destiny as a creature in the image of God. Man's chief end is to glorify God and in joy and thankfulness to have communion with Him. Everything in the universe is designed to point man to that end, whether it be in the ordered movement of the worlds above, or in the wonderful providence manifested among things on the earth. And so God has filled the whole world with evidences of His glory, and attestations of His grace, that by contemplating these through the intelligence which God has given him, man may be induced thankfully to acknowledge the amazing kindness of God and to know Him familiarly as his heavenly Father. The whole of nature images the glory of God,[1] and the lineaments of God's countenance may be traced everywhere,[2] and more especially in the heavens where man who has been made upright may learn to direct his gaze above and beyond himself.[3] There can be no doubt therefore that in the works of nature "God in a manner communicates Himself to us".[4] "God presents before us in His creatures a bright mirror of His admirable wisdom so that every one that looks upon the world and the other works of God must of necessity break forth in admiration of Him, if he has a single spark of sound judgment. If men were guided to a right knowledge of God by the contemplation of His works, they would know God in the exercise of their wisdom, or by a natural and proper method of acquiring wisdom."[5] At the same time, Calvin admits that, were it not for the Word and Voice of God which accompany His works, the contemplation of the dumb and mute works of nature would profit but little. However, even if God did not utter a single Word, there is abundant testimony in the universe to the glory of God, by whose hands

1 *Instit.* 1. 5. 1; *Comm. on Isa.* 40 : 21; *on Heb.* 11 : 3, *etc.*
2 *Instit.* 1. 5. 6.
3 *Comm. on Ps.* 19 : 1; *on Isa.* 40 : 26; *Instit.* 1. 15. 3: "When we raise our eyes upwards, God's glory appears nearer to us than it does on earth. True it is that it shines on all sides, but heaven has in itself greater excellence than the whole earth, and the nearer we approach to God, the more conspicuous becomes His image" (*Comm. on Ezek.* 1 : 22).
4 *Instit.* 1. 5. 9: *Comm. on Heb.* 11 : 3. The real value in contemplating the works of God in nature is not that we may thereby probe into the mysteries of God, but that they may induce *wonder*, and incite to *thanksgiving: Comm. on Ps.* 139 : 13; *on Rom.* 1 : 19 f.
5 *Comm. on* 1 *Cor.* 1 : 21. Cf. *on Rom.* 1 : 19: *Quod dicit Deum manifestasse, sensus est, ideo conditum esse hominem, ut spectator sit fabricæ mundi: ideo datos ei oculos, ut intuitu tam pulcræ imaginis ad Auctorem ipsum feratur.*

all things were fashioned, and so men would have no excuse for ignorance.[1] This "manifestation of God's glory" was intended as a "prelude to more ample instruction which was one day to be published".[2] "Had Adam stood upright, the genuine order of nature would have conducted us" to a knowledge of God.[3]

Calvin has no sooner said this than he hastens to add that in spite of this wonderful manifestation of God men are unable to know Him through nature. "Bright, however, as is the manifestation which God gives both of Himself and His immortal Kingdom in the mirror of His works, so great is our stupidity, so dull are we in regard to these bright manifestations, that we derive no benefit from them."[4] "The demonstration of God, whereby He makes His glory apparent in His creatures, in respect of its brightness, is clear enough, but in respect of our blindness it is not so sufficient."[5] Therefore "although the knowledge of God is naturally presented to all men in this world as in a mirror . . . it is impossible for any to call upon Him until they know Him by the teaching of the Gospel".[6] Commenting on the first chapter of Second Corinthians, Calvin says: "Here we have a most beautiful passage from which we may see how great is the blindness of the human mind, which in the midst of light discerns nothing. For it is true that this world is like a theatre, in which the Lord presents to us a clear manifestation of His glory, and yet, notwithstanding that we have such a spectacle before our eyes, we are *stone-blind*, not because the manifestation is furnished obscurely, but because we are alienated in mind, and for this matter we lack not merely inclination but ability."[7] "And surely nothing is more absurd than that men should be ignorant of their Author, who are endued with understanding principally for this use. And we must especially note the goodness of God, in that He doth so familiarly insinuate Himself that even the blind may grope after Him. For which cause the blindness of men is more shameful and intolerable who, in so manifest and evident a manifestation, are touched with no feeling of God's presence.

[1] *Comm. on Ps.* 19 : 2 f.; 104 : 2 f.; *Serm. on Deut.* 5 : 11 f.
[2] *Comm. on Ps.* 19 : 4; see also *on John* 10 : 38; *on Rom.* 10 : 18.
[3] *Instit.* 1. 2. 1. [4] *Instit.* 1. 5. 11; 1. 6. 3.
[5] *Comm. on Rom.* 1 : 20. He adds that "our reason fails before it can obtain who is God or what He is".
[6] *Comm. on Ps.* 19 : 4. Cf. *Instit.* 1. 6. 4: *Nam quum humana mens pro sua imbecillitate pervenire ad Deum nullo modo queat nisi sacro eius verbo adiuta et sublevata, omnes tunc mortales, exceptis Judæis, quia Deum sine verbo quærebant, necesse fuit in vanitate atque erorre versari.*
[7] *Comm. on* 1 *Cor.* 1 : 21.

Whithersoever they cast their eyes upward or downward, they must light upon lively and also infinite images of God's power, wisdom, and goodness. For God has not darkly shadowed His glory in the creation of the world, but He has everywhere engraven such manifest marks that even blind men may know them by groping. Whence we gather that men are not only blind but blockish, when being helped by such excellent testimonies they profit nothing. Yet here arises a question: whether men can naturally come to the true and clear knowledge of God. For Paul gives us to understand that their own sluggishness is the cause that they cannot perceive that God is present; because, though they shut their eyes, they may yet grope after Him. I answer that their ignorance and blockishness is mixed with such frowardness that, being void of right judgment, they pass over without understanding all such signs of God's glory as appear manifestly both in heaven and earth. Yea, seeing that the true knowledge of God is a singular gift of His, and faith (by which alone He is rightly known) comes only from the illumination of the Spirit, it follows that *our minds cannot pierce so far, having nature only for our guide.*"[1]

The next step that Calvin takes in discussion of this problem is to show that, although men cannot in any sense come to God by natural knowledge, for they are blinder than moles as far as that is concerned, yet God has left them in their blindness such sparks of knowledge as to render them inexcusable through the conviction of their own conscience. They have therefore a slight knowledge of sin and a slight knowledge of God, but God has blinded them in such a way that though they are culpable they cannot make their way through to a real knowledge of God.[2] Their wills are perverted and God will not let Himself be known by them in their perversity.[3] "We are not so blind that we can pretend ignorance, to quit us from the blame of naughtiness or perversity. First, we conceive with ourselves there is a God; secondly, that the same, whosoever He be, is to be worshipped. But here our reason fails, before it can obtain either who is God or

---

[1] *Comm. on Acts* 17 : 27.

[2] Cf. *Comm. on Ezek.* 12 : 1 f.: "God pronounces that their blindness is voluntary. When therefore unbelievers pretend that they have not been illumined by the Lord, it may be conceded to them that they are blind and deaf; but we must often proceed beyond this, since their own obstinacy is the fountain of their blindness and deafness: and *God blinds them, because they will not admit the light offered to them, but stop their ears.*"

[3] Cf. *Comm. on 2 Pet.* 1 : 19 f.; *on 2 Cor.* 4 : 4; *on Isa.* 44 : 18; *on Ezek.* 12 : 1 f.; 20 : 1 f.; *on Matt.* 13 : 2-15; *on Mark* 4 : 12.

what He is. Wherefore the Apostle to the Hebrews ascribes this light to faith, that a man should profit truly in the creation of the world. And not without cause, for through blindness we are so hindered that we cannot come unto the mark: we see so far that we cannot pretend any excuse. Paul declares both these things notably, when He says that God in times past suffered the Gentiles in ignorance; nevertheless He left not Himself without a witness, because He gave unto them rain, and fruitfulness from heaven. Therefore this knowledge of God which avails only to take away excuse differs greatly from that knowledge which brings salvation of which Christ speaks, and in which Jeremiah teaches we are to rejoice."[1] Commenting on the same passage from the Epistle to the Romans, Calvin says in the *Institutes*: "When Paul says that that which may be known of God is manifested in the creation of the world, he does not mean such a manifestation as may be comprehended by the wit of man. On the contrary, he shows that it has no further effect than to render us inexcusable."[2] Elsewhere he puts it thus: "Notwithstanding that God shows Himself openly, it is only with the eye of faith that we can behold Him, save only that we receive a slight perception of His divinity, sufficient to render us inexcusable."[3]

Calvin's position would seem to be that God allows sufficient light to reach man in his perverse will that he may see the distinctions between good and evil, but he cannot see his way out to God so long as he remains in his perversity. It is as if the light shines through a frosted glass such that it enables men to walk and order their lives in the world not in total darkness, but such nevertheless that they are unable of themselves to trace the light back to its true source, and so to know God.[4] We see sufficiently to know that it is our own fault that we sin, and in sin we frost and darken the glass, or as Calvin would say, the mirror, so that we are unable to see out. By our own sin we become imprisoned within our own perversity, while the light which we have in our natural intelligence only serves to convict us.[5]

[1] *Comm. on Rom.* 1 : 20.   [2] *Instit.* 1. 5. 14 f.; cf. 1. 5. 1.
[3] *Comm. on* 1 *Cor.* 1 : 21; cf. *on Acts* 14 : 16 f.; 17 : 27; *on Ps.* 19 : 4; *on Heb.* 11 : 3; *on John* 1 : 9; *on Rom.* 7 : 15; *Serm. on Job* 17 : 1 f.; 33 : 14 f.; 34 : 29 f.
[4] That is to say, the light shines in darkness, but "men are so dull that they do not comprehend whence the light proceeds". "What can be more unreasonable than to draw water from a running stream, and never to think of the fountain from which that stream flows?" And so men turned the light into darkness, but, in so doing, they alienated themselves from the fountain of life. (See *Comm. on John* 1 : 4 ff.)
[5] *Serm. on Job* 34 : 29 f.; *Comm. on Rom.* 7 : 15.

Calvin then goes on to elucidate this position by reiterating the fact that we are unable to reach a real knowledge of God because such sparks of light as we do have by nature are perverted by the essential motion of sin. "Accordingly, when Paul declares that God is not known by means of His creatures, you must understand him to mean that a pure knowledge of Him is not attained. For that none may have any pretext to ignorance, men make proficiency in the school of nature so far as to be affected with some perception of deity, but what God is they know not. Nay, more, they straightway-become vain in their imaginations. Thus the light shineth in darkness. It follows, then, that men do not err thus far through mere ignorance, so as not to be chargeable with contempt, negligence and ingratitude. Thus it holds good that all have known God and yet have not glorified Him, and that, on the other hand, no one under the guidance of nature ever made such proficiency as to know God."[1] Though "men have naturally some sense of God . . . so soon as they begin to think upon God, they vanish away in wicked inventions".[2] And though in this perverse state "the first general knowledge of God doth nevertheless remain still in them", "they never make an end of erring until God help them", who "condemns all inventions of men, which disfigure the true nature of God".[3] "But seeing that God doth far surpass the capacity of our mind to comprehend Him, man deforms and transfigures His glory with a wicked and false imagination."[4] Or, again: "Though there has been an opinion of this kind among the heathen, that the world was made by God, it was yet very evanescent, for as soon as they formed a notion of some God, they became instantly vain in their imaginations, so that they groped in the dark, having in their thoughts a mere shadow of some uncertain deity, and not the knowledge of the true God. Besides, as it was only a transient opinion that flit in their minds, it was far from being anything like knowledge."[5] "In consequence of the corruption of our nature, the true light of truth is not to be found among men where revelation is not

---

[1] *Comm. on* 1 *Cor.* 1 : 21; see also *on Rom.* 1 : 21 f.
[2] *Comm. on Acts* 17 : 28-30; cf. 17 : 24.
[3] *Comm. on Acts* 17 : 28-30.
[4] *Ibid.* Cf. *Instit.* 1. 5. 15: *Simul enim ac modicum divinitatis gustum ex mundi speculatione delibavimus, vero Deo prætermisso, eius loco somnia et spectra cerebri nostri erigimus; ac iustitiæ, sapientiæ, bonitatis, potentiæ laudem ab ipso fonte huc et illuc traducimus. Quotidiana porro eius facta ita aut obscuramus aut invertimus prave æstimando, ut et suam illis gloriam, et autori debitam laudem præripiamus.*
[5] *Comm. on Acts* 11 : 3.

enjoyed, but only certain mutilated principles which are involved in much obscurity and doubt."[1] "If men are naturally taught instead of having any distinct, solid, or certain knowledge, they fasten only on contradictory principles, and, in consequence, worship an unknown God."[2]

The *mutilated principles* Calvin also thinks of in terms of a *seed of religion* which continues to exist in fallen man.[3] It is from this that "the religious propensity springs" which we see in "men's uniform belief in God".[4] This is a "sense of Deity indelibly engraven on the human mind",[5] and "it is more difficult to obliterate it from the mind of man than to break down the feelings of his nature".[6] The difficulty is that man's mind and will are so perverted that he uses this divine seed to pervert and suppress the name of God,[7] and no sooner does he form the ideas in his mind than he hurries away on the road to untruth and destruction.[8] Therefore it is impossible for man to dig the truth out of this seed of religion, or to bring it to its true fruition.[9] On the contrary, it only becomes the cause of all his superstitions.[10] "That we naturally possess some knowledge of God, that some distinction between good and evil is engraven on our conscience, that our faculties are sufficient for the maintenance of the present life; that, in short, we are in so many ways superior to the brute beasts, that is excellent in itself, so far as it proceeds from God. But in us all these things are completely polluted, in the same manner as the wine which has been wholly infected and corrupted by the offensive taste of the vessel loses the pleasantness of its flavour, and acquires a bitter and pernicious taste. For *such knowledge of God as now remains in men is nothing else than a frightful source of idolatry and all superstitions;* the judgment exercised in choosing and distinguishing things is partly blind and foolish, partly imperfect and confused; all the industry we possess flows into vanity and trifles; and the will itself, with furious impetuosity, rushes headlong to what is evil. Thus in the whole of our nature there remains not one drop of uprightness."[11] And again: "All have naturally a something of religion born with them, but owing

---

[1] *Comm. on Ps.* 19 : 7.
[2] *Instit.* I. 5. 12; cf. I. 15. 6; *Comm. on John* 4 : 22.
[3] *Instit.* I. 3. 1 f.; I. 4. 1; I. 5. 15; *Comm. on Isa.* 14 : 14.
[4] *Instit.* I. 3. 2; I. 4. 1; I. 5. 1, 4, 15.
[5] *Instit.* I. 3. 3.
[6] *Instit.* I. 3. 1.
[7] *Instit.* I. 5. 1.
[8] *Instit.* I. 5. 15.
[9] *Instit.* I. 4. 1; cf. I. 11. 8; I. 12. 1.
[10] *Comm. on Acts* 17 : 23; *Instit.* 3. 8. 5.
[11] *Comm. on John* 3 : 6; 1 : 5.

to the blindness and stupidity, as well as the weakness, of our minds, the apprehension which we conceive of God is immediately depraved. Religion is thus the beginning of all superstitions, not in its own nature, but through the darkness which has settled down upon the minds of men, and which prevents them from distinguishing between idols and the true God."[1] "Let us then know that religion, separated from knowledge, is nothing but the sport and delusion of Satan. It is hence necessary that men should know with certainty what God they worship. And Christ thus distinguishes the true worship of God from that of vain idols. 'We know', He says, speaking of the Jews, 'whom we worship.' . . . But I call that knowledge, *not what is innate in man*, or what is by diligence acquired, but that which is delivered to us by the Law and the Prophets."[2] "While man must bear the guilt of corrupting the seed of divine knowledge so wondrously deposited in his mind, and preventing it from bearing good and genuine fruit, it is still most true that we are not sufficiently instructed by that bare and simple, but magnificent, testimony which the creatures bear to the glory of their Creator. For no sooner do we, from a survey of the world, obtain some slight knowledge of Deity, than we pass by the true God, and set up in His stead the dream and phantom of our own brain, drawing away the praise of justice, wisdom and goodness, from the fountainhead, and transferring it to some other quarter. Moreover, by the erroneous estimates we form, we either so obscure or pervert His daily works, as at once to rob them of their glory, and the Author of them of His just praise."[3] Indeed, Calvin says that "the human mind in its wantonness is ever and anon inventing different modes of worship as a means of gaining His favour. This *irreligious affectation of religion*, being innate in the human mind, has betrayed itself in every age and is still doing so, men always longing to devise some method of procuring righteousness without any sanction from the Word of God."[4]

The inability on the part of fallen men to bring *the mutilated principles of light* in them to the state of truth is due, on the one hand, to the perverse pride of men, who, "by appropriating as their own that which has been given them from heaven, put out the light intended to exhibit God clearly to their minds",and so "are not afraid to employ the seed of Diety deposited in human nature as a

---

[1] *Comm. on Ps.* 97 : 7.
[2] *Comm. on Jer.* 44 : 1 f.
[3] *Instit.* 1. 5. 15.
[4] *Instit.* 2. 8. 5.

means of suppressing the name of God".[1] On the other hand, this is looked upon by Calvin as a divine punishment for sin. "Because they regarded not to abide in the knowledge of God, which alone directs our minds into true wisdom, the Lord gave unto them a perverse mind which now can allow of nothing. Whereas He saith, they *approved not*, it is as much as if He should say: they followed not the knowledge of God with such study as they ought, but rather purposely turned their cogitations from God. He signifies, therefore, that through their wicked election, they preferred their own vanities before God; and so that error wherewith they were deceived was voluntary."[2] "For they who, of their own malignity, closed their eyes against the offered light of God, that they might not see His glory, deserved to be blinded, that they might forget themselves, and not see what were convenient for them. Moreover, they deserved to have their sight dimmed at noonday who were not ashamed (as much as in them was) to extinguish the glory of God, which only doth enlighten us."[3] Therefore, says Calvin: "God shut up all mankind in blindness, having taken away from the human intellect the power of attaining to a knowledge of God by its own resources."[4] Calvin has an illuminating passage about the words of the Gospel, "For judgment am I come into the world". "The word *judgment* cannot be understood in this passage to denote simply the punishment which is inflicted on the unbeliever, and on those who despise God, for it is made to include the grace of illumination. Christ therefore calls it *judgment* because He restores to proper order what was disordered and confused, but He means that this is done by a wonderful purpose of God, and contrary to the opinion of men. And indeed human reason considers nothing to be more unreasonable than to say that 'they who see are made blind' by the light of the world. This then is one of the secret judgments of God by which He casts down the pride of men. It ought to be observed that the *blindness* which is mentioned here does not proceed so much from Christ as from the fault of men. For by its own nature it does not strictly *blind* any man, but as there is nothing which the reprobate desire more earnestly than to extinguish the light, the eyes of their mind, which are diseased through malice and depravity, must be dazzled by the

[1] *Instit.* I. 5. 4; cf. *Comm. on Eph.* 4 : 17; *Instit.* I. 11. 8.
[2] *Comm. on Rom.* I : 28. [3] *Comm. on Rom.* I : 27.
[4] *Comm. on 1 Cor.* 2 : 10. Cf. *on Gen.* 3 : 6 f.; *on Isa.* 44 : 18; *Serm. on Job* 17 : 1 f.; 33 : 14 f.; *on 2 Cor.* 4 : 4; *on Eph.* 4 : 18; *Instit.* I. 9. 3.

light which is exhibited to them. In short, since Christ is by His own nature the *Light of the world*, it is an accidental result that some are *made blind* by His coming.[1] But again it may be asked by some: Since all are universally accused of *blindness*, who are *they that see*? I reply, this is spoken of ironically by way of concession, because unbelievers, though they are blind, think that their sight is uncommonly acute and powerful; and elated by this confidence, they do not deign to listen to God. Besides, out of Christ, the wisdom of the flesh has a very fair appearance because the world does not understand what it is to be truly wise. So then they *see*, says our Lord Jesus Christ, who deceiving themselves and others under a foolish confidence in their wisdom, are guided by their own opinion, and reckon their vain imaginations to be great wisdom. Such persons, as soon as Christ appears in the brightness of His Gospel, *are made blind;* not only because their folly which was formerly concealed amidst the darkness of unbelief is now discovered, but because, being plunged in deeper darkness by the righteous vengeance of God, *they lose that small remnant of I know not what light which they formerly possessed.* It is true that we are all born *blind*, but still amidst the darkness of corrupted and depraved nature, some sparks continue to shine so that men differ from brute beasts. Now if man, elated by proud confidence in his own opinion, refuses to submit to God, he will seem, apart from Christ, to be wise, but the brightness of Christ will strike him with dismay; for never does the vanity of the human intellect begin to be discovered until the heavenly wisdom is brought into view. But Christ intended, as I have already suggested, to express something more by these words. For hypocrites do not so obstinately resist God before Christ shines, but as soon as the light is brought near them, then do they in open war and, as it were, with unfurled banner, rise up against God. It is in consequence of this depravity and ingratitude therefore that they become doubly *blind* and that God in righteous vengeance *entirely puts out their eyes which were formerly destitute of the true light.*"[2]

That is a clear statement of the thought which is basic to Calvin's whole doctrine of natural theology, as also to his doctrine of the *imago dei*, namely, that it is the act of God's grace in Christ which blinds the wilfully blind. It is the act of revelation or

[1] This is constantly emphasized by Calvin—blinding is God's strange work, and contrary to the nature of His Word (see *Comm. on John* 12 : 31-41).
[2] *Comm. on John* 9 : 39; cf. 8 : 12; 12 : 39 f.; *on Matt.* 31 : 2-13, 15; *on Mark* 4 : 12; *on Isa.* 6 : 10.

illumination that seals the darkness finally upon the minds of those who, when they meet the light, will not acknowledge it with gratitude and obedience. Such natural theology as Calvin envisages is, so to speak, *the shadow side of revelation*,[1] and takes its place within the revelation of the righteousness of God, which becomes the revelation of God's wrath upon men's perversity.[2] If creation exhibits to fallen men the light of God, *it is of no avail*,[3] apart from rendering them inexcusable, for it proves to be but a *deceiving appearance of light that dazzles the eye instead of assisting them*.[4]

Corresponding to the blinding of the perverted mind is the fact that the whole order of creation has been perverted[5] or turned into confusion.[6] Calvin also uses the words *everted* and *inverted* in the same connection.[7] His thought is that God created the world with a beautiful order which is manifest both in the order of nature and in the rectitude or temperature of the human soul. But with man's revolt that order was inverted, in man as we have seen, and also in the sphere of creation itself.[8] Just as Calvin thinks of the perverted blindness of man over against the judgment of God, so Calvin thinks of the perversion of the whole order of creation as bound up with God's curse upon it.[9] Therefore any attempt to know God out of the perverted order of nature can only partake of its perversity. It can only succeed in inverting the truth of God. This means that the essential motion of any natural theology, in spite of the shadow religion which it may involve,[10] can only be perverted from the very start, so that its essential direction is continually away from God, from perversity to perversity, from alienation to alienation.[11] As long as we remain in our fallen nature "we fight against God".[12]

[1] Cf. *Instit.* 1. 4. 4: *shadow religion*. This is also a *cursed knowledge*, cursed by God: *Comm. on Gen.* 3 : 6; on *Ps.* 19 : 8; on *Heb.* 11 : 6; *Instit.* 2. 1. 5.

[2] *Comm. on Rom.* 1 : 17, 18 f.; *Instit.* 1. 5. 14. This *blindness* goes further than that spoken of in 2. 4. 3, where God is said to blind by taking His light away from men.

[3] *Instit.* 1. 5. 11, 14; 1. 6. 3.

[4] *Comm. on 2 Cor.* 4 : 3; on *John* 8 : 12; on *Heb.* 1 : 3.

[5] *Instit.* 2. 1. 5; *Comm. on Gen.* 37 : 27. Therefore no observation of nature can be turned into a general rule (*Serm. on Job* 12 : 14 f.).

[6] *Comm. on Ps.* 8 : 6; cf. *Serm. on Job* 24 : 10 f.

[7] *Comm. on Gen.* 8 : 21; 2 : 18; on *Rom.* 11 : 36; on 1 *Cor.* 1 : 21; *Serm. on 1 Tim.* 2 : 1, 2; cf. also *Comm. on Acts* 14 : 17; on *Gen.* 48 : 17.

[8] *Comm. on Gen.* 8 : 21.

[9] *Instit.* 2. 1. 5; *Comm. on Ps.* 19 : 8; on *Gen.* 2 : 6; on *Heb.* 11 : 6.

[10] *Instit.* 1. 4. 4.

[11] *Comm. on Gen.* 8 : 21; *Instit.* 1. 4. 1; 1. 5. 11 f., 14 f.; 1. 11. 8; 2. 2. 24; *Comm. on Rom.* 1 : 20; on 1 *Cor.* 1 : 21; on *Heb.* 11 : 3.

[12] *Serm. on Job* 28 : 10 f.; *Instit.* 2. 3. 1; 2. 7. 7; 2. 8. 1; 2. 16. 3; *Comm. on 2 Cor.* 10 : 4; on *Rom.* 7 : 7, 15; 8 : 20; *Serm. on Eph.* 2 : 3-6: "L'homme aura bien quelque raison: mais que fera-il estant en sa nature? Il bataillera contre Dieu et contre toute verité."

Calvin lays great stress in this connection on the fact that the will of man has been perverted, so that now it inevitably moves in a direction counter to the will of God. Therefore he is unable to know God as God wills that He shall be known, and that is the only way in which we may know God: according to His will. Though man has been made by God to be such a creature that he is what he is when he knows God, yet he no longer tends to his true end, but goes the way of self-will and presumption with all the inclination of his mind.[1] Therefore though a man may try to know God in this motion of self-will, he cannot do so, for in actuality he is going against God, and refuses to minister to God's glory by thankfully giving Him what is His due in authority and glory. "The sum is that the whole order of nature is everted and overthrown, if the same God who is the beginning of all things is not also the end . . . whereupon it ensues that those cogitations are absurd and far from reason, yea, are mad, whatsoever they be, that tend to the diminishing of His glory."[2] Thus there is a perpetual and irreconcilable difference between fallen man and the righteousness of God,[3] not only because there is a contrary law engraven on the heart,[4] so that he rejects the Word and is unable to hear it, but because nothing is more hateful to God than self-willed action on the part of man.[5] God opens the ears of men if they will turn to Him in humility and repentance, and reveals Himself to them, but if they will not have Him, and insist on being perverted, He opens their ears only so far as to render them inexcusable, refusing to give Himself to their knowledge.[6] It is only when men "regulate the measure of their knowledge by the will of God"[7] that they may know Him, not when they "obey reason by their own motion", but when they are "governed by His Spirit".[8] "The liberty of the human mind must be restrained and bridled, that it may not be wise apart from the doctrine of Christ."[9] "Natural reason will never direct men to Christ."[10]

---

[1] *Comm. on Rom.* 7 : 15.   [2] *Comm. on Rom.* 11 : 36.

[3] *Instit.* 2. 16. 3: *Perpetuum et irreconciliabile dissiduum est quamdiu peccatores manemus.* Cf. *Comm. on John* 3 : 3: *Atque hac loquutione simul docemur, exsules nos ac prorsus alienos a regno Dei nasci, ac perpetuum nobis cum ipso dissiduum esse, donec alios secunda genitura nos faciat.*

[4] *Comm. on Heb.* 8 : 10.

[5] *Comm. on Isa.* 65 : 2; on *Acts* 7 : 42-45; on *Col.* 2 : 18, 23; on 2 *Pet.* 2 : 10; on *Jer.* 44 : 17; on *Jonah* 2 : 8 f.; on *Zeph.* 1 : 5; *Instit.* 4. 13. 2.

[6] *Serm. on Job* 33 : 14 f.; 34 : 19 f.   [7] *Comm. on Gen.* 3 : 5.

[8] *Comm. on Rom.* 8 : 9.   [9] *Comm. on 2 Cor.* 10 : 4.

[10] *Comm. on John* 1 : 5; cf. on *Col.* 2 : 8: *Quicquid in hominum cerebro fabricatum est, non est Christo consentaneum.*

It is basic to Calvin's thought throughout that men in their pride and vanity refuse to know and worship God *as He gives Himself to be known and worshipped*, but "fly off to indulge their curiosity in vain speculations".[1] "Hence they do not conceive of Him in the character in which He is manifested but imagine Him to be whatever their own rashness has devised. This abyss standing open, they cannot move one step without rushing head-long to destruction. With such an idea of God, nothing which they may attempt to offer in the way of worship or obedience can have any value in His sight, because it is not Him they worship, but instead of Him the dream and figment of their own heart."[2] The word *abyss* used by Calvin in this passage is very typical of him. He uses it again and again to express his shuddering horror at the awful pit of natural theology.[3] "In this way (i.e., by natural theology) man plunges himself headlong into an immense abyss, involves himself in numerous inextricable snares, and buries himself in the thickest darkness. For it is right that the stupidity of the human mind should be punished with fearful destruction, whenever it attempts to rise in its own strength to the height of divine wisdom."[4] "All knowledge without Christ", says Calvin, "is a vast abyss which immediately swallows up all our thoughts."[5] On another occasion he says: "All that knowledge of God which men think they have attained out of Christ will be a deadly abyss."[6] It is a deadly abyss because the lofty perverted spirit of man in attempting to probe into the divine majesty commits a serious impiety by overstepping the bounds of God's Self-revelation and is countered by the wrath of God. "The light of nature is stifled sooner than take the first step into this profound abyss."[7]

Another expression that Calvin uses very frequently in this connection is *labyrinth*, which is applied to the inaccessibility of the knowledge of God in relation to the ramifications of the human mind.[8] This is a labyrinth quite "inextricable, if the Word

[1] *Instit.* 1. 4. 1; *Comm. on Rom.* 1 : 21 f.; *Serm. on Deut.* 6 : 1 f.
[2] *Instit.* 1. 4. 1.
[3] Commenting on *Luke* 1 : 78, Calvin says: "These words show that out of Christ there is no life-giving light in the world, but everything is covered by the appalling darkness of death." See *Serm. on Eph.* 2 : 1-5.
[4] *Instit.* 3. 24. 4. Here Calvin is speaking of the futility of natural theology in relation to election.
[5] *Comm. on* 1 *Pet.* 1 : 21: *Omnis cogitatio de Deo extra Christum immensa est abyssus, quæ sensus omnes nostros protinus absorbeat.*
[6] *Comm. on John* 6 : 46.   [7] *Instit.* 2. 2. 24.
[8] *Instit.* 1. 5. 12; 1. 6. 1, 3; *Comm. on* 2 *Pet.* 1 : 19: "All are immersed in darkness who do not attend to the light of the Word. Therefore except thou art resolved

does not serve as a thread to guide our path".[1] "It is necessary to apply to Scripture in order to learn the sure marks which distinguish God, as Creator of the World, from the whole herd of fictitious gods . . . so as to save us from wandering up and down as in a labyrinth, in search of some doubtful deity."[2] This brings us back again to Calvin's firm conviction in regard to the manifestation of God through the works of creation, which he regards as of no avail to us apart from the Word of God's revelation. He even says that God has deliberately suffered things in the world to be "somewhat confused", so that, when looking at "things present and visible" our "natural reason" is unable to perceive God, we "may ascend high and repose our trust in God's Word".[3] Natural theology itself is only a hindrance or a "kind of veil by which the mind is prevented from beholding God".[4] It behoves us therefore to distrust and renounce it, in order to rely only on the Word.[5] "It amounts to this, that God is not properly worshipped but by the certainty of faith, which cannot be produced in any other way than by the Word of God. Hence it follows that all who forsake the Word fall into idolatry; for Christ plainly testifies that an idol, or an imagination of their brain, is substituted for God, when men are ignorant of the true God. And He charges with ignorance all to whom God has not revealed Himself, for as soon as we are deprived of the light of His Word, darkness and blindness reign."[6] "God will not and cannot have Himself separated from His Word."[7] "God could not be separated from His own Truth, for nothing would be left to Him, were He regarded as apart from His Word. Hence a mere fiction is every idea which men form of God in their minds when they neglect the mirror in which He made Himself known. More-

---

wilfully to cast thyself into a labyrinth, especially beware of departing in the least thing from the rule and direction of the Word." See also *on Isa.* 40 : 8; *on Rom.* 11 : 33; *Serm. on Eph.* 4 : 17-19.

[1] *Instit.* 1. 6. 3.
[2] *Instit.* 1. 6. 1: *Sed tantum quomodo ex Scriptura discere conveniat, Deum, qui mundi Creator est, certis notis ab omni commentitia deorum turba discerni . . . ne per ambages incertum aliquod numen quaeramus.* Cf. 1. 6. 2: *Iterum tamen repeto . . . Scripturam unicum et verum Deum quatenus mundum creavit et gubernat, certis notis et insignibus ornare, ne misceatur cum falsa deorum turba.* See *Serm. on Deut.* 4 : 10 f.; 4 : 15 f.; 6 : 1 f.
[3] *Serm. on Job* 24 : 10 f.
[4] *Instit.* 2. 2. 20; 3. 2. 34; *Comm. on John* 5 : 37; cf. *on Deut.* 8 : 3: *Lucet quidem satis clare in usu, qui naturaliter ex creaturis percipitur, tam potentia Dei quam bonitas. Sed facit pravitas humani ingenii, ut quae testimonia erant, quasi vela obscurent claram lucem.*
[5] *Serm. on Job* 34 : 33 f.; *Comm. on John* 8 : 42: *Qualis est ista Dei cognitio, ubi viva eius imago respuitur?*
[6] *Comm. on John* 4 : 22. [7] *Comm. on Jer.* 44 : 17; also 1 : 9, 10.

over, we ought to know that whatever power, majesty and glory there is in God so shines forth in His Word, that He does not appear as God, except His Word remains safe and uncorrupted."[1] It is only when we attend to this Word and know God through it, that we may begin really to behold God's image in the world which He has made.[2] This is the way in which God restores the right order of nature, and rehabilitates the true *rectitudo* in man.[3]

[1] *Comm. on Jer.* 20 : 7.
[2] *Comm. on Heb.* 11 : 3; *Introd. Arg. in Comm. on Gen.; Comm. on Ps.* 19 : 7.
[3] *Comm. on* 1 *Cor.* 1 : 21; cf. *on John* 9 : 6; *Instit.* 1. 15. 3.

Chapter Twelve

NATURAL THEOLOGY (2)

Calvin's teaching on natural theology is summed up in the Introduction to the Commentary on Genesis. *(1) The Word is necessary for the understanding of nature and for the knowledge of God through the manifestation of nature. That was necessary for Adam and Eve even before the Fall. If we would know God, we must not commence with the elements of the world, but with the Gospel where Christ the Word, the lively Image of God, is presented to us. It is thus by faith that we understand that the world was created by God, and it is by faith that we see God's glory mirrored in the world. But the Word does not illuminate our minds in a single day so that afterwards we can see of ourselves. It is only by constant listening to the Word that our ears are formed to hear, our eyes to see, and our minds to understand the Truth and know God. (2) There can be no knowledge of God apart from atonement, for through the death of Christ the perverted order of the world is restored to its original rectitude, and true knowledge of God becomes possible. Apart from this Word of Grace, God's voice only terrifies and numbs us, and no familiar knowledge is possible. Although there is no knowledge of God possible now apart from the reconciliation of the Gospel, it must also be emphasized that there never was since the beginning any communication between God and man, except through Christ. There is no real knowledge of God apart from His gracious Will to reveal Himself. (3) This means that the whole of man's intellectual wisdom must be submitted to the foolishness of the Cross. Nothing is more opposed to the spiritual wisdom of God than the wisdom of the flesh, and nothing is more at variance with the Grace of God than man's natural ability. Thus the Cross depotentiates all natural knowledge and justification by faith alone sets aside all natural theology as a work of the flesh (including the works of the mind). Christ did not come to fill up or eke out our natural wisdom, but to bring us a final revelation that sets aside the natural reason. This does not mean, however, that God mocks us or disappoints us, for He gives us a full illumination through which our minds may know Him truly. This certain knowledge must not be connected up with the so-called knowledge which it sets aside.*

CALVIN'S whole position in regard to natural theology, and the relation of the Word to the manifestation of God in the world of nature, is admirably summed up in his famous

Argument to the Commentary on Genesis: "Now in describing the world as a mirror in which we ought to behold God, I would not be understood to assert, either that our eyes are sufficiently clear-sighted to discern what the fabric of heaven and earth represents, or that the knowledge to be hence obtained is sufficient for salvation. And whereas the Lord invites us to Himself by means of created things, with no other effect than that of thereby rendering us inexcusable, He has added (as was necessary) a new remedy, or at least by a new aid. He has assisted the ignorance of our mind. For by the Scripture as our guide and teacher, He not only makes those things plain which would otherwise escape our notice, but almost compels us to behold them; as if He had assisted our dull sight with spectacles. On this point, Moses insists. For if the mute instruction of the heaven and earth were sufficient, the teaching of Moses would have been superfluous. This herald therefore approaches who excites our attention, in order that we may perceive ourselves to be placed in this scene, for the purpose of beholding the glory of God; not indeed to observe them as mere witnesses, but to enjoy all the riches which are here exhib-ited, as the Lord has ordained and subjected them to our use. And he not only declares generally that God is the Architect of the world, but through the whole chain of history he shows how admirable is His power, His wisdom, His goodness, and especially His tender solicitude for the human race. Besides, since the eternal Word of God is the lively and express image of Himself, he recalls us to this point. And thus, the assertion of the Apostle is verified, that through no other means than faith can it be understood that the worlds were made by the Word of God (Heb. 11 : 3). For faith properly proceeds from this, that we being taught by the ministry of Moses, do not now wander in foolish and trifling speculations, but contemplate the true and only God in His genuine image.

"It may, however, be objected that this seems at variance with what Paul declares: 'After that, in the wisdom of God, the world through wisdom knew not God, it seemed right to God, through the foolishness of preaching, to save them who believe' (1 Cor. 1 : 21). For he thus intimates that God is sought in vain under the guidance of visible things; and that nothing remains for us but to betake ourselves immediately to Christ; and that we must not therefore commence with the elements of this world, but with the Gospel which sets Christ alone before us with His Cross, and holds us to this one point. I answer: it is in vain for any to reason as philosophers on the workmanship of the world, except those who, having been first humbled by the preaching of the Gospel, have learned to submit the whole of their intellectual wisdom (as Paul expresses it) to the foolishness of the Cross. Nothing shall we find, I say, above or below, which can raise us up to God, until Christ shall have instructed us in His own School. Yet this cannot be done, unless we, having emerged out of the lowest depths, are borne up above all heavens, in the chariot of the Cross, that there by faith we may apprehend those things which the eye has never seen, the ear never heard, and which far surpass our hearts and minds. For the earth, with its supply of fruits for our daily nourishment, is not there set before us; but Christ Himself offers Himself to us unto eternal life. Nor does heaven, by the shining of the sun and stars, enlighten our bodily eyes, but the same Christ, the Light of the world and the Sun of Righteousness, shines into our souls; neither does the air stretch out its empty space for us to breathe in, but the Spirit of God Himself quickens us and causes us to live. There, in short, the invisible kingdom of God fills all things, and His spiritual grace is diffused through all. Yet this does not prevent us from applying our senses to the consideration of heaven and earth, that we may thence seek confirmation in the true knowledge of God. For Christ is the image in which God presents to our view, not only His heart, but also His hands and His feet. I give the name of His *heart* to that secret love with which He embraces us in Christ: by His *hands* and *feet* I understand those works of His which are displayed before our eyes. As soon as ever we depart from Christ, there is nothing, be it ever so gross or insignificant in itself, respecting which we are not necessarily deceived."

In this interesting statement there are several elements which can be singled out as basic to Calvin's dogmatic position.

(1) Calvin insists upon the necessity of the Word for the understanding of nature, and of God who manifests Himself in nature. Even Adam and Eve needed the Word of God in order to know God as Creator, apart altogether from knowing Him as Redeemer.[1] And so Calvin thinks in terms of a primitive revelation by means of which men, particularly after the Fall, were able to gain that *familiar knowledge* of the true God as Creator and Redeemer, apart from the certain and evident manifestation of God in nature

---

[1] *Instit.* 1. 6. 1.

which merely rendered them inexcusable.[1] This itself proved
unavailing, because "unbelievers are deaf to all God's Words
when they echo in the air".[2] And so the Word was communicated
in a written form, and was confirmed through the sacraments.[3]
Therefore if we would know God too "we must not commence
with the elements of this world, but with the Gospel which sets
Christ alone before us with His Cross, and holds us to this one
point".[4] "It is doubtless true, that, if we were not very dull and
stupid, the signatures and proofs of Deity which are to be found
on the theatre of the world, are abundant enough to incite us to
acknowledge and reverence God; but as surrounded with so clear
a light we are nevertheless blind, this splendid representation of
the glory of God, without the aid of the Word, would profit us
nothing, although it should be to us as a loud and distinct pro-
clamation sounding in our ears."[5] "Men's minds therefore are
wholly blind, so that they cannot see the light of nature which
shines forth in created things, until being irradiated by God's
Spirit, they begin to understand by faith what otherwise they
cannot comprehend. Hence most correctly does the Apostle
ascribe such an understanding to faith."[6] "In vain does creation
exhibit so many bright lamps lighted up to show forth the glory
of its Author. Though they beam upon us from every quarter,
they are altogether insufficient of themselves to lead us into the
right path. Some sparks undoubtedly they do throw out; but
these are quenched before they can give forth a brighter efful-
gence. Wherefore, the Apostle, in the very place where he says
that the worlds are images of invisible things, adds that it is *by
faith* that we understand that they were framed by the Word of
God, thereby intimating that *the invisible Godhead is indeed repre-
sented by such displays, but that we have no eyes to perceive it until they
are enlightened through faith by internal revelation from God.* When
Paul says that that which may be known of God is manifested by
the creation of the world, he does not mean such a manifestation
as may be comprehended by the wit of man; on the contrary, he

---

[1] *Instit.* 1. 6. 1-4; *Comm. on Acts* 14 : 17.
[2] *Instit.* 1. 6. 4.
[3] *Instit.* 2. 8. 3; *Institutio* (1536) 29; *Instit.* 4. 14. 1 ff.
[4] *Introd. Arg. in Comm. on Gen.*: *Non igitur ab elementis mundi huius sed ab evangelio faciendum est exordium, quod unum Christum nobis proponit cum sua cruce, et in eo nos detinet.*
[5] *Comm. on Ps.* 19 : 7; cf. 19 :8; 104 : 4: "We profit little in the contemplation of universal nature if we do not behold with the eyes of faith that Spiritual glory of which an image is presented to us in the world."
[6] *Comm. on Heb.* 11 : 3; cf. 1 : 3; 6 : 4; 11 : 6.

shows that it has no further effect than to render us inexcusable."[1]
"It is by faith alone we know that it was God who created the
world."[2] "But faith is not conceived by the bare beholding of
heaven and earth, but by the hearing of the Word. Whereupon it
follows that men are brought by the direction of the Word alone
unto that knowledge of Almighty God which brings salvation.
And yet this does not prevent their being made without excuse,
even without the Word, who, though they are naturally deprived
of light, are blind notwithstanding through their own malice, as
Paul teaches in the first chapter of Romans."[3]

The action of God's Word is such that we are almost compelled
to behold nature, and so see there the attestations of His grace
which help us to acknowledge His fatherly love, and live as those
who depend every moment on His sheer grace. But it is "the
faithful to whom He has given eyes, who see the sparks of His
glory, glittering in every created thing".[4] Calvin is quite emphatic
upon the point that we are able to see the glory of God only if
we are *kept to this point*, that is, to the Word.[5] He does not
therefore envisage any natural theology of the type which may
be abstracted from within the realm of faith, and given a rela-
tively independent status. Thus, he says for example, that such a
statement as "He that cometh to God must believe that He is,
and is a rewarder of them that diligently seek Him" (Heb. 11 : 6)
is not to be laid down as an abstract principle.[6] Such procedure would
not be compatible at all with Calvin's essentially dynamic view
of the relations between God and man, and of God as a *perpetual
Deliverer*.[7] It is only when our knowledge of God is based on
the continual anticipation of grace, that we are brought to know
God in such a way that "no corrupt superstition can seduce
us".[8] Such a natural theology, therefore, as is often envisaged in
Roman theology, and is based upon the activity of a reason
"healed by grace", but abstracted from dogmatics as a *præambula*

[1] *Instit.* 1. 5. 14.
[2] *Comm. on Heb.* 11 : 3: *Sola fide percipimus mundum esse a Deo creatum.*
[3] *Comm. on Acts* 14 : 17: *Fides non ex nudo et coeli et terræ intuitu concipitur, sed ex verbi auditu: unde sequitur, non posse nisi verbi directione ad salvificam Dei notitiam homines adduci. Neque tamen hoc obstat, quominus etiam absque verbo reddantur inexcusabiles, qui tametsi naturaliter luce privati propria tamen malitia cæcutiunt, quemadmodum docet Paulus primo ad Rom. capite.*
[4] *Comm. on Heb.* 11 : 3.
[5] *Comm. on Isa.* 48 : 6: "It is therefore necessary that the lamp of doctrine should shine, in order to regulate our judgment; for in considering the works of God, we shall always go astray, if He do not go before and enlighten us with His Word."
[6] *Comm. ad loc.*   [7] *Ibid.*   [8] *Ibid.*

fidei, would also be impossible for Calvin. Commenting on Augustine's view of the inability of the reason to understand the things of God, Calvin says: "He deems the grace of illumination not less necessary to the mind than the light of the sun to the eye (*De Peccat. Merit. et Remiss.* 2. 5). And not content with this, he modifies his expression, adding, that we open our eyes to behold the light, whereas the mental eye remains shut until it be opened by the Lord. *Nor does Scripture say that our minds are illuminated in a single day so as afterwards to see of themselves.*"[1] It is a question of having to wear the glasses of the Word all the time,[2] and of continually transcending our judgments.[3] "Without the Word, our minds go astray the very first moment they begin to reason."[4] The whole continuing motion of knowing God must correspond with the constant motion of God's grace in the Word. God will be known only thus: outside the Word knowledge is cursed.[5] It is thus that Calvin teaches a doctine of *inseparable relation between faith and the Word*, for "these can no more be disconnected from each other than rays of light from the sun".[6] He denies the Roman doctrine of *implicit faith*, at least in the form in which it is commonly held.[7] The Spirit of God is always present with men, but they must give heed to the Word else the presence of the Spirit would be of no benefit to them.[8] Calvin also insists that faith has no strength in itself, and indeed must vanish away, for its substance lies beyond it.[9] "Although, properly speaking, faith rises from Christ to the Father, He intimates that even when it leans on God it gradually vanishes away unless He Himself interpose to give it solid strength. The Majesty of God is too high to be scaled

---

[1] *Instit.* 2. 2. 25: *Neque uno tantum die illuminari mentes nostras docet Scriptura, ut deinde per se videant.* See also *Comm. on Eph.* 2 : 9, 10.

[2] *Introd. Arg. in Comm. on Gen.; Instit.* 1. 6. 1, 4; 1. 14. 1.

[3] *Instit.* 1. 7. 5; 3. 2. 14, 33 f.   [4] *Instit.* 4. 17. 35.

[5] *Comm. on Gen.* 3 : 6, etc.

[6] *Instit.* 4. 2. 6. Cf. 3. 22. 10: *At fidei mutuus est cum verbo consensus*; and *Comm. on John* 11 : 22.

[7] *Instit.* 3. 2. f.; *Comm. on Heb.* 11 : 12; *on Hos.* 6 : 6, 7.

[8] *Instit.* 1. 9. 2; 3. 2. 33 f.; cf. *Serm. on Gal.* 3 : 7 f.

[9] *Comm. on John* 14 : 1 f. Cf. also *Instit.* 3. 2. 3-35. *Docuimus fidem nisi verbo suffultam effluere . . . Sed quia sine verbo evanidum est quidquid concipimus de potentia Dei et operibus, non temere asserimus nullam esse fidem donec gratiæ suæ testimonio præluceat Deus . . . Sine Spiritus Sancti illuminatione, verbo nihil agitur. Unde etiam liquet fidem humana intelligentia multo superiorem esse . . . Quemadmodum ergo nisi Spiritu Dei tracti, accedere ad Christum nequaquam possumus, ita ubi trahimur, mente et animo evehimur supra nostram ipsorum intelligentiam. Nam ab eo illustrata anima novam quasi aciem sumit, qua coelestia mysteria contempletur, quorum splendore ante in se ipsa perstringebatur . . . Ubi fidem vocans opus Dei, negat esse ex proprio hominis motu; neque eo contentus adiungit, specimen esse virtutis divinæ.*

up by mortals, who creep like worms on the earth. Therefore the common saying that God is the object of faith (*Lactantius* 4 : 16) requires to be received with some moderation. When Christ is called the image of the invisible God the expression is not used without cause, but is designed to remind us that we can have no knowledge of our salvation, until we behold God in Christ."[1] Calvin's argument therefore is that unless the full movement of faith is completed, or at least, except faith be engaged continually in that movement towards its completion in its true end, it will inevitably vanish.[2] "Wherefore, if faith decline in the least degree from the mark at which it ought to aim, it does not retain its nature, but becomes uncertain credulity and vague wandering of the mind. The same Word is the basis on which it rests and is sustained. Declining from it, it falls. Take away the Word, therefore, and no faith will remain."[3]

(2) The second element one must note in Calvin's thought is that there can be no knowledge of God apart from atonement. It is only by atonement that the perverted order of things is straightened out, and true knowledge becomes possible. "Nothing shall we find, I say, above or below, which can raise us up to God, until Christ shall have instructed us in His own school. Yet this cannot be done unless we, having emerged out of the lowest depths, are borne above all heavens in the chariot of the Cross, that there by faith we may apprehend those things which the eye has never seen, the ear never heard, and which far surpass our hearts and minds."[4] This is in line with Calvin's constant emphasis on the motion of grace, and the motion of man's knowledge in answer to God's grace. "No one will be in a suitable state of heart to seek God except a sense of the divine goodness be deeply felt, so as to look for salvation from Him. We indeed flee from God or wholly disregard Him when there is no hope of salvation. But let us bear in mind that this is what must be really believed, and not held merely as a matter of opinion; for even the ungodly may sometimes entertain such a notion, and yet they do not come to God; and for this reason, because they have

---

[1] *Instit.* 2. 6. 4.
[2] *Instit.* 3. 2. 33: *Neque enim fidei tantum inchoator est Spiritus, sed per gradus eam auget, donec ea nos in regnum coeleste perducat.*
[3] *Instit.* 3. 2. 6: *Quare si ab hoc scopo in quem collimare debet, vel minimum deflectit fides, naturam suam non retinet, sed incerta est credulitas, et vagus mentis error. Idem verbum basis est, qua fulcitur et sustinetur: unde si declinat, corruit.* Tolle igitur verbum, et nulla iam restabit fides.
[4] *Introd. Arg. in Comm. on Gen.* Cf. *on Heb.* 4 : 16.

not a firm and fixed faith. This then is the other part of faith by which we obtain favour with God, even when we feel assured that salvation is laid up for us in Him."[1] We have already seen that Calvin thought of the world as designed with the express purpose of bringing man to see that the whole of his life depends on the grace of God, and that in Him alone is to be found salvation. It is only in this consciousness, and in a thankful response to this grace, that man can truly reflect or image the glory of God.[2] But that is no longer possible in the perverted order of the world, where the signs of God's grace are enwrapped by His curse upon sin. Consequently, although "God's voice fills the whole world, and spreads itself to the farthest limits, His glory is celebrated only in His Church,[3] because God not only speaks intelligibly and distinctly there, but also it is there that He gently allures the faithful to Himself. His terrible voice which thunders in various ways in the air, strikes upon the ears and causes the hearts of men to beat in such a manner, as to make them shrink from, rather than approach Him: not to mention that a considerable portion turn a deaf ear to its sounds in storms, rains, thunder, and lightnings. As men therefore profit not so much from this common school as to submit themselves to God, David wisely says especially that the faithful sing the praises of God in His temple, because being familiarly instructed there by His fatherly voice, they devote and consecrate themselves wholly to His service. No man proclaims the glory of God aright but he who worships God willingly. He appears therefore after the example of all the godly, for the purpose of teaching us, that in order truly to know God, and praise Him as is His due, we need another voice than that which is heard in thunders, showers, and storms in the air, in the mountains, and in the forests; for if He teach us not in plain words, and also kindly allure us to Himself, by giving us a taste of His fatherly love, we will continue dumb. It is the doctrine of salvation alone, therefore, which cheers our hearts and opens our

---

[1] *Comm. on Heb.* 11 : 6.   [2] *Comm. on Rom.* 11 : 36.

[3] See *Introd. Arg. in Comm. on Gen.* Calvin thinks of the whole of creation as designed from the very beginning to foster and serve the *Church*. The whole of history revolves around God's purpose which is enshrined in the Church, within which His familiar Word may dwell as in a temple, and through which God may be known as a loving Father. Cf. *The Secret Providence of God, Introd.* It is in the Church that God gives us a "nearer view of Himself . . . as Father of His family. The Church is the great workroom of God, wherein, in a more special manner, He displays His wonderful works; and it is the more immediate theatre of His glorious providence."

mouths in His praises, by clearly revealing to us His grace, and the whole of His will. It is from thence that we must learn how we ought to praise Him. We may also unquestionably see that at that time there was nothing of the light of godliness in the whole world, except in Judea. Even philosophers, who appeared to approach nearest to the knowledge of God, contributed nothing whatever that might truly glorify Him. All that they say concerning religion is not only frigid, but for the most part insipid. It is therefore in His Word alone that there shines forth the truth which may lead us to true piety, and to fear and serve God aright."[1]

Calvin holds, then, that if we are to reach a real knowledge of God we must not just know that God is, but we must know His will toward us.[2] "It concerns us not only to know what He is in Himself, but also in what character He is pleased to manifest Himself to us. We now see therefore that faith is the knowledge of the divine will in regard to us, as ascertained from His Word."[3] Accordingly, it is not just the bare will with which we are concerned, for "the Law of the Lord kills its readers, when it is dissevered from the grace of Christ, and only sounds in the ear without touching the heart".[4] "Hence there is need of the gracious promise, in which He testifies that He is a propitious Father; since there is no other way in which we can approach to Him, the promise being the only thing on which the heart of man can rely."[5] "God justly regards us all as objects of His displeasure, as we are all by nature under His curse, and we have no remedy in our own power. It is hence necessary that God should anticipate us by His grace; and hence it comes that we are brought to know that God is, and in such a way that no corrupt superstition can seduce us, and also that we become assured of a certain salvation from Him. . . . No one, except he be blinded by presumption, and fascinated by self-love, can feel assured that God will be a rewarder of his merits. Hence this confidence of which we speak relies not on works, not on man's worthiness, but on the grace of God alone; and as grace is nowhere found but in Christ, it is on

---

[1] *Comm. on Ps.* 29 : 9; cf. *Instit.* 1. 6. 4; *Comm. on Ps.* 93 : 5; *Serm. on Deut.* 32 : 44 f.
[2] *Instit.* 3. 2. 2.   [3] *Instit.* 3. 2. 6.   [4] *Instit.* 1. 9. 3.
[5] *Instit.* 3. 2: 7. 3. 2. 30: *Firmus ergo fidei status non erit, nisi in Dei misericordia sistatur. Comm. on Heb.* 11 : 11: *Semper enim tenenda est mutua inter verbum Dei et fidem nostram relatio. Sed quia in Dei benevolentia præcipue fundatur fides, ideo non quodlibet verbum, quamvis profectum ex eius ore, sufficeret: sed requiritur promissio gratiæ testis.* But even grace can make us tremble (*Instit.* 3. 2. 17).

Him alone that faith ought to be fixed."[1] It is through the Cross that we see this grace,[2] for there we have a "Mediator who delivers us from our fears, and who alone can tranquillize our conscience, so that we may dare to come to God in confidence".[3] It is only through the death of Christ, by which the whole order of things has been restored, and only within this circumscription of our minds by His grace and reconciliation,[4] that we may reach a true knowledge of God in an order corresponding to that in which He graciously reveals Himself to us. "There is no other way in which God is known, but in the face of Jesus Christ — that is, by the intervention of a Mediator . . . that knowledge which forms us anew into the image of God from faith to faith, or rather, which is the same with faith, by which, having been ingrafted into the body of Christ, we are made partakers of the divine adoption, and heirs of heaven."[5] "Therefore let us set this down for a surety: that there was never since the beginning any communication between God and man, save only by Christ; for we have nothing to do with God, unless the Mediator be present to purchase His favour for us."[6] The conclusion one must draw here is that if there is no real knowledge of God apart from the gracious will of God to reveal Himself, and apart from God's gracious action in restoring the disorder of nature, then there is no real knowledge that is not also saving knowledge.[7] "One thing is certain, that these two things, salvation and the knowledge of the truth, are always *inseparably* joined together."[8]

(3) The third element which we must discuss in Calvin's handling of natural theology is his stress on the fact that the essential motion of true knowledge entails "the submission of the whole of intellectual wisdom to the foolishness of the Cross".[9] The Cross *depotentiates* all natural theology, and entails a change in the natural man which is complete and entire.[10] "The Kingdom of Christ cannot be set up or established otherwise than by throwing down everything in the world that is exalted. For *nothing is more opposed to the spiritual wisdom of God than the wisdom of the*

---

[1] *Comm. on Heb.* 11 : 6.   [2] *Instit.* 3. 2. 2.
[3] *Comm. on* 1 *Pet.* 1 : 21; *on Hos.* 3 : 2-5.
[4] *See Instit.* 1. 14. 1, 20; 2. 6. 1-4; 2. 12. 5; *Serm. on Job* 11 : 7 f.
[5] *Comm. on John* 17 : 3.
[6] *Comm. on Acts* 7 : 30; *on Gen.* 48 : 16; *on Isa.* 25 : 9; *Instit.* 2. 6. 11; 3. 2. 1; 3. 11. 9; *Comm. on John* 14 : 1; *on Eph.* 2 : 12.
[7] *Instit.* 2. 6. 4; 2. 12. 1; *Comm. on Heb.* 11 : 6; *Serm. on* 1 *Tim.* 1 : 17-19.
[8] *The Doctrine of the Secret Providence of God,* Art. 1 (Eng. tr. p. 277).
[9] *Introd. Arg. in Comm. on Gen.; Comm. on* 1 *Cor.* 1 : 21; *Instit.* 2. 6. 1.
[10] *Serm. on Eph.* 4 : 20 f.; *Comm. on* 1 *Cor.* 15 : 51.

flesh; nothing is more at variance with the grace of God than man's natural ability, and so as to other things. Hence the only foundation of Christ's Kingdom is the abasement of men."[1] "For so long as we rest in our own judgment, and are wise in our own estimation, we are far from having any approach to the doctrine of Christ. Hence we must set out with this: that 'he who is wise must become a fool' (1 Cor. 3 : 18), that is, we must give up our own understanding, and renounce the wisdom of the flesh and thus we must present our minds to Christ empty that He may fill them."[2] This is, for Calvin, the essential act of faith corresponding to the death and resurrection of Christ: it is the act of self-emptying as opposed to the act of the natural man which is self-affirmation.[3] Faith robs us that we may seek from God what we need.[4] The beginning of wisdom in the school of Christ is to renounce ourselves.[5] "As men arrogate to themselves more than what is right, and even inebriate themselves with delusions, He strips them naked, that after having known that all they think they have either from nature or from themselves, or from other creatures, is a mere phantom, they may seek true glory."[6]

This was not the original order of things, nor the original life-movement of man, but all that has been perverted — and so it is entirely due to the fault of man that he must now be stripped and abased, in order to enter the true order of acknowledgment and worship of God.[7] "The right order of things was assuredly this, that man, contemplating the wisdom of God in His works, by the light of the understanding furnished him by nature, might arrive at an acquaintance with Him. As, however, this order of things has been reversed through man's depravity, God designs in the first place to make us see ourselves to be fools before 'He make us wise unto salvation' (2 Tim. 3 : 15), and secondly, as a token of

---

[1] *Comm. on 2 Cor.* 10 : 4.   [2] *Comm. on 2 Cor.* 10 : 5.
[3] *Comm. on Hab.* 2 : 4; *on Phil.* 2 : 5 f.; *on Eph.* 2 : 8 f.; *Instit.* 3. 7. 1 f.; 3. 8. 1 f.; especially *Comm. on John* 6 : 29: *Fides nihil ad Deum affert, quin potius hominem vacuum et inopem sistit coram Deo, ut Christo eiusque gratia impleatur. Quare passivum est opus ut ita loquar, cui nulla potest rependi merces. Nec aliam confert homini iustitiam nisi quam a Christo recipit.*
[4] *Comm. on Hab.* 2 : 4. See *Comm. on Acts* 15 : 19; *on* 1 *Cor.* 1 : 21 f., etc.
[5] *Serm. on Job* 37 : 1 f.; 32 : 4 f.; *Instit.* 3. 2. 24.
[6] *Comm. on Jer.* 9 : 24. Cf. *on* 2 *Pet.* 1 : 19: "Peter condemns all the wisdom of men in order that we may learn humbly to seek, otherwise than by our own understanding, the true way of knowledge; for without the Word nothing is left for men but darkness."
[7] *Instit.* 2. 2. 1. And yet this is in accordance with the original state of man. "For as soon as man begins to be, even by the right of creation, he is so bound to his Creator, that he has nothing of his own" (*Comm. on Rom.* 11 : 35).

His wisdom, He presents to us what has some appearance of folly. This *inversion of the order of things* the ingratitude of men deserved. By the *wisdom of God* He means the workmanship of the whole world, which is an illustrious token and clear manifestation of His wisdom: God therefore presents before us in His creatures a bright mirror of His admirable wisdom, so that everyone that looks upon the world, and the other works of God, must necessarily break forth in admiration of Him, if he has a single spark of sound judgment. If men were guided to a right knowledge of God by the contemplation of His works, they would know God in the exercise of wisdom, or by a natural and proper method of acquiring wisdom; but as the whole world gained nothing in point of instruction from the circumstance that God has exhibited His wisdom in His creatures, He then resorted to another method for instructing men. Thus it must be reckoned as our own fault, that we do not attain a saving acquaintance of God, before we have been emptied of our own understanding."[1]

Calvin argues also that this self-emptying motion of faith is not just bare *submission* to authority, such as is often demanded in the Church of Rome, and indeed to the Church of Rome. "Faith consists not in ignorance, but in knowledge; knowledge not of God merely, but of the divine will. We do not obtain salvation either because we are prepared to embrace every dictate of the Church as true, or leave to the Church the province of inquiring and determining; but when we recognize God as a propitious Father through the reconciliation made by Christ, and Christ as given to us for righteousness, sanctification, and life. By this *knowledge*, I say, not by the submission of our understanding, we obtain an entrance to the Kingdom of Heaven."[2] Calvin's point is that it is because we "must seek in Christ not the half, nor merely the part, but the entire completion" of our redemption, that we must seek all our wisdom in Him. *Christ has "not been given to us by way of filling up or eking out . . . wisdom,* but there is assigned to Him exclusively the accomplishment of the whole".[3] In other words, it is the positive wisdom of God's revelation in Christ

[1] *Comm. on* 1 *Cor.* 1 : 21.
[2] *Instit.* 3. 2. 2. *Serm. on Eph.* 1. 17 f.; 4 : 11 f.; 5 : 11 f.
[3] *Comm. on* 1 *Cor.* 1 : 30. *Instit.* 3. 16. 1: "Christ cannot be divided." Cf. *Comm. on Col.* 2 : 3; 2 : 9: "In Christ there is a perfection to which nothing can be added. Hence everything that mankind of themselves mix up is at variance with Christ's nature, because it charges Him with imperfection." 2 : 8: "Hence philosophy will be nothing else than a corruption of spiritual doctrine, if it is mixed with Christ." See also *on John* 3 : 6.

which sets aside our natural wisdom, and relativizes the natural reason.[1] Therefore "while God acts contrary to human reason, He never mocks us, nor disappoints us".[2] There are innumerable passages in the *Commentaries* and *Sermons* where Calvin insists on the necessity of putting off the image of the natural man, and putting on the image of the new, and where he declares that the new image in point of fact destroys the old image, and that the new nature is not a completion but a real destruction of the old, inasmuch as it is entirely new.[3] "The whole man, and everything that he can call wisdom is set aside."[4] There can be no doubt that Calvin views the fallen man as so thoroughly perverted that he needs a complete renewal[5]—though that does not involve any heightening of his physical nature which in itself is neutral. There is a sense in which he would agree with the Thomist doctrine that grace does not destroy nature but perfects and completes it, provided that *nature* is to be understood in a neutral sense; and sometimes Calvin does use it in that sense. But he takes a more profound view of salvation than St. Thomas, and takes seriously the new creation in Christ.[6] This he thinks of as so total and complete that there can be no patchwork in man's salvation. The new creation destroys the old, but only in that it replaces it with a new nature. "The Word of God leaves no half-

---

[1] *Instit.* 1. 1. 2 f.; 1. 5. 13; 1. 9. 3; 1. 11. 1; 2. 1. 2; 2. 8. 1; *Comm. on* 1 *Cor.* 11 : 10 f.; *Serm. on Job* 32 : 4 f.; etc.

[2] *Comm. on John* 5 : 4.

[3] *Instit.* 2. 3. 6.   Cf. *Comm. on Eph.* 2 : 3.   [4] *Comm. on Eph.* 2 : 9.

[5] *Comm. on Rom.* 6 : 6: "By 'old man' Paul means the whole nature which we bring out of our mother's womb, which is so incapable of the Kingdom of God that it must perish, so far as we may be restored to true life." Cf. also *on Rom.* 7 : 6; and *on* 1 *Cor.* 5 : 7: "That is said to be old which we bring with us from the womb, and must perish as we are renewed by the grace of the Spirit." And *Instit.* 4. 16. 17: "We must part with our own nature before we have any access to the Kingdom of God."

[6] See *Comm. on Ezek.* 11 : 18, 19: God's grace does not just "follow out and perfect what we have willed". Before God even our good is in the wrong (*Serm. on Gal.* 1 : 8). See also *on Eph.* 1 : 17-18: "*S. Paul monstre que la raison de l'homme est du tout aveugle, iusques à ce que Dieu l'ait renouvelee, et non pas comme s'il y avoit une partie de vertu en nous, et qu'il ne fist sinon suppleer à quelque defaut. Autrement S. Paul eust dit que Dieu aide à nostre clairté, ou qu'il l'augmente, ou qu'il adiouste ce qui est requis. Il ne parle pas ainsi: mais il dit, Qu'il vous donne des yeux illuminez: monstrant que c'est un don gratuit, et qu'il faut nostre Seigneur supporte non seulement nostre infirmité et y adiouste quelque portion: mais qu'estans aveugles nous ne pouvons rien voir, iusques à ce qu'il nous ait donné ouverture et que nous soyons conduits et gouvernez par ceste revelation.*" And also *on Eph.* 5 : 11-14: "*Ce n'est pas seulement que nous soyons debiles en nostre veuë, et qu'il nous aide et qu'il supplee au defaut qui est en nous: mais c'est que nous sommes povres aveugles, que nous sommes trespassez: bref, nous sommes aux abysmes d'enfer: comme un corps qui sera ietté au sepulchre, on luy aura beau apporter des torches et des chandelles, on ne le fera pas voir pourtant. Ainsi donc nostre Seigneur Jesus Christ nous communique sa clairté, non point pour nous faire voir plus clair que nous ne voyons auparavant: mais pour nous rendre du tout la veuë, d'autant que nous sommes aveugles du tout.*"

life to man, but teaches that in regard to life and happiness he has utterly perished. When Paul speaks of our redemption he does not say that the half-dead are cured but that those who are dead are raised up. He does not call the half-dead to receive illumination of Christ, but those who are asleep and buried."[1] Thus it is the revelation of the Word of grace which completely undercuts natural reason and natural knowledge, and puts them out of court. That is to say, this motion of faith by which man is declared empty and impotent in himself, is through and through the action of grace.[2] "God bestows His grace upon us that we may know that we are nothing; that we stand only in the mercy of God."[3] It is only thus that a man can be stripped and not degraded, for the degradation and slandering of man are an insult to God.[4] "Men are not so stripped of all glory that they may lie down in disgrace, but that they may seek a better glory, for God delights not in the degradation of men."[5] Again: "For God does not despoil us with a view to leaving us bare, but forthwith clothes us with His glory — yet on this condition, that whenever we would glory we must go out of ourselves. In short, man, brought to nothing in his own estimation, and acknowledging that there is nothing good anywhere but in God alone, must renounce all desire for his own glory, and with all his might aspire and aim at the glory of God exclusively."[6] In self-abasement of this sort "man is in no danger of taking too much from himself, provided that he learns that whatever he wants is to be recovered in God".[7] No doubt there is a great deal that is excellent in man,[8] and all these gifts are from God alone,[9] but we have to renounce them nevertheless because they are inextricably bound up with human pride. "The wisdom of this world has become a kind of veil by which the mind is prevented from seeing God."[10] The only way to the knowledge of God is by a return to His grace,

---

[1] *Instit.* 2. 5. 19: *Neque enim dimidiam homini vitam relinquit Dei Verbum, sed penitus interiisse docet, quantum ad beatæ vitæ rationem. Non semivivos dicit sanatos Paulus, dum loquitur de nostra redemptione; sed, quum mortui essemus, suscitatos; non semivivos inclamat ad recipiendam Christi illuminationem, sed dormientes et sepultos.*

[2] Cf. *Serm. on Job* 37 : 1 f.: "We must be sacrificed unto God by means of the Gospel. There must be a kind of dying in us or else God's Word will never prevail in us. We must renounce ourselves and whatsoever is of our own nature must be cast down."

[3] *Instit.* 2. 2. 11; 2. 3. 6; *Comm. on Isa.* 40 : 7.

[4] *Instit.* 2. 1. 10, 11; 2. 2. 15; *Comm. on 2 Pet.* 1 : 3.

[5] *Comm. on Jer.* 9 : 24; see on *Gen.* 1 : 26.

[6] *Comm. on 1 Cor.* 1 : 31; *Serm. on Job* 33 : 1 f.   [9] *Serm. on Job* 32 : 4 f.

[7] *Instit.* 2. 2. 10.   [8] *Ibid.*

[10] *Instit.* 2. 2 20; 3. 2. 34; *Comm. on John* 5 : 37; cf. *on Ps.* 29 : 5; 119 : 17.

and a complete undoing of our own wisdom. The new knowledge of God refuses to have anything to do with naturally acquired knowledge, for this "is not acquired in a natural way, and is not attained by mental capacity, but depends entirely on the revelation of the Spirit. . . . The Spirit of revelation, which we have received, is not of the world, so as to be merely creeping on the ground, so as to be subject to vanity, or to be in suspense, or vary, or fluctuate, or hold us in doubt or perplexity. On the contrary, it is from God alone and hence is above all heavens, of solid and unvarying truth, and placed above all risk of doubt."[1] "Without faith it is impossible to please God. . . . It is hence evident that men in vain weary themselves in serving God except they observe the right way, and that all religions are not only vain, but also pernicious, *with which the true and certain knowledge of God is not connected.*"[2]

[1] *Comm. on* 1 *Cor.* 2 : 12. Cf. *on Heb.* 8 : 11: "For the right knowledge of God is a wisdom which far surpasses the comprehension of man's understanding; therefore to attain it no one is able except through the secret revelation of the Spirit . . . God does not promise what is in our power but what He alone can perform."

[2] *Comm. on Heb.* 11 : 6: *Sine fide autem impossibile est placere Deo . . . Unde patet, frustra homines in colendo Deo fatigari, nisi rectam viam teneant: nec vanas modo, sed vitiosas quoque esse omnes religiones, quæ certam Dei notitiam coniunctam non habent.* Cf. *on Jas.* 2 : 19.